The art of record

The art of record

A critical introduction to documentary

JOHN CORNER

MANCHESTER UNIVERSITY PRESS Manchester and New York

distributed exclusively in the USA and Canada by St. Martin's Press

Copyright © John Corner 1996

Published by Manchester University Press
Oxford Road, Manchester M13 9NR, UK
and Room 400, 175 Fifth Avenue, New York, NY 10010, USA

Distributed exclusively in the USA and Canada
by St. Martin's Press, Inc., 175 Fifth Avenue, New York, NY 10010, USA

British Library Cataloguing-in-Publication Data
A catalogue record is available from the British Library

Library of Congress Cataloging-in-Publication Data
Corner, John.
    The art of record : a critical introduction to documentary / John Corner.
      p.   cm.
    ISBN 0–7190–4686–6. (hardcover : alk. paper).—ISBN 0–7190–4687–4
    (pbk. : alk. paper)
    1. Documentary films—History and criticism.   I. Title.
    PN1995.9.D6C57   1996
    070.1′8—dc20   95–47212

ISBN 0–7190–4686–6 *hardback*
ISBN 0–7190–4687–4 *paperback*

First published 1996
00 99 98 97 96   10 9 8 7 6 5 4 3 2 1

Typeset in Photina with Frutiger
by Northern Phototypesetting Co Ltd, Bolton
Printed in Great Britain
by Redwood Books, Trowbridge

For my parents
John Leonard and Vera May Corner

Contents

Acknowledgements

A number of people have greatly aided my preparation of this book, either by discussion during the writing period or by commenting on drafts. In particular, I would like to thank my immediate colleagues, Julia Hallam, Len Masterman, Kay Richardson and Maggie Scammell. At other institutions in Britain, I am indebted to Sylvia Harvey, Richard Kilborn, Karen Lury, Derek Paget, Julian Petley, Paddy Scannell and Brian Winston, whilst abroad I have benefited from discussion with Peter Dahlgren in Stockholm, Ib Bondebjerg in Copenhagen and Dave Mckie in Perth, Western Australia. Twenty years of students on various 'documentary' courses which I have taught have undoubtedly been the most important contributors – their enthusiasm, judgements and points of disagreement providing me with a steady strand of development.

I would also like to thank the British Film Institute, British Gas PLC, the Post Office, the BBC, Central Television, Trade Films, Clarity Films and Black Audio Film Ltd for their assistance, and Sage Publications for allowing me to reproduce in Chapter 4 material which first appeared in Paddy Scannell (ed.), *Broadcast Talk* in 1991.

A note on availability of the films and programmes discussed

Coalface and *Housing Problems* can be hired from the British Film Institute, 21 Stephen Street, London W1P 1PL, as can the programmes from the *Look In On London* series. *Cathy Come Home* is available from the Concord Video and Film Council, 201 Felixstowe Road, Ipswich IP3 9BJ. Enquiries about hiring *Living On the Edge* should be made to Central Television, Birmingham. *Roger and Me* is available through Warner. Trade Films Ltd, of 36 Bottle Bank, Gateshead NE82AR, will hire copies of *When the Dog Bites*; the Black Audio Collective, 7–12 Greenland Street, London NW1, hire and sell copies of *Handsworth Songs*. *The Life and Times of Rosie the Riveter* is currently distributed by Metro Pictures, 79 Wardour Street, London W1V 3TH. The British Film Institute's *Films on Offer* is an invaluable guide to the current state of distribution and addresses for all the above organisations can quickly be found either from this or from the BFI's *Film and Television Handbook*.

Introduction

Within film and media studies, there is an increasing interest in documentary work. This is often accompanied by practical film-making but it sometimes proceeds as an entirely academic pursuit, paralleling the established lines of enquiry into fiction cinema. The growth in attention has been stimulated by a number of recent studies, of which Bill Nichols's *Representing Reality* (Nichols 1991), a comprehensive theoretical review, must be the most notable and influential. The discursive complexity of much documentary and the often unique way in which its directness of reference and expositional purpose connect its articulations to the social are of obvious analytic interest and significance, but to explain the new academic enthusiasm we need perhaps to look at broader intellectual shifts. An intensified concern with the nature and means of knowledge, with the ethics of social inquiry and with the relations between subjectivity and public culture, has been displayed across the humanities and social sciences. It is possible to see this, at least in part, as being produced by the range of broader debates on rhetoric, reason and truth which, often under the general heading of Postmodernism, have been a focus of theoretical discussion for a decade or more.[1] The new interest in documentary may indicate a kind of critical response, a measured reassessment, to be set against the more comprehensively sceptical and pessimistic accounts of knowledge which have been in circulation.

Certainly, this book is offered as a development of documentary inquiry, partly in appreciation of a range of achievements, partly in further questioning of aims and means. A further impetus is given to it by the sense which I have that documentary is in the process of quite significant shifts. Although some of the factors lying behind these shifts are a cause for concern; for instance, the newly constrained and ratings-competitive character of much television output, many of the inter-generic mixings and explorations which are occurring give reason to believe that, as well as it having new pressures to confront, there are also new imaginative possibilities for documentary. I discuss these, with examples, in my final chapter. Here, by way of introduction, I want to look at the broad character of my study, at some of the general issues which it addresses and at the organisation of its contents.

'Documentary' is the loose and often highly contested label given, internationally, to certain kinds of film and television (and sometimes radio programmes) which reflect and report on the 'the real' through the use of the recorded images and sounds of actuality. Just how the transformation of bits of real appearance into image is managed, and then just how the images and sounds are combined into exposition and argument, are questions which have a considerable history. Although the project of using film in the service of a depictive and/or reportorial realism goes back to the first pioneers of the medium, and the 'realist' capacities of film had excited the early theorists of the cinema,[2] the British film-maker John Grierson is credited both with the coinage of the term 'documentary' in 1926,[3] and with the elaboration of the first principles of documentary cinema in the late 1920s and 1930s. In fact, as later discussion in this book will show, Grierson's 'principles' constituted a highly partial and strategic perspective on non-fiction cinema, one which was suited to his own particular ambitions and context. However, his formulations have had what may be considered a suprising longevity given the specific conditions which produced them, attracting appraisal and critique some sixty years later.

During this period, documentary has undergone two crucial shifts. It has, first of all, become a generic category of international television, where it has a 'public' profile far exceeding that of contemporary documentary cinema (which survives according to the differences of national circumstances for production and distribution). The nature of television's relationship to its audiences and the kinds of economy (direct economies of resource and production but also, more indirectly, of representation) upon which the television industry is based often differ radically from those of cinema, especially 'minority' cinema.

Secondly, although documentary began as a form of the *cinematic essay* (impressionism put to promotional ends; an exploration of the modern and the changing through the evocative, metonymic use of images and sounds), documentary television has been dominated by the journalistic – the use of the documentary form as a means of *expanded reportage*.

I shall regularly return, both in general comment and specific analysis, to these two axes of development in documentary history.

My title, *The art of record*, is meant to indicate what is by now a widely recognised and problematic duality in documentary work – its character as both artifice and as evidence. Engaging critically with both these aspects requires close textual attention and what is, certainly for film studies, a more than usual thoroughness of address to the specifics of reference, to what a given documentary is *about*. It is in my chapters on particular films and programmes that this pull in two directions is examined most intensively, but even where I have done little more than indicate a number of selected formal and thematic elements, I hope to have done justice to the precarious nature of this duality (which can be both complementary and contradictory) and to have opened up further possibilities for analysis and debate.

I have already noted that documentary work is almost always premised on a certain epistemology which itself is grounded in the recording of the particular, physical real by camera and microphone. Thus a very specific kind of fidelity to the real obtained by cinematographic or electronic technology becomes subsumed within more ambitious levels of possible 'fidelity' (that of a speaker's testimony to the events described, for instance, or that of one shot of a city centre to its general appearance). Finally, these more ambitious levels of fidelity comprise the general 'truthfulness' of the documentary's various depictions and assessments as this is projected within the film or programme (perhaps implicitly in its narrative sequencing or explicitly through commentary) and then, with variation, attributed to it by viewers. Of course, documentaries vary radically in the way in which they organise their truth claims as well as in the strength and nature of these claims, which have often been open to doubt and vigorous critique. However, it seems to me that as one moves away from work using elements of the recorded real, the term 'documentary' becomes more problematic. So, for instance, although one may talk of 'prose documentary', the work of writers such as George Orwell poses rather different problems of depiction and of discursive subjectivity from those associated with films and television programmes.[4] This may be contested, and certainly drama-documentary reconstructions (discussed in detail in Chapter 2) put considerable pressure on such a distinction, as do certain kinds of 'second-order' historical documentary where no direct visualisation or sound is available. Nevertheless, the whole epistemic identity of documentational discourse, its appeal as well as its discursive capacity, changed when the indexicality of recorded image and/or sound was introduced.[5] This is quite clear from the history of early documentary photography and the later and influential antecedent of radio actuality features,[6] where interview speech was used in ways which sometimes prefigured cinematic and televisual formats.

My intention in this book has been to avoid the 'easy' resolution of documentary epistemology. That is to say, I have adopted a critical position which is properly sceptical of the less qualified type of truth claim made on behalf of documentary, a truth claim which has often served the purposes of political and social management. Yet it is a position which is also unhappy with the kind of criticism which rests content with 'suspicion' and which seems to find its fulfilment in exhaustively proving the fraud and deceit of the documentary enterprise. For not only does such an intellectual endeavour quickly become repetitive, it also has a habit of becoming insensitive to the variety of documentary form and to the specific and often highly modifying (i.e. de-universalising) circumstances of production and reception.

Even more important is what I see to be a failure to recognise the continuing need of public culture for a cinema and a television of engaged non-fictionality which, despite its recognition of the problems of representation, continues to regulate its activities by a discipline of principles and codes of practice. That these should be more openly declared, and therefore more available to contestation as the rules of a prominent kind of public knowledge, is highly desirable for the health of the public sphere generally as well as for the health of documentarism itself.

So as a generic label, documentary is a very loose one, the name now encompassing a very wide range of depictive styles and depictive aims. Formatively institutionalised around the very specific promotionalist project of Griersonian factual cinema in the 1930s, an institutionalisation which allowed some emphasis on the 'creative', 'artistic' aspects of the enterprise as well as on its informative and, indeed, propagandist possibilities, its character has since become strongly shaped by the conventions and purposes of broadcast journalism. At the same time, an independent documentary cinema has flourished internationally, a cinema which is perhaps primarily defined in terms of its use of film for the radical questioning of dominant political and social systems and for the putting forward of alternative and oppositional views. This latter strand of work can be seen as the one with the longest lineage in so far as it picks up on the productive mixing of film aesthetics and politics which accompanied the first phase of post-revolutionary redevelopment in the Russia of the 1920s.[7]

Although it receives detailed treatment on a number of occasions in the chapters which follow, it is perhaps worth saying something here about the relationships of documentary work to 'fiction' since this issue comes up, in various ways, in most debates about documentary. A little simplistically, one can see such relationships as being placed between the two poles of sharp contrast and virtual indistinguishability. Bill Nichols (1991) catches at this awkward positioning with both wit and perceptiveness in a section of his book entitled 'A fiction (un)like any other'. For to claim a clear division between documentary 'fact' on the one hand and 'fiction' on the other is to move to a position of epistemological confidence which not only runs counter to that scepticism about knowledge – its grounds and means of production – which has so characterised contemporary academic inquiry but also ignores the very wide range of narrative, dramatic and imaginative devices which have been employed in documentary-making. Yet simply to collapse documentary into a kind of rhetorical variant of fiction fails to do justice to the specific, if troubled, nature of its referentiality and to the particular kinds of self-constraint which documentarists have chosen to work within in order to achieve a level of evidentiality, of expository accuracy and of general truth to circumstances not normally required in fictional works (and often seen as an unwelcome limitation of their imaginative capacities). To note, for instance, that many documentaries employ a narrative structure to organise their expositions and/or observations does not by itself provide an obstacle to differentiation unless it is supposed that narrative organisation is an exclusive property of fiction – a very limited and limiting view to take (a point well argued in Winston (1995: 113–19)).

In the first chapter, on documentary theory, I attempt to show how the fact/fiction argument has often had a 'see-saw' character in which untenable claims for factuality have been countered by unhelpfully broad ideas about fictionality. I noted at the start of this introduction how, quite recently, more considered and closely argued accounts have emerged and how beneficial these have been to the development of documentary studies and to the appreciation (and also at times to the defence) of documentary practice.

If one 'bad' reason for the relative lack of media studies interest in documentary has been an inclination towards dismissiveness (an inclination which has also had the effect of reducing interest in the qualities of documentary discourse in comparison with fictional discourses), there have also been some 'good' reasons for neglect. The difficulty of (legally) obtaining primary texts for screening and study has limited the place of documentary on the syllabus. This is particularly true of broadcast television output, but even the work of independent cinema groups has been harder to assemble than, say, international feature fiction. It is also true that the very modest, if increasing, size of the academic literature, particularly that usable in teaching, has until now dissuaded many lecturers from attempting much more than the most selective and brief of treatments.

The organisation of the book

The book is organised around a core of chapters which deal with specific films and programmes. These latter have qualities which make them of interest in themselves but they have also been selected both to illustrate the range of documentary work and to illuminate a number of major issues concerning aims, methods and forms. There is a continuity of approach across these analytic chapters, which provides the basis for making comparisons and contrasts and for recognising that which is distinctive. In developing my own accounts, I have variously drawn on contextual information, on interview material, on contemporary reviews and on the existing academic literature.

I start with a chapter which looks at documentary theory, attempting to explore some of the principal directions taken by ideas about the forms and purposes of documentary work. In order to provide some sense of historical development here, as well as in the interests of conceptual clarity, I have used the categories of 'foundations', 'critique' and 'reconstruction' to organise my critical review, subdividing further where necessary. This chapter will, I hope, provide a broad intellectual entry to the themes taken up in more detail and specificity elsewhere.

My second chapter looks at two of the most controversial of documentary approaches – the uses of dramatisation and the variants of the 'vérité' (or 'fly-on-the-wall') mode. Both have a considerable and lively history but both are still very influential in mid-1990s documentary. I attempt to distinguish between the different kinds of thing which the term 'dramatise' can mean in relation to documentary and to register the ways in which the appeal of directly observational material has been organised at the level of method and form. Throughout, debates about the value and propriety of particular ways of using images and sounds, including speech, as a means of documentation are cited and discussed.

Eight chapters on particular films and programmes follow. Here, I have drawn both from cinema and television, from mainstream and 'independent' production, from Britain and the United States, and I have included a range of formats variously using dramatisation, observationalism, interview, archive film, presenter address, music, and so on.

Chapter 3 looks at two classic and contrasting films from the British documentary movement of the 1930s, *Coalface* and *Housing Problems*, and sets their depictive aesthetics, their distinctive 'realisms', in the social and political circumstances of the period.

Chapter 4 takes the documentary series *Look In On London* from 1956, the first full year of commercial television in Britain, and concentrates on its extensive use of interview method in a format which mixes social inquiry with an attempt at popular appeal through lively presentation and lighthearted tone.

Chapter 5 focusses on *Cathy Come Home*, often regarded as one of the most significant productions of 1960s British television and a major development in drama-documentary 'mixing'. This programme gave rise to a much more general debate about the legitimacy of dramatised form as well as showing how imaginatively powerful it could be.

Chapter 6 takes an ambitious television film from the mid-1980s, Michael Grigsby's *Living on the Edge* – an attempt to portray the state of Britain at that time and 'reading' it against post-war British economic and political history by using archive images and soundtrack. Employing a wide range of depictive methods and often beautifully rich in its imagery, this film was networked across the ITV national system.

Chapter 7 looks at a film which has become celebrated both for its use of archive material and for its attempt at a popular feminist historiography. Connie Field's 1980 film *Rosie the Riveter* explores the experience of women in industry during the Second World War, setting interview testimony off against official propaganda. It raises

The art of record

questions about the use of history in documentary, about ways of being political and about the specific issue of feminist documentary practice.

Chapter 8 examines a boldly innovative film from the independent sector, screened on Channel Four in 1988. Penny Woolcock's *When the Dog Bites* investigates life in a northern town a few years after the closure of its main industry, the steelworks. By a variety of unconventional means (some of which indicate a 'postmodern' attitude towards inter-textual borrowings and referential stability), this film constructs a portrayal which raises interesting questions about the future possibilities and pitfalls of documentary discourse. This chapter concludes with an interview with the film-maker.

Chapter 9 is about *Roger and Me*, Michael Moore's 1989 film on the gradual shutdown of General Motors' manufacturing in a Michigan town. This is one of the most widely screened, reviewed and discussed documentaries of recent times (though made on a small, independent budget it was later distributed by Warner). The changes which Moore introduced into the chronology of his account became the subject of controversy, particularly after a strongly critical notice by the New Yorker's film critic Pauline Kael. Moore's film must stand as a marker in the development of contemporary documentary, not least for its breezily biographical style and calculated amateurism.

Chapter 10 looks at a British film produced in 1986 by the Black Audio Film Collective, *Handsworth Songs*. Made, self-declaredly, in a 'Griersonian spirit', this is a multi-stranded and sometimes oblique exploration of the black community in Britain and of racial inequality, focussing on the violent civil disturbances in the Handsworth district of Birmingham in the mid-1980s. *Handsworth Songs*, like other films in the book, brings a deconstructive pressure to bear on the very idea of documentary depiction, on the relation between the subjective and the objective and on 'political' film-making.

Chapter 11 brings a number of earlier themes together by looking at the future of documentary and at some of the strongest new tendencies discernible in the mid-1990s, such as the hybridisations of the 'emergency services' series, and the rise of do-it-yourself camcorder formats initiated by the BBC's *Video Diary* programmes.

As can be seen from this brief description of the selected material, there are many productive overlaps and contrasts in the works discussed. By adopting a loosely chronological approach, I hope to have allowed some sense of implicit history to have come through as well. Interconnection between the substantive analyses and the more general theoretical questions occurs regularly and, in relation to some of the key themes, frequently. Many of the chapters use a system of subheads and regular itemisation to organise the mix of brief description, analysis and commentary in the most effective, concise and clear manner. At the bottom of the acknowledgements page I have indicated where copies of the films I discuss in detail might be hired or bought.

Documentary is an extremely rewarding object of study, leading enquiry to questions about the picturing of the social which lie at the very centre of a changing, troubled modernity. I hope this book helps to increase awareness and appreciation.

Documentary theory

1

In this chapter, I want to examine some general ideas about documentary, ideas which are taken up in more detail in the chapters on individual works, in the next chapter (which looks at drama-documentary and vérité forms) and in the final chapter on future developments. General ideas about documentary have often been generated in critical debate about particular films and programmes but there also exists a body of commentary which seeks to address the whole genre of documentary work. This is often referred to as 'documentary theory', indicating a set of connected propositions and concepts concerning the socio-aesthetic nature of documentary practice. It is my view that the use of the word 'theory' in the social sciences and the arts in currently prone to abuse, such that a relatively modest if suggestive idea or two may often lay claim to the status of 'theory' in a way that is pretentious as well as imprecise. And since being theoretical is now quite widely thought to be a good thing, probably better than being analytical and substantive if one has to choose, this is not surprising. However, in many other areas (for instance, the cognate ones of film and literature) the development of theoretical work has often increasingly divorced itself from attention to specific practices and artefacts, setting up as a relatively autonomous discursive activity 'above' the level both of practice and practical criticism. It has frequently sought 'horizontal' connections with theories in other fields (particularly big theories like Postmodernism) at the cost of maintaining good 'vertical' relations. Given the marked (if problematic) referentiality of work in documentary, it would be a great pity if this happened to documentary studies.

In fact, compared to many other areas of media production, 'theories' about documentary are quite few and most of them maintain a strong connection with specific practice, either by way of critique or recommendation. The sheer range of practices to come under the 'documentary' heading, together with the specific contingencies of documentary representation, perhaps work against the kind of flourishing self-sufficiency which has occurred elsewhere. I hope so, anyway.

Documentary is also distinguished by the degree of 'self- theorising' which accompanied pioneer work in the area. John Grierson's early deliberations on the nature and role of documentary in society (collected in Hardy 1979) provide it with an eloquent, ambitious (and often highly misleading) 'mission statement'. The theory of this early advocacy still provides a primary target for that body of much later theory (mostly, though not exclusively, academic in origin) which projects itself primarily as 'critique'. So whilst the main aim of the early theory is to make the case *for* documentary, quite often with a strategic focus on those practices and forms which the author wishes to advance, the main aim of much recent theory is to make the case *against* it, with some variation on the question of whether or not documentary can reconstruct itself into a project with a future.

Undoubtedly, the main issue around which recent theory has organised its 'deconstructive' interests in the documentary canon and the documentary enterprise has been the question of realism. Or perhaps one should say questions of realism since, as it is part of this book's purpose to demonstrate in some detail, the ways in which relations to the real are posed in documentary discourse vary considerably as well as being complex. Nevertheless, it is the claim, made in different ways throughout the history of documentary work, that a special relationship to the real is being achieved (indexical, evidential, revelatory) and, on the basis of this relationship, that 'truths' are being communicated, which excites the energies of critique and refutation. To many students of the media and film, documentary has seemed to be so bold and complacent in its epistemological assumptions and its devices of showing as to be, in itself, an *offence* to theory, an outrageous act of naivety, frequently compounding its philosophical and aesthetic shortcomings with a social and political complicity which trades on them.

There are a number of different ways in which a brief account of the variations and the historical shifts in theorising about documentary might be organised. I propose to work primarilywith three broad classifications which have a 'developmental' logic. First of all, I want to look at some of the principal aspects of 'foundational thinking'. Secondly, I want to examine the major variants of 'critique' to emerge (amounting at times to the putting forward of an 'anti-documentary' position). Finally, I shall look at what is currently on offer by way of guidelines for the future of documentary, for its social, imaginative and discursive reconstruction. There is no doubt that those currents of aesthetic and social ideas gathered (precariously) together under the heading of Postmodernism have had an impact here. And as documentarists themselves have become more reflexive and more inclined to recognise the contingincies of their practice, the consequences of engagement with Postmodernist ideas have often been energising and productive.

In looking at 'theory' according to my scheme, three related themes will regularly emerge, each one of which can be represented in the form of a couplet of tension and potential conflict. These are *art/reportage* – the status of the documentary as aesthetic artefact and as referential record; *truth/viewpoint* – the perennial question of documentary veracity in relation to the subjective dimension of its methods and discourses, and *institution/forms* – the 'embedding' of documentary-making within different political, economic and social orders, within different landscapes of public knowledge which, though they may not be directly visible, carry implications for practices and usage.

Foundational thinking

I sketch out a brief account of the work of the 1930s British documentary film movement in Chapter 3, where I concern myself with two important films of the period.[1] Here, I want to look at some of the ideas which were advanced in support of the documentary project at this formative period of its institutionalisation as a generic enterprise. My purpose is to bring out the major theoretical themes which were articulated rather than to look at the contemporary literature of commentary and debate surrounding particular films. These themes occur mostly in the writings of John Grierson, by far the most significant figure in the movement. Grierson was active at every level in the formation of the documentary project – as a producer and director but also as an organiser, campaigner and manifesto-writer.

I undertake this acccount knowing that recent academic work on the 1930s movement, including that on its philosophy and guiding principles, has contributed substantially to what is now a detailed literature of scholarship and commentary. In particular, Ian Aitkin's study of John Grierson (Aitkin 1990) sets his ideas about the documentary in the context of a detailed intellectual biography, whilst Brian Winston's important revaluation of the documentary tradition (Winston 1995) brings out the extent to which Grierson's approach to definitions, aims and objects was shrewdly tactical and not to be taken at face value.

Of all Grierson's many essays on documentary form, 'First Principles of Documentary' (written between 1932 and 1934) is most often cited. In it, Grierson makes both the social and the aesthetic case for documentary by comparing possibilities in the 'new form' with two other kinds of film-making. First of all, with the fictional cinema, primarily that of Hollywood, and secondly with the earlier tradition and the current conventions of the factual film. Grierson finds documentary superior to the former in so far as it engages with the real rather than encouraging fantasy and superior to the latter in so far as it works imaginatively and dramatically, rather than confining itself to the limited aesthetics of the newsreel and the illustrated lecture. Before considering his arguments further, it

Documentary theory

might be useful to quote a few of the more familiar and more important formulations from the 'First Principles' essay. Here is Grierson arguing that the category of 'documentary', though it has become attached, in its short history of usage, to a wide range of films, should be applied much more specifically:

> So far we have regarded all films made from natural material as coming within the category. The use of natural material has been regarded as the vital distinction. Where the camera shot on the spot ... in that fact was documentary. This array of species is, of course, quite unmanageable in criticism, and we shall have to do something about it. They all represent different qualities of observation, different intentions in observation, and, of course, very different powers and ambitions at the stage of organising material. I propose, therefore, after a brief word on the lower categories, to use the documentary description exclusively of the higher. (Hardy (ed.) 1979:19. My italics)

In talking of one of the 'lower' species, the 'lecture film', Grierson goes on to identify limitations in further detail:

> They do not *dramatize*, they do not even dramatize an episode: they *describe*, and even expose, but, in any aesthetic sense, only rarely *reveal*. (Hardy (ed.) 1979:20. My italics)

By contrast, he notes the way in which 'documentary proper' goes beyond these limits:

> one begins to wander into the world of documentary proper, into the only world in which documentary can hope to achieve the ordinary virtues of an *art*. Here we pass from the plain (or fancy) descriptions of natural material, *to arrangements, rearrangements, and creative shapings of it*. (Hardy (ed.) 1979:20. My italics)

In further, prescriptive commentary on the 'vital art form' which the documentary offers, Grierson notes how, in contrast with 'studio films', documentary would 'photograph the living scene and the living story'. His antipathy to current fictional cinema can be seen in this comment on the benefits of working with 'the raw':

> We believe that the materials and the stories taken from the raw can be finer (more real in the philosophic sense) than the acted article. Spontaneous gesture has a special value on the screen. Cinema has a sensational capacity for enhancing the movement which tradition has formed or time worn smooth. Its arbitrary rectangle specially reveals movement; it gives it maximum pattern in space and time. Add to this that documentary can achieve an intimacy of knowledge and effect impossible to the shim-sham mechanics of the studio, and the lily-fingered interpretations of the metropolitan actor. (Hardy (ed.) 1979:21.)

Drawing on the work of Robert Flaherty,[2] Grierson pursues the 'distinction between description and drama':

> but it is important to make the primary distinction between a method which describes only the surface values of a subject, and the method which more *explosively reveals* the reality of it. You photograph the natural life, but you also, by your juxtaposition of detail, *create an interpretation of it*. (Hardy 1979 (ed.) 22–3, My italics)

Finally, we can note how he introduces the idea of documentary aesthetics carrying 'sociological' responsibilities which are not easy to discharge:

> This sense of social responsibility makes our realist documentary a troubled and difficult art, and particularly in a time like ours. The job of romantic documentary is easy in comparison: easy in the sense that the noble savage is already a figure of romance and the seasons of the year have already been articulated in poetry ... . But realist documentary, with its streets and cities and slums and markets and exchanges and factories, has given itself the job of making poetry where no poet has gone before it, and where no ends, sufficient for the purposes of art, are easily observed. *It requires not only taste but also inspiration, which is to say a very laborious, deep-seeing, deep-sympathising creative effort indeed.* (Hardy (ed.) 1979:25. My italics)

These quotations variously indicate key aspects of Grierson's documentary philosophy, and I think that a more extended citation of them than is usually offered brings out the distinctive character of this more directly than does a focus exclusively on particular phrasings. Of all the phrases that have been used in discussion of 'foundationalist thought', the one which is cited most often is 'creative interpretation of actuality' but as Andrew Higson points out (Higson 1995:191), this is hard to find anywhere in Grierson's extensive writings, although 'creative treatment of actuality' occurs. Higson cites a 'first found use' for this in an article on 'The Documentary Producer' written by Grierson for *Cinema Quarterly* in 1933. However, in the penultimate quote we can see the elements out of which a paraphrased comment about 'interpretation' might easily be made. Such a degree of exegetical interest in Griersonian formulations might seem beside the point (in fact, I think it often turns out to be so), but the question of precisely what kinds and degrees of intervention Grierson is introducing into his favoured generic formula, and how these serve to distinguish documentary from other practices (especially from fiction) has been a matter of great practical as well as theoretical interest in the subsequent history of factual film-making.

What is absolutely clear is that, in the advocating of his ideas about documentary method and the documentary 'mission', Grierson is not in the grip of a naive realism. What he says may not always be either clear or consistent but the kind of practice which he is putting forward is grounded in a considerable degree of discursive skill and creative 'vision' (revelatory, 'deep-seeing'), it is not simply a result of any 'capturing' performed by the camera. It is therefore thoroughly and self-consciously aestheticised, a symbolically *expressive* activity, and Grierson portrays it as such except on those occasions where his polemical purpose is best suited by emphasing the nature of documentary as public information. Here, he is inclined to marginalise the 'creative' and 'transformative' factors and, indeed, sometimes to perform a complete U-turn and describe the project as being essentially 'anti-aesthetic' in character (see, for example, the claims in Hardy (ed.) 1979:112). Aitkin brings out extremely well the error of many previous critics in accusing Grierson of a far stronger commitment to mimetic realism or illusory naturalism than was the case, mostly due to an unawareness of the philosophical sources (including British Hegelian) of many his ideas. So, for instance, in extract D. above, the phrase 'more real in the philosophic sense' points not to an empirical grounding but to an idea of underlying essence to which the documentarist's creative seeing provides access. Of course, thus to excuse Grierson from a charge of empiricist realism does not remove at all from the problems caused by the metaphysical abstraction of his remarks or by their irritating inconsistency.

Documentary is *authorial* in that it is about creativity and transformation based on vision. In being this, it is also emphatically *dramatic*, as part of its bid for the public imagination, although we should note that the term 'dramatic' can mean something to do with intensity of narrative shaping and also something to do with 'enactment'. Although both are relevant, it is useful to differentiate between the two (see Chapter 2 for a more extended discussion of this point). However, the 'raw material' for the creative endeavour is provided by 'reality' and it is the address to this, albeit with transformative intent, which provides documentary with its claimed superiority over fictional cinema. It also provides Grierson with the basis for his social democratic theory about film as an agency of citizenship and reform, since only to the degree that it has a 'core' of *reliable referentiality* in its depictions can the documentary film be argued to be a key agency of modern public information. We are still a very long way from the time when, within television, documentary would be regarded as primarily a form of *journalism*, with all the constraints and obligations which this entails, but an informational role was central to the foundational enterprise. It would be difficult for documentary to discharge its responsibilities simply as 'Art', whilst to emphasise a licence to propagandise and promote would also be to undermine its public informational value. Grierson was, in fact, a believer in the need for state publicity, and indeed, not suprisingly given their source of funding, many documentaries of the 1930s and wartime performed a highly instrumentalist role in this respect (again, unrestrained by journalistic convention). Making this role a defining feature in the official 'manifesto' was, nevertheless, a different thing entirely. A bedrock of veracity was essential.

Winston's reassessment of Grierson finds the play-off between creativity and realness unconvincing:

> Grierson's taxonomic triumph was to make his particular species of non-fiction film, *the* non-fiction genre while at the same time allowing the films to use the significant fictionalising technique of dramatisation. (Winston 1995:103).

This is a usefully provocative point, though agreement with it will largely rest on certain, contestable ideas about 'fictionalisation'

The art of record

and 'dramatisation'. The issue is dealt with directly in Chapter 2, as part of considering the debate around drama-documentary forms, and it occurs in relation to specific works throughout this book. Not suprisingly, it also forms a main strand in that large body of documentary theory which is primarily intended as 'critique'.

Before turning to examine that strand, however, I want to conclude this very brief examination of Grierson's view of documentary by attempting a summary evaluation of its main features.

We can see the Griersonian position as a combination of two rather precariously positioned sets of ideas – one concerning the social purposes of the form and one concerning its nature as a filmic practice. The social purposes of documentary are not journalistic nor are they propagandistic – they are promotional, certainly, and didactic, but they are interwoven with the development of citizenship in modern society and with the cause of social democratic reform. As a practice and a form, documentary is strongly informationalist (and therefore requires a level of 'accuracy') but it is also an exercise in creativity, an art form drawing on interpretative imagination both in perceiving and using the sounds and images of 'the living scene' to communicate 'the real' (not finally a matter of phenomenal forms but of structures and relationships).

We have already seen how the often uncertain (and sometimes strategically inconsistent) terms in which Grierson develops his case on both these counts make his general position a vulnerable one. Moreover, they mean that any attempt to apply the principles as direct guidelines for practice or even for critical judgement (the constituents of 'good documentary') is likely to be faced with a stiff challenge.

Grierson's legacy to subsequent documentary film-making has been considerable but it has been much 'looser' than the handing-down of a prescriptive clustering of social and aesthetic ideas. It essentially amounts to the varied practice of the 1930s and wartime film-makers (most of whom worked under Grierson at one time or other) together with the broad linking of socially realist depiction to public informational goals. We can see the legacy coming through clearly in the comment made by Paul Rotha in 1954, about the new BBC television documentary department of which he had been appointed Head – 'To those who still believe that documentary has a specific social job to do, this mass access ... is of paramount importance' (Cited in Bell 1986:71).

But the transmission of Griersonianism in any more direct form was inhibited by a number of factors. First of all, there were the specific, philosophical origins of his views, in which much of the distinctiveness of his vocabulary as well as his strong sense of 'totality' lies. Secondly, there was the reconstitution of documentary within television as a major extension of journalism, introducing social and aesthetic requirements and expectations quite different from those with which Grierson had worked. Finally, there was the introduction of new, lightweight equipment which allowed for extensive location shooting and which brought a new drive towards directorial minimalism and against self-conscious elaboration.[3] One can see these last two changes as involving new forms of *empirical* emphasis – journalism's concern with *inquiry and analysis*; vérité and direct cinema's concern with *observation* – displacing Grierson's loftier engagement with the imaginative capturing of a non-phenomenal 'real'. However, in many films of the early period, including those made within Grierson's units, at least partial precedents for these newer modes can be found.

Critique

As I noted earlier, the very broad range of theories which can be classified as critique engage with documentary mainly in denunciation of what they see to be its failings and dangers. At the cost of a little over-simplification, we can usefully classify these theories into two types. There are those which address themselves primarily to a *critique of documentary evidentiality*, to its claimed capacity to reference the world. These can be comprehensive 'denials' of documentary but they can also be offered as form-specific critiques; for instance, vérité or commentary films may be singled out for primary attention, with other forms shown more tolerance, if only implicitly. Then there are those theories which address themselves primarily to a critique of the *institutional character of documentary*, to its specific location within political, economical and social systems. Clearly, this latter approach will show a degree of national variation. It will also vary in the extent to which the critique is offered as 'terminal' or put forward with the implication that a *re-institutionalised* documentarism might be able to perform an acceptable and useful communicative function. Since I am going to look at 'reconstructive' ideas in the next section, I will concentrate here on the deconstructive aspect of the two strands, which can of course often be found in combination.

Critiques of documentary evidentiality

I observed in the above section how Grierson's own ideas on documentary are vulnerable to a misreading which regards them as empiricist when in fact they are strongly idealist. In some of the criticism of documentary realism written during the 1970s, under the influence of Structuralist film theory, Grierson was quite often seen as a primary source of 'bad' thinking about documentary evidence. So, for instance, in his short essay on the documentary in Britain for the 1978 British Film Institute catalogue, Julian Petley reviews the work of the 1930s movement in terms which are strongly critical of Griersonian naivety. Petley's piece, and the subsequent commentary on individual films which follow it, was a very helpful aid in directing critical attention to the non-fiction film and to its distinctive history in Britain. However, although it contains much shrewd assessment, the way in which its appraisal of Grierson inclines towards *dismissal* is very much of its time. For instance, having noted some of Grierson's main formulations, Petley goes on to observe:

> This was probably the closest Grierson ever got to a theoretical statement on documentary, and its lack of sophistication reveals his mistrust not only of narrative cinema and formal innovation, but also of theoretic formulation. (Petley 1978:5)

Elsewhere, in his commentary on the film *Housing Problems* (1935) (see my discussion of this in Chapter 3), he develops the point further:

> Unfortunately, because of Grierson's empirical anti-theoretical bent the problems of 'realism', the problematic notion of 'reality', were never fully recognised and centrally never fully discussed in print. It is only now – in this country – in journals like *Screen* that the issues are being raised. (Petley 1978:13)

Whilst, as I have suggested, Grierson's thinking may well stand accused of obscurity, inconsistency and of self-promotion (the nub of the assessment in Winston 1995), it is hard to find it guilty of the kind of unreflective belief in the 'transparency' of film which Petley seems to find. For Grierson's accounts are dense with ideas precisely about how documentary-making is a creative intervention and about the need for 'formal innovation'. A critique of his views gets off to a much better start, and is able to develop a more productive engagement with post-Grierson practice, if it recognises the extraordinary *elaboration* of his ideas and his commitment to reference points beyond the appearances 'captured' in individual shots.

Winston's critique, which I have touched on earlier, takes a rather different tack. Here, Grierson is accused of producing an *apparently* coherent documentary philosophy which in fact includes a number of rather drastic inconsistencies, not least those surrounding the guiding idea of 'the real'. The main worry which Winston has concerns the key formulation about the 'creative treatment of actuality'. Just how much 'actuality' might we expect to survive 'creative treatment'? he asks. What kind of balance or play-off is Grierson himself assuming? Winston's own judgement is that the phrase effectively works as a self-accorded licence to fabricate. Thus the central tension between documentary as artefact and documentary as record is, in practice, resolved in favour of the former without the genre relinquishing the special status which derives from the latter.

Taking Winston's argument, at least for the time being, as a convincing one, there are three issues which seem to me still to require attention. For a start, there is the difference between regarding the 'actuality' *as* the real itself, which the film-maker perceives and creatively relays, and regarding it as *primary* representation, the recorded sounds and images from which the film is constructed. From the evidence of his usage, it does not seem altogether clear which meaning Grierson intended. The 'raw material' of documentary film-making is seen to be both 'reality' and the primary recorded units. If we give emphasis to the first, then the whole question of the indexical fidelity obtaining between particular image and element of reality, the whole question of documentary as *evidential representation*, is bracketed out. If, however, we give emphasis to the second, then it follows that this fidelity is simply assumed and, moreover, that no 'creative' intervention in the 'primary' production of image and sound is admitted, creativity being applied only at the 'secondary' stage of construction.

It is worth noting here how large a part conflations of 'primary' and 'secondary' stages (or contested versions of differentatiation between these stages) play in dispute about documentary. The referential values of primary depiction are essentially to do with the fidelity of images and sounds to specific features of physical reality. As well as involving technical accessibility, this is a matter of conventions of shooting (e.g. the degrees of directorial intervention and assumed levels of behaviour modification in the speech and action of filmed subjects). However, the truth claims of documentary exposition reach well beyond this level of specific, rendered appearances to encompass abstract propositional/argumentational matters. The whole textual system of the film or programme, its expositional organisation, forms of argument, modes of adducing visual and verbal evidence and the lines of causality indicated in the narrative scheme are all implicated here. General truth claims in documentary cannot be seen to be fully grounded in primary fidelity since such fidelity underdetermines them, even within the particularistically focused (sometimes, indeed, obsessed) project of vérité. Nevertheless, as all the chapters in this book variously demonstrate, it is on the warrant provided by the integrity of their 'raw materials' that most documentaries base their discursive status. The relationship between the two levels has to be perceived by the viewer as having a strongly *inductive* element for this to be accepted. Should the employment of the primary level be regarded as too heavily a function of secondary level discursive requirements, then there are problems of credibility *even though the primary veracity of the material remains undisputed*. Different documentary forms pose the relationship in different ways; the Griersonian form, as we have seen, has a quite distinctive – by turns emphatic and evasive – rhetoric of combination (see Vaughan 1976 for an analysis of the relationships obtaining in vérité, and Branigan 1992 for a brief but suggestive discussion of the determination of reference in non-fiction).

A second problem following from Winston's critique, illuminating though it is, involves the assumption which I think he is inclined to make that allowance of 'creative treatment' necessarily collapses the documentary project into 'fiction'. What is needed here is more attention to the case-law apparent in 1930s documentary practice, where it is clear that the gravitational pull of actuality is registered in a number of different ways, most of which

A fly on the wall: filming *Police*
(BBC 1982)

require that the textual system of the films be organised in a manner distinct from narrative fiction. So, for instance, the poetic–dramatic shaping of *Coalface* (1935) is in tension with the indexical appeal of the particular images of miners, mining machinery and minework, whilst the to-camera testimony of *Housing Problems* (1935) grounds the socially reformist rhetoric of that film in representations of situated individuality. Winston's deconstruction of the Grierson holistic vision usefully problematises phrasings that have too often been allowed to carry a self-evident grandness, but the requirement is still to explore further the *different levels* at which documentarist practices relate to the 'real' and the different ways in which 'creativity' can operate, within various political and social conventions of representational propriety.

A third problem is much more general. Winston's assumption is that the precedent of Griersonian thinking has served to mislead much subsequent documentary practice. But, as I have argued above, once documentary came to be regarded primarily as a form of extended journalism – a development concurrent with its emergence as a television genre – it was subject to a wholly new set of discursive constraints within which the lofty imperatives of Griersonianism could only survive as little more than fragments of rhetorical decoration, as 'lineage'.

The case against 'evidentiality' has been more tightly and more productively pursued in relation to later models of documentary, where indexical claims are often much stronger. Television documentary has often made these claims in seeking to fulfil journalistic criteria concerning 'factuality', whilst the vérité or 'fly-on-the-wall' sub-genre (See Chapter 3) has made them as part of its project of purist observationalism, the mere 'relaying' of an ongoing real. Although I pursue questions of vérité style in some detail later, including the criticisms which have been made of its epistemology, it may be useful here to look at some of the broader theoretical issues which it raises. In his valuable (and somewhat under-recognised) study *Television Documentary Usage* (1976), Dai Vaughan presents what is finally a rather ambivalent, if brilliantly perceptive, assessment of the vérité mode, noting the possibilities of the viewing experience it offers at the same time as being concerned about the opportunities for bad faith which it presents to the filmmaker. Among these, the dependence of the whole project on the illusion that the viewer is watching social action in which the actors are unaware of being watched is central. This produces, as Vaughan says, a problematic fusing of putative event (what things *would* have been like without the camera there) with pro-filmic event (what happened when the camera was there). Commitment to a practice of minimal intervention in the direction of the pro-filmic does not address this fusion. Nor does it address the question of the 'authorial' function of editing, in which shot material (however 'pure' in its immediate referentiality) is turned into the basis for a narrative and a diegesis. It is the very lack of *discursive ambi-*

tion in much vérité work, its interest in (at times, its fetishisation of) the observational rather than the expositional, which has made it so vulnerable to criticism in a way which contrasts with the particular vulnerabilities of Griersonian views. Vérité has often been championed as 'bedrock' documentary, not merely drawing on evidential materials but making its entire project the production of them. Vaughan also anticipates the later criticism of Nichols (1983) and Winston (1995) in seeing this emphasis, one in which any overtly sense-making function – critical, analytical, argumentative – is displaced by the activity of 'showing', as encouraging an abnegation of responsibility on the part of the film-maker. An innocence is assumed towards the world and this is either feigned (a mask for persuasive strategies) or genuine (naive). In neither case is the viewer encouraged to develop any self-consciousness in the act of conferring meanings to what is seen and heard (e.g. *whose* meanings, related to *what* larger view?). It is part of Nichols's argument that such discursive 'shyness' (such lack of 'voice' as he puts it) is politically dangerous and, more recently, it figures within Winston's (1995) critique as a retreat from the *intellectual* rigour of documentary practice which has had an influence stretching wider than the vérité form alone. Winston believes that varieties of intensive and engagingly watchable 'showing' have too often replaced investigation, analysis and argument in contemporary television. Of course, for advocates of vérité, it is this 'unvoiced' character which guarantees its 'openness', its apparent placing of the viewer 'in the driving seat', as Nichols deftly puts it.

So that line of critique which is primarily interested in questions of representational form has aimed to 'uncouple' the relationship between putatative reality, pro-filmic reality and screened reality which much documentary depends upon, if not exclusively. It has done this by raising questions about the way in which the pro-filmic is variously modified by the very act of filming, whether through conscious management or otherwise. It has seen the practices of shooting as 'authorial' in themselves (primarily through the positioning, angling, settings and movement of camera) and regarded the phases of editing as involving major transformations not easily distinguished from the transformations of conventional fiction. Since narrative organisation provides a principle of coherence for many documentaries, the links with fiction have been given added emphasis. From the perspective of the strongest of these critiques, documentary is nothing more than a sham – a fraud – which needs exposing. A connection is often made with theories of ideological reproduction, in which relationships of power are variously naturalised and displaced in public communications in such a way as to encourage (if not enforce) a misperception of the real terms within which economic, political and social 'life' is structured. However, theories of ideology have often been prone to miss the actual complexity of representational practice (visual and verbal) in public forms as well as drastically to ignore the processes by which viewers use television in forming their views and dispositions. From this perspective, documentary is just one more cognitively contaminated genre of television, but perhaps one more culpable than most in its claimed and seeming fidelity to the real. I shall come back to the question of ideology in discussing 'reconstructive' theories below, since the ways in which power relations bear on depiction are still of great importance and require far more inquiry. The inadequacy of much recent and current theorising about ideology and documentary points towards the need for greater attention to the issues, not less.[4]

There is no doubt that the project of vérité, with its sometimes extreme epistemological claims, has drawn the most vigorous and perhaps the most cogent critical attacks. But few if any documentaries would want to relinquish the 'indexical warrant' of their images and sounds and therefore few if any documentaries escape the implications of the representational critique.

I want to look now at criticism which has concentrated more on the particular conditions of documentary production (political, economic and socio-cultural) rather than on its forms, though in fact attention to conditions bears finally on questions of form. This kind of criticism may or may not regard *documentarism itself* as a suspect practice – what it concerns itself with is the specific interests being served, the specific voices being heard and being silenced.

Such concern has been expressed about the British Documentary Movement of the 1930s; in fact it is a line of criticism which goes back further than the debate about 'evidentiality'. Much of that work of that movement was done within the essentially 'civil service' setting of film units working on government sponsorship of one kind or another (Grierson was involved in activities, successively, at the Empire Marketing Board, GPO films and later, less directly, at Crown Films (see Aitkin 1990: Chapters 4 and 5). Quite apart from the extent to which this source of funding positioned the documentary film as a form of 'official information' (and therefore as a form of propaganda) rather than a form of independent critical communication, Grierson's own ideas about the 'social purpose' of documentary show, as we have had opportunity to see, the same degree of tension and potential contradiction as do his ideas about documentary's depictive practices. A commitment to imaginative civic education and to the revelation of the 'real' went along with doubts about the efficacy of the democratic process and a belief in the need for national morale to be strengthened and opinion to be 'directed'.[5] Although the films can by no means be read off as simply reflecting their immediate circumstances of funding and production, there has undoubtedly been a considerable degree of taint perceived in these circumstances. This is made more noteworthy by its contrast with Grierson's own inclination to celebrate and ennoble his enterprise. Again, Winston's study (1995) provides an excellent, sceptical commentary on the relationships between ideas, practices and institutional settings at the time.

Broadcast documentary poses the 'institutional' question very differently, as I have noted earlier. It is not usually any direct sponsorship that provides the grounds for suspicion but the location of broadcast production within a set of quite tight, if often implicit, conventions concerning the 'public interest' and 'due impartiality'. Documentary practice exists within the same general climate as news production – encountering problems of non-cooperation from official sources, anxious monitoring from interested parties and potential self-censorship from nervous production executives. It has been argued that the working practices which result from this climate are 'skewed' systematically towards reproducing a dominant view of the political and social world and marginalising where not actively traducing other views. This is documentary as a tool of the established order. In previous writing (Corner 1995a) I have distinguished between the 'univocal' and the 'multivocal' functions of factual programming and such a distinction may be useful here. 'Univocal' functions primarily involve the speech of presenters and commentators, and perhaps the directorial viewpoint as established visually. 'Multivocal' functions involve the selection, combination and weighting of the different voices and viewpoints which a programme may 'access'. Argument that documentary works *for* certain groups and *against* others may choose to highlight one or both of these functions, but they involve rather different communicative methods and (as I shall show in many of the chapters which follow) documentaries use them in very different ways, implicitly and explicitly – sometimes developing a strong univocal strand, sometimes working exclusively through multivocality. All this can greatly increase the complexity of questions about *what* view a programme privileges over others, let alone questions about *how* this privileging is done.

Although the 'Tool of State' perspective has often been expressed in refutably simplistic terms, more subtle commentaries have undoubtedly shown the degree to which documentary accounts – particularly those directly concerning State affairs – *are* frequently subject to considerable circumscription through a mixture of straightforward censorship and an unwillingness to offend senior political figures. This, despite the fact that a strong strand of independent inquiry exists within British current-affairs programming and that it is by no means to be regarded as acting as a straight relay device for the interests of the State. We can see some of these issues exemplifed in the debate surrounding programmes like *Death on the Rock* (Thames Television 1988) which went out on the ITV network despite a strong request from the British Foreign Secretary that it be banned for being in contempt of court. The programme offered a critical investigation of the circumstances surrounding the recent killing of three IRA members by British security forces on Gibraltar. An independent inquiry finally cleared the programme of any substantial breach of propriety in production and format, but not before a strong campaign had been developed against it, a campaign which was to have its influence on the subsequent climate of programme-making.[6] Many other examples from the most confident period of Thatcher government in the 1980s could be cited too, including the siezure of tapes from broadcasting premises by Special Branch police when it appeared that certain 'sensitive' material was about to be aired.[7] Of course, whilst pointing unambiguously to 'pressures', these examples also point to a measure of 'independence'.

A final institutional criticism often made against television documentary should be noted here, although I alluded to it earlier when talking about the influence of vérité's success on the broad character of programming. This is that in the interests of maximising audiences (and profits) television documentary is essentially a part of the entertainment industry and thereby 'generically' lacks the investigative energy and argumentative rigour to offer 'proper' critical analysis. Such a judgement could simply not be upheld against much of British television at the moment, but there are increasing signs of documentary being put under pressure to win larger audiences by becoming 'lighter'.[8] Moreover, some of the most significant hybrids in recent programme development have had a marked 'infotainment' character (see Chapter 11), a trend which is likely to persist. A general, if gradual, movement in the identity of documentary television can therefore be seen to be under way.

Having established a sense of the range of positions from which documentary has been subject to criticism, I want to turn finally to the recipes for reconstruction which have been suggested.

Reconstruction

Those who offer guidelines for redevelopment often do so selectively and with very different aims for documentary in mind. For instance, some are concerned primarily with the documentary as a vehicle for critique operating largely outside of mainstream broadcasting – placing reconstructive ideas in the context of a political and aesthetic development of the 'independent cinema' sector. Others engage with the changing nature of broadcast journalism and relate their recommendations to this. It is important to be clear about purposes, since, as the above discussion has shown, although there is no unity of intention which all the forms of documentary share, this has not stopped much critical debate from carrying a universalistic ring. My own sympathies are with those suggestions making a firm connection with existing broadcast practice rather than with those which are premised on 'alternative' models. For whilst a great deal of innovative work has been done within the 'independent sector' of small units, ones sometimes arranging their own distribution and mostly much less constrained politically and aesthetically by matters of institution and audience, the public significance of documentary work is at its highest when it forms part of the major national and international currency of symbolic exchange.

Perhaps we can start by noting that there are no proposals for somehow strengthening the 'indexical warrant' of documentary, of providing its images and sounds with a surer referential guarantee. Indeed, many reconstructive theories treat 'vérité' formats as beyond redemption. So the attempted reconstruction of documentary starts with the vulnerability of *documentary as record* and does not seek to remedy this. What it does seek to remedy is the nature of *documentary as a discursive practice*. In doing so, ideas vary in the emphasis and role they give to the 'evidential'.

Across different writers, the most common general recommendation has been for documentary work to become more *reflexive*, to 'show its hand' more openly to its audiences. Not suprisingly, enthusiasm for discussing and then for implementing this has been strongest in the independent documentary sector, where the resulting aesthetics of self-consciousness have been perfectly congruent with the minority audience's understandings and expectations concerning political Modernism and the reconfigurations of Postmodernism. Within broadcast television, strong journalistic codes as well as acute anxiety about ratings present problems for self-reflectiveness except when pursued in the most token and minimal of ways (e.g. the occasional shot of the sound-recordist; the brief inclusion in the commentary of remarks about the particular circumstances of the film-making).

Bill Nichols's much-cited article, 'The Voice of Documentary' (1983), gives clear indications of what a more comprehensive approach would entail. Suprisingly, Nichols draws his examples not from Modernist fictional film (e.g. Godard) but from the experimental work of anthropological film-makers like Timothy Asch and David and Judith MacDougall.[9] This work employs such devices as intertitles marking off one scene from another, the regular appearance of the film-makers in the film, the calculated breaking-up into parts of scenes which might conventionally have been constructed in 'narrative continuity' form, and the use of titles as a level of discourse which can placed against speech (as, for instance, in the rendering of the questions and answers of an interview).

Perhaps one of the most important questions raised by reflexive notions of documentary construction concerns just how, and in what way, audience perceptions of the material are changed. Underlying some of the more naive versions of reflexionism there appears to be the suggestion that, *unless it is explicitly indicated otherwise in the film or programme*, audiences will hold to a firm and comprehensive trust in the 'truth' of what they see. They will become the subjects of illusion in a way which produces faulty understanding. Audience research suggests that there are strong grounds for doubting this.[10] As in fiction cinema, 'reminding' the audience that thay are watching a film can carry strong tones of vanguardist condescension. A second problem here is the extent to which reflexive practices work only as occasional, peripheral indicators of the problematic status of the main depiction or, conversely, are integrated into the very *production* of that depiction.

In the latter case, apart from exercises in 'anti-documentary' or exercises in simply advertising the difficulty of doing documentary, the issue is soon raised of how slender the referential claim can be for a depictive discourse which still wants to engage an audience with the 'worldly' status of its sounds and images. A thoroughly self-destabilised documentary may not only have problems of intention and address (it sounds formidably hard viewing), but it may also suffer from problems of regression – how can it deconstruct its own discourses of deconstruction, how can it stop the contribution which untested assertions and assumptions make to its portrayal?

Rather than advocating a specific line of formal development, Brian Winston (1995) switches attention to viewers. He notes that: 'Grounding the documentary idea in reception rather than in representation is exactly the way to preserve its validity' (Winston 1995:253). This will produce a situation in which '[T]he relation of image to imaged depends not on the image's instrinsic quality guaranteed by science but on our reception of it as an image of the real guaranteed by (or corresponding to) our experience' (Winston 1995:253). But this radical shift from 'indexical warrant' to a notion of correspondence grounded in reception effectively subjectivises depiction to the point where it is beyond argument because, in many respects, it is beyond arguable criteria of veracity and adequacy. Documentary becomes radically relativised, placing terminal limitations on its role as one of the key discourses of the public sphere. Such a movement is quite often claimed as a progressive bringing-back of documentary into the ambit of 'fiction' after having its distinctiveness honoured for far too long, though just how this works progressively in the context of specific political and social structures – in, for instance, the formation of consensus and the articulation of conflict – is far from clear.

Winston moves to this position because of what I regard to be a too uncompromising assessment of the play-off between 'actuality' and 'creative treatment' in the traditional version of documentarism. I have referred to his useful discussion of Grierson earlier, but it is interesting to note how, in advancing his ideas on reconstruction, he sees the Griersonian mode in relation to the audience: 'The Griersonian idea of "actuality" depends on an assumption of a particular naivety in the audience. Without such naivety, the audience could not believe that anything of the real would survive "creative treatment"' (Winston 1995:253). '*Anything*' of the real? Isn't it possible for audiences to believe in factors of degree and interplay here rather than to be caught between two absolutes? And isn't it possible (even allowing for more discursive complexity in the production of the referential than might ever become generally realised by audiences) for them to be right?

Factors of degree and of interplay are clearly going to be of the greatest importance in the future of documentary, whatever the tenor of critical debate, reflecting in part the broader hybridisations of television's generic system. Part of the interplay will continue to involve referentiality, the appeal of the indexical, the authenticity of testimony, the revelation of the shot, and so on. It might be useful for those who wish to argue the case for reconstruction to hold all of the above to be problematic without rejecting them entirely as principal modes not only of established image–viewer relations but also of image–imaged relations. This is especially true if recommendations are to have some outcome in changed practice.

A rejection of referential 'purism' (as found very differently in, for instance, versions of vérité and authoritative commentary) and a heightening of the expressive and dramatic element in documentary are to be found extensively in contemporary work and are variously indicated in the works chosen for discussion in this book. The narrative structuring of exposition, providing chronology and causal connections as well as a principle of coherence and engagement, has long been a feature of documentary. Moving close to the conventions of dramatic fiction in some productions, its usage has been partial and less prominent in others. A general shift towards making documentary more attractive is likely to produce narratively prominent formats. It will, indeed, be one of the most interesting aspects of documentary in the late 1990s to see how increased symbolic densities relate to the continuing requirement for realist literalism and to the newer, urgent modes for presenting ongoing actuality (a matter taken up in the last chapter).

Modalities of documentary language

I want to finish this critical survey of theoretical questions by looking more closely at some of the principal depictive modes of documentary discourse. Clearly, these have been a primary element in most, if not all, of the issues and disagreements discussed above, made explicit in my discussion of 'levels' of discourse, but it might be useful to give their formal character more attention and to note significant variations. This is different from attempting a generic typology although it clearly relates to typological matters; it is to identify some of the principal ways in which communication is organised in documentary. Although not strictly speaking 'theory', such identification provides a useful analytic basis for the more intensive investigations of documentary vocabulary and syntax in my subsequent chapters.

I want to suggest that we can divide use of the image up into four modes and speech into three. Simplistic though this may be, it seems to me to catch adequately at the range of existing and emerging practice. In most of these modes, the 'evidential' is variously privileged, a point which unsuprisingly follows from the tenor of the discussion above.

Taking the image first, I would identify as follows:

Evidential mode 1 (reactive observationalism)

This is the mode of minimal directorial intervention in respect of pro-filmic events. It is the mode of 'fly on the wall', which I shall explore with examples in the next chapter, although it is also used outside that particular format. It is an indirect mode, placing the viewer in the position of vicarious witness to ongoing events and often requiring of them a high level of interpretative work in converting the particularity of what is seen and heard into 'significance'. Given the circumstances of filming, it often has very limited scopic mobility (for instance, the filming of an ambulance crew attending a road accident) and cannot offer the range of close-ups, matching shots, complementary shifts of perspective and anticipatory shots by which other modes can enhance their visuality. It is often edited in such a way as to emphasise durational values, temporal sequentiality and immediacy – the use of real-time segments within an overall strategy of time elision being important here. This provides a visualisation of process which is akin to the diegetic plane of dramatic fictional narrative, though without the authorial controls of the latter and therefore far more dependent on the comprehensibility, interest and visual 'strength' of the pro-filmic events themselves. If this is not forthcoming, loss of depictive coherence as well as of viewer engagement can occur.

Evidential mode 2 (proactive observationalism)

Here, a scene or sequence adopts the basic mode of observationalism, but with management of the pro-filmic allowing increased scopic mobility (including continuties of depicted movement), a more discursive use of *mise-en-scène* and smoother time-compressions. One might image a student being filmed boiling an egg in their cramped bedsit as part of a documentary on student loneliness – the fundamental mode is still indirect but the depiction has been more heavily coded, perhaps more richly inflected, as a result of the increased management of movement and space as well as of shooting. Whether these codings of *mise-en-scène*, composition and shot type are marked in the depiction (as self-conscious *styling*) or whether, conversely, they are collapsed into observational 'transparency', will vary with their kind and degree, with directorial choice and with the function to which the sequence is put in the overall documentary design.

Although I do not propose to deal with it here, it is interesting to consider how this mode, when pushed further, can be transformed into that of dramatised reconstruction (not only in one-off productions but also, for example, in recently successful series like the BBC's 999). Here, of course, considerable narrative and depictive controls can be exerted, including that over characterisation (see the next chapter for further development of this point).

The art of record

Evidential mode 3 (illustrative)

This is a mode used widely in current-affairs documentaries. The visualisation is subordinate to verbal discourses, acting in support of their propositions or arguments, which they can frequently only partially 'confirm'. Often, the narrative drive is visually weak (as in many news stories) with low levels of continuity and little if any attempt at achieving the durational values of observationalism. At times, distinguishing between the evidential claims of image and speech in a given combination of the two can not only be difficult but also controversial, as later chapters will show.

Associative mode

Here, the visualisation is primarily engaged in the making of second-order meanings, producing a kind of visual exposition or visual evaluation. This exploitation of the connotations and symbolic resonances generated by pro-filmic, shot type and editing can reinforce, and coexist with, the use of the images for more directly referential purposes. So, for instance, a sequence in a report on life in a South African town can use elements of the pro-filmic (the homes of black and white families, farm implements, children playing, a civic occasion) within a depictive rhetoric of marked symbolic purpose. But some uses of the associative may be primarily aesthetic rather than cognitive, aiming to produce a pleasing representation not necessarily one with increased informational yield. Of course, if this goes beyond a certain point, it may bring a charge of impropriety, a privileging of form over content. Again, a number of the chapters which follow document such charges.

The three modes of speech are somewhat simpler both to identify and describe, at least in the broad terms I am adopting here. I would classify them as follows:

Evidential mode 1 (overheard exchange)

This is the speech of observed subjects, whose ostensible reason for speaking is to be located in pro-filmic action. The way in which action is 'objectified' within the visualisation varies (see reactive and proactive modes above) and the proximity of overheard speech to the coherence and pointedness of dramatic dialogue will vary too, as will the speaker's indications of self-consciousness and of performance.

Evidential mode 2 (testimony)

This is interview speech, variously obtained and used. The marking of interview speech along the axis objective/true – subjective/partial can be achieved by visual editing (including subversive juxtaposition) as well as by sound editing. In the chapters which follow, a number of ways of using interview material will be examined. These include its use as voice-over in a manner which can serve to 're-focalise' visual portrayal (see Branigan 1992) and encourage empathetic feeling from the viewer.

Expositional mode

The 'classic' mode of documentary speech, including full and partial commentary, occasional out-of-frame bridging, presenter direct address, etc. Although eschewed by many recent documentarists as an unacceptably authoritarian mode, expositional voice is still necessary in a range of television productions which require to engage with abstract, propositional matters and to link across disparate visualisations. It is inevitably given to objectification (hence the use of the term 'voice of God' to describe the classic, 'heavy' commentary) but recent documentaries have also used subjectivised exposition effectively, including the dispersal of the expositional function across a number of speakers, seen or unseen.

All these modes are to be found at work within different textual systems in contemporary documentary; my typology is provisional and heuristic. It is clear that it holds implications not just for documentary form, however, but also for the affective and cognitive character of documentary reception, understanding and use. Both implications will be taken up at points throughout the book, in respect of particular forms and, indeed, of specific films and programmes.

In this chapter, I have reviewed some of the more important ways in which ideas about documentary – organised at the level of 'theories' – have posed it as a particular kind of discursive practice. I have looked at the inconsistencies and difficulties of terminology in its foundational phase, a phase of rather grand claims-making, and then at the ways in which it has been situated as a practice to be exposed and denounced. I have considered some theoretical reflections on its future, on its reconstitution (more substantive comments on current tendencies and future possibilities are given in Chapter 11). Finally, I have put forward a basic schema which can inform more detailed attention to the communicative modes of documentarism.

Throughout, I have tried to retain awareness of the fact that the practice has always been more various than the theory and, indeed, that it has often belied theory. That the shapes of documentary-to-come will be determined by a mix of factors amongst which theoretical commentary is unlikely to figure should also 'go without saying'. However, many of those currently writing about documentary regard it as an exciting and an essential form rather than something simply to be either championed or attacked, and I take this to be a very good sign indeed.

Action formats: drama-documentary and vérité

In this chapter I want to explore some of the issues raised by two forms of documentary which have perhaps attracted more critical attention – both from the public and from academics – than any other. These are 'drama-documentary' and 'fly on the wall', or 'vérité'. I realise that to call these 'forms' may suggest a clarity of differentation from other methods and styles and a degree of internal homogeneity which simply is not there. The 'boundaries' between the various modes of documentary are often blurred and they are becoming more so. Nevertheless, both terms indicate broad, but I think useful, groupings within documentary-making internationally, and both indicate clusterings of work with a sufficient level of internal commonality in respect of aims, methods and formal features to justify categorisation. That such categorisation has to be applied with caution when discussing and judging specific documentaries is a point I am very willing to concede.

British drama-documentary has its origins in the 'story documentary' formats used by the documentary film movement in the 1930s and during the Second World War.[1] Its early use in television (from the 1940s) partly compensated for the difficulty and even impossibility of getting 'actuality' footage in certain location settings, given the lack of lightweight equipment and the consequent degree of disruption to pro-filmic activities which filming might cause.[2] 'Reconstruction', often using professional actors, was a means of overcoming the limitations (some of them physical, some of them the product of social and institutional conventions) placed on the camera's access to certain 'real events'. However, the particular dynamics of narrative which 'dramatisation' allowed, together with the distinctive aesthetic and affective properties of the viewing experience offered, also suggested themselves as advantages in gaining and holding a popular audience. Nowadays, an element of dramatisation, including full-scale reconstruction, can be found in many documentary formats, including mainstream, investigative programmes. Dramatisation has become a standard element in the popularisation of documentary journalism, and has been controversially prominent in the shift towards merging 'actuality' with 'entertainment' values in the newer styles of programme concerned, for instance, with the reconstruction of accidents and of crimes. The use of dramatisation as the primary or exclusive mode of depiction also continues within the television schedules, making connections with a variety of fictional narrative styles and often looking and sounding very different from work produced during the 'classic' period of the 1960s, when the development of dramatised documentary ran alongside (and partly merged into) that of the realist television play (see the discussion of *Cathy Come Home* in Chapter 5).

In any discussion of documentary 'dramatisation', it is important to register straight away the difference between using the term 'drama' to indicate the exciting, intensive character of an event (as in conversational and journalistic phrases like 'the drama unfolded', 'things then took a dramatic turn') and as indicating *enactment* – the production of an event precisely for the purpose of spectatorship. In fact, the two usages are often in an awkward relationship with one another both in everyday speech and in television (e.g. dramatic reconstruction is used to give a journalistic report a more 'dramatic' character; our ideas of what is 'dramatic' owe a strong debt to cinematic and televisual fiction). In what follows, however, I shall be mainly interested in 'dramatisation' as involving one form or other of self-conscious enactment, frequently employing professional actors. But I shall be aware of the other meaning, and also aware of the difficulty of distinguishing where 'enactment' can be judged to stop in the necessarily creative and transformative business of documentary-making, which may encourage varieties of 'performance' even where there is no intent to dramatise.

'Fly-on-the-wall' or 'vérité' formats have enjoyed considerable critical attention and ratings success for several years. This kind of documentary minimalism, grounding the account in the following-through of specific pro-filmic events (actions and talk), recorded without directorial intervention and often without use of interview or commentary, has its origins in various French and American experiments of the early 1960s and is predicated on the use of light-weight camera and sound equipment. Though they have now lost their generic novelty (and have thus been increasingly driven to innovation in visual and verbal organisation, often with a need to be popular viewing), vérité programmes are still well represented in the schedules, mostly in series form. As I noted in the previous chapter, over the years, a considerable literature of critical disapproval has developed around the vérité idea, centred upon the general charges of naivety and of 'illusionism'. I shall discuss this more fully below but it worth noting how, despite this, vérité forms remain a potentially powerful way of placing viewers in the position of vicarious witnesses to events at the same time as providing

them with the frisson of social voyeurism. Witnessing and voyeuristic functions have been encouraged and organised in a number of
rather different ways and development continues within television
all over the world, albeit with a reduced sense of orginality. One of
the problems from which vérité work suffers, quite apart from the
self-imposed austerity of its discourse (mostly organised to offer *revelation* rather than *exposition* and generally disinclined to 'tell' the
viewer much directly), is its heavy reliance on a certain type of pro-
filmic circumstance for both the interest and the narrative shape of
the account. That is to say, vérité programmes have frequently projected themselves as 'interesting' in direct relation to the fascination
which certain kinds of (often institutionalised) circumstances hold
for viewers – hospitals, police stations, army training camps and
schools have, for instance, all been well represented. Of course,
every documentary is to some extent dependent on its subject-
matter for generating viewer interest, but it is the precise form
which this dependence takes in the vérité programme, and then the
way in which it manifests itself formally (through, for instance, the
management of chronology and the according of durational values)
which is distinctive. I shall say more about this later. Just as
'dramatisation' cannot be firmly separated off from that low level of
enactment which is a potential factor in nearly all documentary
production, so vérité styles cannot be neatly separated from that
much more general mode of observation (the business of onlooking
and overhearing) which has been one of the defining modalities of
documentary production since the earliest pioneers. Moreover, in its
concern to present to the viewer the sense of an ongoing plane of
action (mostly of social interaction) located within given spatial and
temporal limits and apparently unmodified by the camera's presence, vérité has a paradoxical relationship with 'drama'. This has
been a key point of debate in critical analysis both of particular films
and programmes and of the general philosophy (essentially, a social
epistemology) of vérité. It is also interesting to note how, like
dramatisation, vérité has been a central strand informing the newer
styles of 'infotainment' internationally.

In what follows I want to offer some thoughts on the separate, if
sometimes related, histories of dramatisation and of vérité documentary on British television. I shall need to be highly selective,
since the range of material defies comprehensive treatment in the
space available. In my historical references, I shall draw extensively
on the primary studies that have so far been made of the written
and visual archive (much more work of this kind needs to be done).
My main concern, though, is not so much to offer a concise history
of productions as to trace the development of the debates surrounding both forms. These are clearly acknowledged and contributed to by documentarists themselves as well as by critics,
viewers and by those various representatives of official and institutional life (often governmental, public or corporate) who have felt
the need to protest at particular depictions using the dramatic or

the vérité form, and who have often questioned the general legitimacy of the approach. I want to address the overall socio-textual character of both bodies of work and to set this in a context of development, but in order to do this effectively I shall regularly draw on particular examples.

First of all, dramatisation.

The drama-documentary mix

I noted above how the term 'drama' could be applied in two rather different ways to documentary material, even if both ways are finally related. One of these ways, the one with which I am most concerned, is to do with enactment, the bringing to documentary work of the scripting, acting and directional approaches of fiction. It is also possible to see the combination of dramatic with documentary approaches as being organised within the terms of one or other of two main kinds of 'recipe'. The approach of 'dramatised documentary' begins with a documentary base or core and uses dramatisation to overcome certain limitations and to achieve a more broadly popular and imaginatively powerful effect. The other approach, 'documentary-drama', is essentially a form of *play*, but a form which is seen to develop a documentary character either as a result of its scale of referentiality to specific real events (private or public or both), *or* because of its manner of depiction. These different reasons for making an attribution of 'documentariness' to a play need to be kept apart in discussion.

In fact, quite apart from the general problem of critical subjectivity in using such classifications, maintaining a clear distinction between the two 'models' becomes hard to do when confronted with certain examples (of which *Cathy Come Home* (BBC 1966), discussed in Chapter 5, is one). Nevertheless, the differentiation still seems to me to have analytic value, even where it is finally confounded.[3] We can apply it to the earliest television work to use a 'mixed' approach.

Television documentary and 'dramatisation' in the 1950s

I have noted above how the 'story documentary' was one of the forms used by the official film documentarists of the Second World War. Although there were stylistic variations between the films, the essential idea was to take a documentary theme (the submarine service, for example, or the nightly bombing raids of the Royal Air Force) and treat this by 'particularising' it around a storyline with characters which could be given an intimate rendering using the depictive methods of feature fiction. The result mixed informational throughput with narrative satisfactions, allowing for empathy with the main figures of portrayal, whose experiences and whose personal qualities were projected with far greater intensity and focus than more conventional documentary formats could have achieved.

One can usefully talk here of the *proxemics* of the dramatisation – its capacity to 'bring us close' to the local human detail within the larger themes and sphere of action being addressed. This is in contrast to the necessary, and sometimes emphatically maintained, 'distance' at which a conventional documentary works, through its mixture of observation and commentary. Viewers were invited not to an exposition but to the witnessing of an 'imitation of an action', to use Aristotle's classic phrase about the character of drama.

As with later forms of 'story documentary', the difference from the range of conventional feature fictions was discernible in a number of ways. Apart from the intermixing of the dramatic material with 'actuality' sequences, perhaps the most obvious of these was the relationship between the 'story' core of the film and the wider project of 'documentation'. Although feature films (including wartime features) frequently provided a strong 'real life' context for their stories, the 'story documentary' had an economy of depiction which required it continuously to register the nature of circumstances – both local and general – which were happening 'to the side' of the main narrative. This might mean closing in to focus on particular procedural matters (aircraft bomb loading; the adjustment of course on a warship's bridge) or pulling back to look at the more general circumstances and processes of which the dramatised events were simply one part. The movement out from story to documentation and back (sometimes smoothly achieved, sometimes awkward) is nearly always of a kind which would be considered deviant within the conventions of realist feature film-making; there is simply *too much* time spent 'out of story' looking at detail or establishing context. Only when one assumes an audience coming to the film with *some* expectations about being informed as well as entertained would the subsequent dispersal effect exerted on character interest and plot development be considered justifiable. I shall return to these points about the early 'story documentary' later, since the precedent has exerted a considerable influence not only on realist tendencies in subsequent British cinema but on developments in television fiction.

The television documentarists of the 1950s were well aware of the 'story documentary' mode; indeed many of them had worked on wartime productions themselves. However, their own use of 'dramatisation' was initially prompted by a different set of requirements. Paramount here was the need to produce documentary television about circumstances and processes which could not be filmed directly either because of restrictions on television access or because of the technical limitations placed on 'live' broadcasting. Without the option of videotape recording and with the expense of location shooting on film, the obvious 'solution' was dramatic reconstruction in the studio. Within these exigencies, the kinds of narrative intensity and explorations of person, action and space available to the wartime film productions were simply not a possibility. In the more modest productions, the situation was in many ways akin to

Drama-documentary and vérité

that of the 1930s documentarists, who had frequently resorted to 'scenic reconstruction' (e.g. the cabin of a fishing vessel; the 'sorting office' of a mail train) within films having no continuous dramatic diegesis. There was still the emphasis on the 'imitation of an action'; the procedures of drama were allowing relations of proximity and offering an experience of witnessing. But the simulacrum was often a means of making up for the non-availability of the original, rather than a means of managing affective power and scopic field for full dramatic satisfaction. In her excellent account of BBC documentary production during this period, Elaine Bell notes the general character of this kind of studio-based work:

> Among topics dealt with in this period were hooliganism, borstal, drugs, working women, children in care, problems of youth, marriage and old age, prostitution, industrial relations and declining industries, while such series as *Made By Hand*, *I Made News*, *Pilgrim Street* (about police methods) and the much praised *Course of Justice*, which illustrated legal procedure by individual cases, were made. (Bell 1986:74)

Interestingly, Bell also notes how the BBC regarded this kind of work with some anxiety as to the status attributed to it by audiences. For instance, an internal memo notes with disappointment that an issue of the *Radio Times* had included a cast list for such a production, a practice which its author thinks will 'kill the reality of the programme'. There was anxiety too about repeating dramatised documentaries. Whilst it was common practice for plays to be repeated 'live' (i.e. the same cast going through the whole thing again in front of the cameras), it was thought that this might greatly reduce the status of documentary output. It is hard to credit the level of condescension towards the audience suggested by some of these attitudes. They indicate both a full awareness of the extent to which artifice has replaced reality in the production but a concern not to let this knowledge spoil the 'illusion' for the viewer. In this early phase of engagement with the issues of creativity and truth generated by the 'mix', there are clear signs of the themes which would become more contested and more complicated in later documentary and 'realist' developments.

In a 1956 discussion of 'The Story Documentary', Caryl Doncaster, an experienced television director of such programmes, gives some interesting glimpses of the view from the production end. One section is worth quoting in full:

> The story documentary, however, has little in common with the straight drama, which depends for its effect on what the writer has to say, the strength of his plot with which he captivates our interest while he is saying it, and that 'suspension of disbelief' which his audience must feel when watching, be it on the television set at home, at the theatre or in the cinema. The writer of the story documentary should never allow his own opinions on the subject he interprets to deflect him from impartiality. He must try to present each facet of the problem in true perspective.
>
> As for plot, he is trying to present a cross-section of life; therefore, what plot he uses must only exist to give shape and cohesion. He can

never make use of deus ex machina, the happy ending, the numerous other theatrical devices which untie the knots. On the other hand, he is not trying to suspend the disbelief of his audience for, through his technique both as writer and producer, the viewer is presented with reality itself. (Doncaster in Rotha 1956, cited in Goodwin *et al.* (eds) 1983:8)

The self-denying character of the production ethos is here apparent, though we might well think the claims about showing 'reality itself' and the maintenance of a 'true perspective' to beg several very large questions.

Related to the issue of 'artifice', its legitimacy and modes, are the issues of generic distinction and generic blurring and therefore of audience perceptions and expectations. Even in the 1950s, a clear differentiation between what was and what was not 'dramatised' could be hard to make. Bell cites the example of Maurice Wiggin, television critic of *The Sunday Times*. Wiggin had stated his dislike of the dramatised documentary method in terms which were to become familiar: 'The whole point of a documentary is that it is literally true ... . If it is not literally true, it is not documentary but something else ... a kind of play-writing ... . We have had too much fact-based fiction cooked up in the studio and played by professional actors.' Later on in his article, he had contrasted such productions with a recent documentary about a London hospital at night. Of this he commented: 'we saw the real thing, directly. It was more impressive than any documentary done in the studio.' However, as Bell points out, drawing on other contemporary sources:

[This programme] was a 'built OB' [Outside Broadcast], a totally scripted and rehearsed programme in which the people concerned were speaking lines learned by heart and performing movements worked out by the producer. The performers were actually playing the roles they played in real life, in the setting in which they actually worked, but nevertheless were acting in a scripted programme. (Bell 1986:76)

This raises the question of the different levels of fabrication which a production can employ, some perhaps being seen as more significant for the status of the programme than others (the use of actors is clearly a major factor here). Wiggin may have been naive, but his wish to differentiate between studio-based, professionally acted productions and location-shot ones employing people in their 'real' roles is not undercut by the example, even if the terms in which he expressed it are problematised. We can also see here how the notion apparently lying behind his comments, a desire for television access to a reality which is not only free of the studio and of professional artifice but also of *any* modification introduced by television's presence, connects directly with the later project of vérité.

The arrival of new technology in the form of lightweight 16mm film cameras and subsequently of videotape removed most of the conditions which had made early dramatised documentary on television an expedient and popular response to limitations. Dramatisation was no longer quite so 'necessary' and projects of the kind described above were less frequently found in the schedules. However, as the wartime experience had shown, the dramatisation of documentary material was still an effective way of performing certain communicative functions, of producing certain 'effects', and new types of function and new depictive modes were to emerge. Nor did the problem of 'access' disappear; it simply moved to a higher level as television developed more ambititous notions about where it might 'go' and what types of rendering of the real it might present to the viewer (see Kilborn 1994b on this point).

Documentary and the realist play

Dramatisation of varying kinds continued to be used in documentary work but there is no doubt that the return to prominence of drama-documentary as an issue had much to do with developments in the realist play during the 1960s. To some extent following tendencies in literature and then cinema (charted in Laing 1986), a number of television playwrights became more concerned with using character and story to explore aspects of social change and social class. Plays were often based on intensive research and their stories were given an extensive grounding in social circumstance, frequently realised in location shooting. Character and action were located in a contingent universe of work, home and environment which often departed from established dramatic conventions, not only in the emphasis placed on 'context' but also in the degree to which this context was 'ordinary' and often 'working-class' – introducing strong themes of class difference and class tension into the dramatic mix. There was, in much of this work, a 'sociological' seriousness and commitment which, in some people's perceptions, gave it a thematic proximity to documentary productions quite apart from questions of depictive style. In their earlier years, the hugely popular serials *Coronation Street* (Granada 1960-) and *Z Cars* (BBC 1962-65) were also seen to have at least an element of this 'documentarist' ambition informing their construction.[4] In the case of Z Cars this is immediately obvious both in theme and form; the series idea was actually developed by the BBC Documentary Drama Group (whose change of name from the Dramatized Documentary Group is significant (see Goodwin *et al.* (eds) 1983:3).

Much of the debate through the 1960s and into the mid-1970s surrounded productions which, drawing on a variety of recipes for their 'mix', offered radical, critical portrayals of contemporary British political and social life. These productions not only showed a convergence with the work of radical television drama noted above, they increasingly emerged from *within* this strand of work. Allowing for the caveats I have placed on the use of the distinction, one can say that here it was the drama which was increasingly given a documentarist articulation, rather than the reverse. *Cathy Come Home* (BBC 1966), about the housing shortage in contemporary Britain, is perhaps the most celebrated of the 1960s hybrids and since I have given an entire chapter over to its analysis and significance, I shall be very brief in my comments here. *Cathy* is based on detailed research into the kinds of circumstances depicted in the film. It dramatises these circumstances through the use of a single narrative concerning 'one case' – fabricated from material drawn from a wide range of real cases and developed into a dramatic fiction. The portrayal of this constructed 'typical' instance is grounded in the then developing conventions of realist dramatic fiction but it also uses a number of more directly documentary conventions, such as the use of anonymous 'testimony' to camera, the use of expert and vox-pop voice-over, the occasional use of a visual field and mode of cutting imitating the modes of television reportage. The extent to which it circumscribes plot and character development in the interest of maintaining a connected thematic address to housing problems marks it out as 'different', even for socially realist drama. The amount of research which informs its thematic aspects also suggests a documentary project, although, as such, it is invisible to the viewer. Finally, the frequent use of documentary conventions within the depiction itself, including voiced-over statistics and other information, seems to anticipate and encourage a level of documentary reading, without thereby deceiving the audience that it is watching actuality footage.

Yet, on the other hand, the programme went out in the weekly *Wednesday Play* slot, is titled as 'a film by Jeremy Sandford' in the opening credits, uses an established actress as its lead and includes a large number of scenes which both in terms of the social space they explore (private encounters, arguments, love-making) and the mode of this exploration (close-ups, shot-reverse-shot sequences, continuity matches) draw on the language of realist fiction. Given all these factors, *Cathy* is something of a one-off event – a television 'original' – in the development of British drama-documentary, putting pressure on the conventions derived from both sides and, not suprisingly, acting as a frequent focus for debate about television's capacities as a medium not only for engaging with the real but, reflexively, with the dominant modes of its own representations. I say more about this in Chapter 5.

Peter Watkin's *The War Game* (BBC 1965, not transmitted) is another highly original programme which deserves mention here. This depiction of a nuclear attack on a British town was banned from transmission at the time (though distributed to certain cinemas) for reasons which have now been clearly established as to do with the politics surrounding government nuclear deterrence policy.[5] As with so many other 'controversial' drama-documentaries, objections which were primarily about the substantive content and viewpoint expressed were strategically displaced into becoming objections about the unacceptability of the form itself. Thus disagreement over *issues*, risking an engagement around specific evidence and argument, becomes disguised as a fear about 'deception' in communicative *style*. As we have already seen, this frequently involves considerable condescension towards ordinary viewers, who are often regarded as being at serious risk of miscognition and duping. *The War Game* is certainly a very disturbing film. Using a sort of 'time-capsule' approach, it places the viewer as witness to catastrophic events in the future, as Britain enters a nuclear war. The passage from frantic preparation for possible attack through to the strike itself and the phases of physical, pyschic and social deterioration which follow, is depicted in a brilliantly edited mix of newsreel, vérité and interview sequences. Continuity is provided by keeping the main focus on one locality. Unlike *Cathy*, *The War Game* contains few depictions which draw on conventional dramatic portrayal. Its entire visual and aural system reproduces the immediacy and rawness of actuality materials. In this respect, it is not so much a dramatised documentary as an imitation documentary. However, the work of the imitation draws upon historical and contemporary sources in order to put forward an argument about the 'way it would be' were a nuclear conflict to occur. This use of a researched base, not to inform a propositional discourse of prediction but a dramatic discourse of imagined occurrence, lies at the heart of *The War Game*'s distinctiveness and power. Of course, as with *Cathy*, the programme was freed from the normative constraints of 'balance' affecting conventional documentary production and was able to organise its 'imitative coverage' of future events around the implicit point of view that the nuclear deterrent policy was senseless and likely to end in disaster. In part it did this by showing the *horrific particularity* of a nuclear strike and by placing the viewer as a vérité observer of it, utilising television's most potent ways of coding actuality (including present-tense reportorial commentary). This approach works on the assumption that although people know that such a conflict would be horrible, they can still be so 'shocked' by looking at its specific manifestation as to be caused to reject their previous 'abstract' acquiescence in nuclear deterrent policy. This 'power of the particular' is a major factor in assessing the public profile and capacity to disturb of drama-documentary work and I shall refer to it again at other points in the book.

In the mid-1970s, the public debate about hybrid forms flared up again in discussion of *Days of Hope* (BBC 1975), a series of four plays by the writer Jim Allen about the working class and class politics from 1914 to the General Strike of 1926. The series was produced by Tony Garnett and directed by Ken Loach, the same team behind Sandford's *Cathy*. The depictive approach was grounded in dramatic realism. This was overlaid in certain scenes by a 'documentary naturalism' which shot actions as if the camera was following them spontaneously (hurried and often awkward composition within the frame, adjustments of focus and occasional 'blocked' shots) and used dialogue which was only part-scripted, allowing for improvisation.[6] Certainly, these codings of reportage (some of them comparable to devices used in Cathy) gave heightened immediacy values to the drama without encouraging the viewer to believe that they were, indeed, watching actuality. What seemed to have caused the 'problem' was the coincidence of a sense of historical authenticity with a radical left-wing view of the politics of the period. Although the plays were conceived throughout in terms of narrative fiction, the tightness of their referentiality to certain real events, the emphasis they put on political and social setting and then the radical intepretation they worked with, caused some people once again to remark on the illegitimacy of mixed forms. A *Times* leader on the series noted:

> In a documentary political objectivity and historical accuracy are essential qualities; in a play they can have a depressing effect on the creativity of the author or producer. So it is important to retain a clear distinction in the mind of the viewer. (*The Times*, 30 September 1975)

This ponderous advice was really unnecessary – it is very hard to imagine any viewer believing that the detailed rendering of often very personal events set in the 1920s was a 'documentary' in *any* conventional use of that term. But viewers *were* presented with a critical treatment of political history surrounding and informing the personal story. Once again, anxiety over the substance of what was being 'said' became displaced into claims about deceit in the 'saying'. As in the case of *The War Game*, the extent to which these complaints were made from a position of strategic bad faith should not be underestimated.

The mid-1970s also saw important developments at the other end of the spectrum from documentary drama, in Granada's dramatised documentary department. Here, the emphasis was on the dramatic treatment of specific circumstances, involving the 'reconstruction' of particular incidents from all available evidence, including tape recordings, court transcripts, other contemporary documents, and research with the co-operation of participants and witnesses. In 1970, Granada had produced *The Man Who Wouldn't Keep Quiet*, based on detailed documentation of a Russian dissident's imprisonment in a mental institution. With Leslie Woodhead as director and/or producer, it continued to do dramatised work on East European themes throughout the decade, with perhaps the most notable productions being *Invasion* (1980 – about the invasion of Czechoslovakia) and *Strike* (1981 – about the Polish shipyard strike at Gdansk and the development of 'Solidarity' as a political movement). These productions drew extensively on dramatic imagination, but the degree of documentary evidence which went into the script and the tightness of relationship to real events and to real people gives them a distinctive character, more constrained in its use of conventionally dramatic language (Woodhead has highlighted the prioritising of documentary values in his striking comment: 'we made bad plays'[7]). It is worth noting how the attempted 'reconstruction' of specific real events in local detail continues to gives certain drama-documentary projects a special socio-discursive profile. This is in contrast to the more loosely referential 'based on' formulas which often attract playwrights and the even looser relationship of contextual circumstances to historical reality in mainstream realist fiction. Of course, this is not to make any judgements about the 'social truth' contained in a depiction, documentary or dramatic, but simply to note the different kinds of referential relation which are claimed, against which questions of 'accuracy' may be raised, as well as questions of interpretative acceptability. ATV's *Death of a Princess* (1980), concerning romantic affairs within the Saudi Arabian Royal Family, is an interesting example of a reconstructive narrative using 'modernist' devices to play off various accounts of 'what happened' against each other. The programme, press commentary on it and the controversy it caused are well explored in Petley (1983).

In recent British television, documentary dramatisation has used a wide range of styles. For instance, it has employed the model of the international thriller (as in Granada's *Why Lockerbie?* (1990) about the Pan-Am aircraft bomb) and the disaster movie (as in the BBC's *Valdez* (1993) about the Alaskan oil spill). The dramatised use of the depictive codes of documentary, so evident in 1960s work, has given way to more consistent and conventionally dramatic modes of portrayal, if with plot, characterisation and action constrained by informational and contextual requirements (Kilborn (1994b) and Petley (1996) explore these shifts further). So, for instance, in *Shoot To Kill* (Yorkshire TV 1990), a drama-documentary about the operation of armed police units in Northern Ireland, although referentiality was established by a tightly specific indication of names, places and dates, and although the drama opened out to include a whole range of 'procedural' sequences in order to carry the indirect exposition, the depiction did not at any point 'imitate' documentary portrayal.

At the end of this chapter, I want to look briefly at the future both for drama-documentary fusions and for vérité on television, but it may be useful to conclude here by noting again the key issues around which the drama-documentary issue has turned. These can be itemised as follows:

1 The 'referentiality' issue. What tightness of relationship does the programme claim with real events? Is it using a 'based on' licence or attempting as faithful as possible a 'reconstruction'? 'Based on' formulas can either allow dramatic transformations of specific events or, as in *Cathy*, allow the fictive construction of a 'typical' case from research on real incidents.

2 The 'representation' issue. How does the programme look and sound? Is there an attempt to imitate the codes of documentary and thereby generate (if only 'in play') reportage values? Is there a mix of dramatic with more conventional documentary material? What are the possibilities for 'deception', for a viewer attributing an incorrect status to the depiction at any point?

3 The 'manipulation' issue. This relates to 1 and 2. The charge is made that viewers are encouraged to give truth status to unsubstantiated or purely imaginary elements, and, furthermore, that the commu-

nicative, affective power of the dramatic treatment is likely to install accounts in the mind of the viewer with force and depth.

4   The 'thematic' issue. In what ways does the point of view given prominence in the programme relate to 'official' positions and attitudes? How is a 'debate' of ideas set up within the programme? As we have seen, behind some of the apparent concern expressed about hybrid forms lies the straightforward objection to views being aired which run counter to dominant dispositions and policies.

Perhaps the most important aspect of drama-documentary as controversial form, across its various manifestations, is the linking together of a 'viewpoint' discourse with discourses of strong referentiality and of high imaginative potency. I have suggested that a distinction between the dramatising of documentary accounts and the 'documentarising' of drama can be analytically useful, although I have also suggested that firm distinctions are hard to draw and that certain programmes confound them altogether. As television's generic system shows an increasing tendency towards hybridisation and reflexiveness, this 'blurring' is likely to continue, but so is public debate about programmes which combine dramatic with journalistic values in relation to sensitive political and social themes.

For the student of non-fiction television, one of the most engaging aspects of these formats is the way in which they pose more general questions about the transformative character of television–reality relationships. These questions concern presumed epistemologies, research and production methods, depictive forms and modes of viewer engagement and understanding. The history of the more controversial programmes also offers us a valuable insight into specific instances of the political and social formations within which television's 'knowledge' is formed and distributed.

Vérité as method and form

I noted in my introduction that the minimalism of vérité has its origins in the kinds of innovative film-making which followed the introduction of lightweight 16mm cameras in the 1960s. The distinctive viewing experience which it offers and its often strong truth claims have made it perhaps the most discussed of contemporary documentary formats, attracting a range of excellent commentary and criticism.

Although its lineage is often unified, two distinctly different 'traditions' of early work can be traced. In his recent, richly documented, account of documentary history, Brian Winston (1995) reminds us of this and reflects on its implications. The French *cinéma vérité* movement, with which the work of the anthropologist Jean Rouch is most often associated, was in fact very *un*like modern television vérité in its approach. Far from wishing to render the camera 'invisible' and to project what happens before it as some magical capturing of the spontaneous, Rouch and his associates showed the film-making process intervening in the events filmed, with participants not only looking at, but also addressing, the film-makers. The most famous of Rouch's films is *Chronique d'un été* (1960), shot in in co-operation with the sociologist Edgar Morin and involving several groups of people, who are seen discussing contemporary political issues in various 'casual' settings. Winston describes the way in which its project is a reflexive one:

> It is at constant pains to remind us that filming is in progress. For instance ... Morin is seen closing a window, and thereby revealing the reflection of a light, prior to questioning Marilou.
>
> Rouch and Morin manipulate and condition the film at every turn, most importantly by insisting that the topics they think significant are dealt with by the other participants. If something was being missed they arranged a meal and, again on camera, bullied the others into discussion. (Winston 1995:185)

Despite this open interventionism and declared 'authorship', however, Winston sees the film's project as finally grounded in a firm commitment to the 'evidentiality' of film (even if, here, the evidence includes that of the film-making) and in that regard as open to criticism. What I want to do here, though, is simply to follow him in noting the difference between this strand of work and the activities of the 'direct cinema' directors in the United States, the most famous of whom were Don Pennebaker, Richard Leacock, Frederick Wiseman and Robert Drew. There are considerable variations in the work of these directors (again, Winston's account is both thoroughly researched and suggestive on this issue) but their film-making practices shared the common principle of 'following' ongoing action through a method which worked, precisely, to render the film-making itself invisible and to give viewers the sense of unmediated access to the contingencies of an actuality uncompromised by the camera.

Vérité television in Britain

I can do no more than indicate just some of the modes and the shifts which have occurred in the development of 'vérité' as a sub-genre of documentary within British television. However, no account could leave out two series – *The Family* (BBC 1974) and *Police* (BBC 1982), since these atttracted a popular audience, became the subject of widespread comment and attracted a useful critical literature. In surveying more recent work I want to give some attention to *The Living Soap* (BBC 1993–94), since this attempt to present aspects of student domestic life became caught up in a number of problems, in a sense putting the vérité form into near-crisis as a result of attempted innovation.

The new forms of documentary depiction explored by the 'pioneer' work in France and the United States quite soon provided British television documentary teams with possibilities for their own shooting and editing. As Winston points out, however, it was the non-interventionist, observationalist, 'direct' cinema which was used as the primary model, rather than the reflexive approach of the *cinéma vérité* movement, even though the term 'ciné-vérité' and then 'vérité' became used interchangeably with 'fly on the wall' to indicate the developing strand of television work.

A 1968 *World in Action* programme, 'The Demonstration' (edited by Dai Vaughan, also a distinguished writer on documentary), is a good early example of vérité being used at the level of a significant programme component. The programme focuses on a London demonstration against the Vietnam War, a demonstration which eventually becomes a major confrontation between protesters and police in Grosvenor Square, in front of the United States' embassy. Coverage of this confrontation becomes the core of the programme, lasting some ten minutes or so and having no soundtrack save the noise of the conflict itself. Surrounding it are much more clearly structured sequences, connecting together different spaces and times in order first of all to present a 'build-up' to the Grosvenor Square events and then to present an 'aftermath' in which various assessments are made of it. The core sequence is explicitly placed as 'evidence' within this overall structure, a chance for the viewer to make up their own mind about events which have, in the gap between shooting and screening, become a matter of debate in Parliament and an issue of public interest and concern. This sequence combines (1) shots which place the viewpoint 'in' the crowd, being jostled in out-of-focus proximity to police and protesters, with (2) mid-range shots showing specific incidents (scuffles, arrests, the throwing of smoke-bombs) and (3) long-range shots taken from the top of adjacent buildings which serve to locate the whole event. Thus the movement is between an overall sense of the event's scale and appearance and more local perceptions of activity.

Shown to students today, this is still a powerful piece of footage for reasons which are both substantive and formal. The absence of commentary and the marked durational quality of the sequence (although, of course, considerable time-lapse is employed) project a remarkable quality of 'rawness'. It is interesting, too, how it can be used to support readings both of police brutality and of the unacceptability of the protesters' behaviour. Such variant readings depend partly on the relative emphasis given to certain shots (e.g. police dragging a protester along by the hair; protesters attempting to knock a policeman off his horse with a banner pole) and partly on interpretative variation in reading more 'open' shots (e.g. of crowd scuffles with no clear indication of causality). However, few of the students to whom I have shown the sequence over the years have wanted to question its basic reliability as 'evidence'. For a start, the very fact that it is such a large public event seems to work against any idea of people producing a 'performance' for the cameras, as does the very intensity of their participation. As I shall bring out more fully later, anxieties about 'behaviour modification' constitute a major ground for audience suspicion of vérité. Another ground for such suspicion is the manipulative possibilities provided by editing, particularly where high shooting ratios require considerable selectivity to be exercised. Here though, the relative 'unity' of the event in space and time does not suggest cause for worry in the way that a more dispersed pro-filmic event might do. That the film-makers could have *intentionally* omitted certain scenes and emphasised others (the question of the perceived balance between 'police violence' and 'crowd violence' is pertinent) is sometimes raised in discussion, but is generally seen to require too extreme a view about calculated deception for it to be plausible in this context. Moreover, what degree of depicted 'police violence' there is has enough force to persuade viewers who might have held this view that it is not applicable here. It is worth mentioning, finally, the question of coherence and 'watchability', since this will also arise later as a more general issue. Were the sequence to go on much longer than it does, it is clear that problems would emerge. As the informational yield of the sequence starts to provide diminishing returns, the shots having explored a certain number of aspects of the incident and been 'shocking' in different ways, then engagement begins to slip away. Without a commentary to generate propositional and descriptive meanings (not usually admitted within the vérité mode) or 'overheard' conversation to provide a degree of narrative continuity in terms of character and interaction (usually present, and often primary, in vérité) the sustainability of the sequence is seriously threatened.

Although not properly an example of television 'vérité' in so far as it is only a section of a programme, this *World in Action* sequence sets up some useful ideas about the strengths and limitations of the approach and I shall refer back to it in what follows.

The Family (1974)

In 1974, *The Family* was made for BBC television by Paul Watson. This was a twelve-week series looking at the daily lives of one family in Reading, the Wilkins. The Wilkins were a working-class family and their relationships included some elements that were to prove significant in the response to the series. Mr and Mrs Wilkins were living together but one child had been fathered by another man during a temporary separation. The eldest son had married his pregnant girlfriend, the eldest daughter lived in the house with her boyfriend, the youngest daughter had a half-black boyfriend. For several weeks, the BBC team filmed them selectively throughout the day, without using lights. They had keys to the house and came and went according to their own schedule. The 'observationalist' material shot in this manner was organised within the programmes into a chronologicial sequence of episodes, with fades indicating the passage of time.

A number of interesting questions are posed by *The Family*, some of which have a more general import. Like much vérité the series is *institutional* in focus in so far as observed particularity gets its significance from the *kind* of activities being observed – here 'family life'. This does not provide such a tight connection between particular and general as does, for instance, *Police* or other successful series like *The Duty Men* (on customs officers) or *Sailor* (on life at sea) since the 'typicality' by which such a connection is made is more obviously open to dispute. In fact, it was hotly disputed by some television critics and by members of the public writing to newspapers (see the commentary in Young 1974). Nevertheless, it is clear from the film-maker's own remarks that it was aspects of contemporary family life and the reflection of larger political and social shifts within it rather than a specific interest in the Wilkins themselves which was considered to be of primary interest.

The idea of 'domestic vérité' clearly raises a number of special problems. For a start, the question of 'performance', of behaviour modified in response to the camera's presence, is likely to become much more acute than in instances where the situations which are shot involve large public groupings (as in 'The Demonstration') or the carrying out of official duties (as in *Police*). There is simply more individual space for performance in the domestic setting: less rigidity in the requirements of the professional/occcupation function to serve as a counterbalance to the self-conscious status of the observed as an 'observee'. Against this might be set the claim (actually made by the programme team) that by their routine presence, the film-crew became semi-naturalised into the Wilkins's home life and that, as a result, normative patterns of behaviour were quickly re-established. A further line of argument is to claim that viewers quickly learn to recognise modified behaviour and to 'allow' for it variously in their interpretations of persons and actions. I want to return to this issue of the modifying presence of the camera in different kinds of vérité.

A further, distinctive aspect of the domestic focus is the particular kind of viewing relation entailed by the proximity in which viewers are placed to personal matters. The question of social 'voyeurism', of taking a kind of prying and snooping pleasure in what is seen and heard, is never very far away in vérité. Clearly, a series which spends so much time depicting the 'private' is likely to raise it in a strong form. The modes of viewing which result are then likely to relate directly to those which are entailed in the viewing of popular drama series – character interest (involving identification, empathy and dislike), the following of fluctuations in personal relationships, the more general movements of emotional life. That the series was a 'real-life soap opera' was often suggested in critical commentary on the series (this would become a far more prominent and intentional element of later versions of domestic vérité). Defenders of the series (including Roger Graef, who had been an early proponent of the general method in his own *The Space Between Words* series for the BBC in 1970 and who was later to make *Police*) argued not only for its sociological integrity but also its therapeutic value. Graef interpreted criticism of the series as often stemming from the 'unnerving' effect which the programmes had both on viewers' sense of conventional family life and on their conventional expectations of television portrayal. Collapsing together substantive and formal aspects of the series in a rather risky way, Graef concluded that

> They [viewers] could cope, I think, if the films were heavily narrated; or packaged with analysis before, during and after the events; or, better yet, set in remote tribal lands, in which our taboos would not be touched. But to present to British families other British families, unexplained, is to confront them most uncomfortably. And they panic, lest the box turn into a mirror. (Graef 1974: 772–3)

The Family raises, then, a number of questions about the application of the vérité method to the domestic sphere. These concern the effect of the camera's presence on behaviour, the relationship projected between particular and general, and the play-off between the kinds of knowledge, pleasure (including voyeuristic pleasure) and indeed discomfort which viewing can generate. In some reviews of the series, the idea of 'access' also figured – in the suggestion that the very ordinariness of the Wilkins, their difference from the usual run of people appearing on television, was a factor in some of the criticism which it received. This was interpreted positively, as at least pointing towards a more comprehensive accessing of the 'ordinary' on our screens (both Graef 1974 and Young 1974 put this case well). The interconnection of 'access' ideas with the vérité approach, an interconnection which alters the kinds of enunciative relations at work within the depiction, also occurs in later programmes, as I shall show.

Police (1982)

The 13 part series *Police*, directed by Roger Graef for the BBC and screened in early 1982, was perhaps the most watched and the most controversial of vérité applications on British television. The series was made with the co-operation of the Thames Valley Police and involved Graef and his team in regular and lengthy attendance at events in Reading police station and various locations at which the police were either patrolling or operating in response to a crime. The police had an opportunity to see the final version of material at a stage at which it was practical to make alterations. They also had an agreement with the BBC that the Corporation would undertake to correct matters of fact, would preserve professional and private secrets, and would take account of police comment on fairness of presentation. Although some critics initially interpreted this as effectively giving a right of veto to the police, it was never agreed that the permission of the police was necessary before transmission, and the actual level of intervention seems to have been minimal (these details are taken from the 1992 BBC *Arena* programme on the series). After the first few episodes, the idea that the series was a managed 'public relations' exercise became very hard to sustain in view of the variety, complexity and controversiality of the material being transmitted.

Working on very high shooting ratios (over 30:1), Graef and his cameraman Charles Stewart shaped the footage into thematic and narrative coherence in post-production. However, the identification of possible 'story' routes through the material began during the shooting itself, as Graef indicates in an interview comment:

> We would discuss as we launched into it, what we were doing, and there's a lot of exploring with the camera, really, and the sound recording ... the sound recordist produced as many ideas for a film ... a story as anyone did, by listening, and so did other members of the team. (Graef in *Arena* (BBC2, 7 February 1992)

The titles of the programmes in the series indicate the kind of temporal, thematic (and implicitly spatial) frame being used – for instance, 'New Year's Eve', 'Traffic', 'A Busy Saturday Night', 'Pop Festival', 'A Complaint of Rape', 'A Suspicious Death'.

Like most vérité series, *Police* was projected as a fascinating exercise in revelation ('TV's candid camera presents the police as you have never seen them before', said the *Daily Express*). The three questions routinely asked of work in this mode were regularly raised. These are (1) selectivity in editing (what we don't see and the durational values of what we do); (2) modification of behaviour for the cameras ('acting up'); and (3) typicality of incident shown (the generalisability of the particular). In respect of (2), it is interesting to note that the makers of Smirnoff vodka ran a concurrent advertisement in which one man is shown saying to another: 'I wanted to be actor, but luckily I joined the Thames Valley Police'! Arguments about (1) were frequently brought up by police and police spokesmen during the course of the series. Concern was expressed not only about the way in which editing selectivity narrativised events in a manner which was distortive of their 'true complexity', but about the failures of the vérité method itself adequately to contextualise action and interaction within a broader framework of knowledge (about previous incidents, about procedures, etc.). Of course, such a framework could only be supplied through the very devices which Graef's approach eschewed – commentary, interview and expositional visualisation. It was precisely the sustaining of the 'naive' perspective (in the sense of an unaddressed gaze at ongoing events) which gave the programmes their particular appeal and evidential effect. Graef makes no attempt to disguise the artefactual character of his work in post-production, but he casts himself in the role of a discoverer, an organiser and relayer of various stretches of indexical record in response to which a viewer's attribution of significance must be made. There is no consistent 'point of view' within the programmes to be assessed, no propositions about policing to be weighed. In Graef's judgement on his own practice (BBC, *Arena*, 1992 again), the viewer is offered the means of secondary cognition, framed with no inflection either of celebration or critique.

Incompetence of various kinds was frequently on display. In 'Pop Festival' the police make a seizure of what they believe to be drugs only to find that the suspect packets contain macaroni! (This programme brought a charge of 'untypicality' from police authorities as well as of selective editing.)

Undoubtedly the most controversial programme in the series was 'A Complaint of Rape', in which a young woman is shown enduring an extremely unsympathetic interview with two policemen, following her making of the complaint. Although the camera crew left the room at points, the interview sequence develops strong durational values as the two investigators 'work over' the main features of the allegation and subject both it and the women to increasing pressure (the shooting ratio for the interview itself was extremely tight, about $1\frac{1}{2}$:1). The projected spectator position is one of acute discomfort, with principal point-of-view behind the woman (largely to preserve anonymity). All three of the issues I noted above – selective editing, behavioural modification and untypicality – were subsequently taken up by police spokesmen in an attempt to limit the damage which it was thought this programme would cause to the public image of policing. The public and political response was, in fact, so strong that it eventually led to changes being introduced into police procedures for the initial interview of rape complainants. Winston has recently noted how this is a rare example of a documentary actually having a 'demonstrated effect' as a result of its indexical, evidential power (Winston 1995:210). As he also remarks, this power is partly to be attributed to the sheer scale of the series, with its thirteen hours of screened material and huge shooting ratios. Within the durational scheme permitted by such a venture, a level of integrity can be achieved in relation both to the local representativeness of the depicted particular and, though less securely, to particular–general relationships obtaining in the topic field as a whole (here, 'policing'). The status of the *Police* episodes as 'films of record', to use Graef's own phrase, has a logistical as well as a formal basis.

In its putting of major television resources (including airtime) behind the application of a 'purist' observational style to a principal institution of civil society, *Police* is a vérité 'classic' in ways which, for a variety of reasons, are unlikely to be eclipsed. Its combination of large audiences with a high degree of self-imposed sobriety of address was, quite apart from anything else, the product of a particular conjuncture in British public service television. Many other examples of 'institutional vérité' have drawn more on the exotic qualities of their topic and the possibilities for conventional narrative excitement which it offers (e.g. *Duty Men, Murder Squad*) even where a strong 'public knowledge' function has also been evident.

'Neo-vérité'

I use the term 'neo-vérité' to indicate broadly the way in which television has recently attempted to mix a primarily vérité approach with elements drawn from other areas of programming. It is important to distinguish my use of this term (loose though it inevitably must be) from two other kinds of shift detectable in vérité 'usage'. First of all, there was the shift towards offering more exposition. The 'purist' form of observationalism practised by Graef was always hard to sustain and many television series of the 1980s, though they followed the general approach and projected themselves as 'fly on the wall', also used interview and occasionally voice-over to provide a continuity of information throughput and to provide an additional means of obtaining coherence and structure (for instance, in bridging between widely disparate scenes). Secondly, there was the increasing use of 'fly-on-the-wall' sequences in documentaries organised principally through exposition. This merely pushed the conventional use of observational scenes in such documentaries a little further in the direction of durational values and the use of footage for primary, evidential rather than secondary, illustrative purposes (it could be argued, of course, that it is unhelpful to use the term 'vérité' of a scene rather than of a whole programme or film – let us, then, refer to 'vérité-*like*' scenes.

Important though these shifts have been, by 'neo-vérité' I mean to indicate those much more thoroughgoing attempts to re-work the terms of the idea so as to align it better with changing notions of 'good television', attempts increasingly anchored in ideas about entertainment. Series like *Blues and Twos* (Carlton 1994) have done this in respect of that popular 1990s genre – the emergency services programme, offering short but intensive depictions of accidents and rescues (see Chapter 11). *The Living Soap* (BBC 1993/94), as its title suggests and as I noted earlier in this chapter, tried it in a more sustained way in respect of popular series drama. In doing this, it was to some extent drawing on the earlier *Sylvania Waters* (BBC 1992) in which Paul Watson (who had made *The Family* twenty years earlier) revisited domestic vérité. In his new project he depicted the everyday life of a wealthy Australian family in terms which moved away from detached observationalism, connecting directly with the 'good television' values of the exotic, the dramatic and the farcical. The shift of enunciative position is clearly signalled in the first episode of *Sylvania Waters*, when the son of the household introduces us cheerily to the characters we are 'going to get to know'. This opening sequence bridges brief 'tasters' of each person with exterior shots, underneath a musical soundtrack, of the neighbourhood and the relevant homes. The possibility, clearly there in *The Family* twenty years earlier, that the intensity of the vérité gaze when applied to a small domestic group would begin to produce high levels of self-consciousness, such as to generate at times a markedly histrionic 'virtual performance' from the participants (see Nichols 1991: 122), here becomes much more fully realised.

Sylvania has attracted extended critical comment, not only for its hybridised formal features but also for the distinctive and symptomatic way in which ideas of 'family' are at work (and play) within it.[8] I am more interested here in the even more radical modifications made to vérité in *The Living Soap*.

If 'virtual performance' can be a problem when the participants' social identity and space have a prior and independent status in respect of the 'documenting' process, then this is even more so when television is involved in their construction. In making *The Living Soap*, the BBC hired a house in a Manchester suburb and 'cast' six students from Manchester University as its tenants. Life in the house was then used as the basis for a series promising a 'fly-on-the-wall' experience but introducing considerable innovation into the terms on which this was offered to the viewer. Not only were the general pro-filmic circumstances themselves largely the product of television's need to 'observe' but there was routine management of local action such that 'occurrence', though not usually *initiated* by the crew, often had to be arranged in order to fit in with shooting convenience. One of the 'replacement' students (there was a steady loss of the original 'cast' during production; one replacement was elected by a television poll!) talked to a newspaper reporter about the way in which a routine task became 'complicated' by its being 'observed': 'On the floor is a borrowed vacuum cleaner. "They came to film me borrowing it and it took nearly an hour. Simple things like that take a long time on television"'. (O'Kane, *Guardian* 9 March 1994). Another student speaks of the more general requirements imposed by 'role': 'There is a lot of competition between the different camera crews. They ask you to start doing loads more things and you know that they haven't got enough for that week's programme.' (O'Kane, *Guardian* 9 March 1994).

In addition to this unprecedented interventionism, the programme also aligned itself to three other kinds of programme. In terms of its topic, it played off the soap/sitcom potential of the idea of 'student group as family' (the successful zany sitcom series of the mid-1980s *The Young Ones* (BBC) was never very far in the background). In terms of its form, it connected both to the rhythms and styles of 'youth' television which emerged in the mid- to late 1980s (bright colours, loud music, eclectic graphical design, a deliberate instability of look and tone) and to the new 'access' modalities established by camcorder programmes like the BBC's *Video Diaries* in the early 1990s. It did the latter by including sequences in which students used a (garishly decorated) 'video room' to address the viewer directly, often about incidents which the viewers had 'observed' in an earlier sequence. This mixture of 'objectivist' and 'subjectivist' positions was also sustained by the use of participant voice-over in many of the observationalist sequences.

At one level, *The Living Soap* can be seen as deconstructing the principal elements of the vérité approach, replacing the epistemology of evidence with a mixture of discursive effects, stylishly self-reflective as the students cope with their roles in the show. However, I think such a view would be a mistaken one, since strongly referential claims to wider realities (student life today) were a major feature of the publicity for the series and can be seen to be a factor in the thematic organisation of the programmes. The paradox of the project is the extent to which it is prepared to fabricate and manage in order to secure its evidential suggestiveness. It is as if the extent of the interventions made in the construction of an 'observational opportunity' go unmonitored in the implications they carry for the status of the depiction. Such uncertainty can be seen, too, in that interrelation of 'objectivist' and 'subjectivist' aspects noted above. Getting the 'look', or rather a certain combination of different 'looks', becomes paramount. However, an appeal to a modern reflexivity, to wacky self-regressiveness, is always available as a way of covering the inconsistencies of aims and means, the discrepancies of programme philosophy, which ensue.[9]

The series also encountered severe problems of 'publicity effect', due to the fact that early programmes were being transmitted as later ones were being made. This (as in Watson's *The Family*) allowed the impact of the series to be fed back into the terms of its making, significantly increasing the levels of self-awareness of the participants as 'stars'. Not only that, it also generated strong reactions from within the locality, resulting not only in personal abuse to the students but also to attacks on the house.

The Living Soap's experiment in a hybridised form of vérité was messy and unsuccessful, certainly it did not get the audience which it had hoped for. Among its many other problems, it fell a (predictable) victim to 'typicality' debate – with widespread complaint from student groups that it distorted contemporary student life, particularly in terms of the relative wealth of the participants and their attitudes. There appears to have been a fundamental lack of coherence in production aims, so many possibilities being entertained and allowed an under-monitored presence within the series' procedures and discourses. That it originated from within a 'youth programmes' rather than a documentary department is important to an understanding of its character. Nevertheless, in its very uncertainties and confusions, its mix of appeals, the significance of the series is considerable – pointing to a broader configuration of tensions and innovatory imperatives currently surrounding observationalist work and, indeed, non-fiction television more generally.

Future perspectives for drama-documentary and vérité

The various combinations of drama-documentary and the varieties of vérité have developed distinctive 'problem agendas', as I hope to have shown above. These agendas bear back on the full range of work in documentary since they tend, in different ways, to raise questions about the credentials which documentaries of whatever sort can claim to have in their renderings of the real.

In the case of drama-documentary, it could be argued that 'pseudo-problems' have taken up more time than anything else, given the levels of strategic political interest, bad faith and inflated fears about 'deception' which have been apparent in arguments about programming. Nevertheless, the use of dramatic form to reconstruct real incidents in detail is bound to put into tension the distinct conventions and proprieties of dramatic depiction and documentary journalism. Directors know this, and have frequently 'played' with the tension in productive ways. Where the actual subject-matter of the programme is itself controversial, either in its specificity or in its implications, then it follows that anxiety about a form of depiction allowing high levels of creative licence will be the focus of suspicion. This will be true for political groups and for professional, occupational or other social groups who have a stake in the depiction. To point out the 'constructed' character of conventional documentary and the long history of drama as a means of social commentary has not, will not, and should not, change regular disagreements about the accuracy of elements of drama-documentary depiction and the validity of the interpretative position which informs scripts and direction. So, to take a recent instance, the portrayal of particular circumstances in Granada's programme *Hostage* (1992) – about Western captives in the Lebanon – brought accusations of distortion from one of the men whose plight was depicted. Drama-documentary offers itself as a 'tool' of public debate and it is therefore only to be expected that its own procedures and rhetoric as well as its content will be routinely subject to critical attention.

Vérité's problems have both a more philosophical and a more technical aspect. Although some directors have been keen to qualify the claims made for their work, the publicity given by many television companies to the 'transparency' of programmes, to their unproblematically evidential status, has caused a considerable critical backlash. As I suggested in the previous chapter, the 'purer than thou' element in the vérité project has prompted a deconstruction of its assumptions from which new work can only proceed with caution and qualification.

Dai Vaughan identified the 'paradox of vérité' very well twenty years ago:

> Television vérité presents us with a paradox; that the most exciting form to develop in reaction against television's impoverishment of documentary usage should itself, by placing all its trust in the integrity of the diegesis, be uniquely vulnerable to subversion. (Vaughan 1976: 34)

This 'integrity of the diegesis' is, as we have seen, communicated to the viewer via the illusion that the camera is not there – creating an insincerity in the terms of the depiction which, as Vaughan explores in some detail, provides the conditions for forms of concealed 'slippage'. More recently, Brian Winston has argued that the evidential values upon which vérité depends have become terminally impaired not only by established conventions of dissembling but by the new technology of image manipulation. I noted in Chapter 2 how Winston believes that the emphasis given to the 'vérité look' has served to weaken the structure and rigour of organisation of television documentary generally and that the aesthetics of optimum transparency and of indexical trust need to be abandoned if documentary is to develop.

'Neo-vérité' has *not* put 'all its trust' in diegetic integrity but has, instead, supplemented itself with other, more direct, modes of address. However, it has done this without letting go of its basic claim to 'transparency', even where (as in *The Living Soap*) this claim is in contradiction both with the level of television's intervention in the production of the pro-filmic and with the degree of self-consciousness of the filmed subjects. It remains to be seen what further modifications will, or can, be made to the vérité approach as documentary attempts, within an increasingly competitive context, to renovate itself both as 'good viewing' and as 'socially significant television'.

Drama-documentary and vérité put pressure on documentary's 'look' and 'truth' by developing specific generic characteristics and aspirations to an extreme degree. It is therefore interesting that both of them are major, and often complementary, constituents within what are perhaps the most significant new forms of factual television programme to be scheduled in Britain – the 'emergency services' series and the camcorder, do-it-yourself formats. Indeed, vérité is involved in what can be seen as a third strand of current development, the use of hidden micro-cameras in series like Granada's *Disguises* (1993) and Channel Four's *Undercover Britain* (1994).

I shall talk about these developments, and the further shifts they suggest, in Chapter 11, but we can note here the continuing imaginative appeal of the dramatised rendering (of a crime, as in the BBC's *Crimewatch*, or of an accident in *999*) and also of the spontaneous/evidential (as in *Video Diaries*, or differently, in *Undercover Britain*). As well as the question of their separate development, then, drama-documentary and vérité have now to be addressed as staple and convergent elements of the new 'reality television', ingredients in what might be regarded as a new and eclectic symbolic economy, where the very assumptions carried by the idea of a 'mixed form' might quickly come to seem naively inappropriate.

3 Coalface and Housing Problems (1935)

These two short films, both made in 1935, are impressive and contrasting works. They show the British documentary movement of the 1930s being innovative in distinctly different directions, with respect not only to the use of sound and image but also to the social functions of documentary cinema. *Coalface* was directly a product of the 'Grierson' school, being produced by John Grierson himself for the GPO film unit (see Chapter 1) with the footage (some of it 'stock footage') coming from a number of directors and the editing carried out by the brilliantly innovative Brazilian Alberto Cavalcanti. In many respects something of a 'test run' in depictive styles for what was to become perhaps the most famous 1930s film *Nightmail* (1936), *Coalface* is an exercise in experimentalist realism which is at least as much an achievement as its more famous successor. *Housing Problems* was also produced by John Grierson and directed by Edgar Anstey and Arthur Elton. It was sponsored by the gas industry and attempted to examine the problem of the slums, with considerable emphasis being placed on the slum-clearance solutions being adopted by 'the more enlightened councils'. Instead of being organised in terms of that 'poetry of fact' which characterises so many documentaries of the period, *Housing Problems* develops a reportorial naturalism which has been widely seen to make it, at least in part, a precursor of the contemporary television documentary. In a way which was then highly original and even 'radical', this naturalism is grounded in the testimony of 'ordinary people'.

Taking *Coalface* first, I want to look at each film's organisation in some detail before considering it critically in relation both to its formal and its substantive aspects.

Coalface

Coalface is an eleven-minute-long look at coal-mining, organised in terms of a topic progression from the visual establishing of the surface plant, through the geography and productivity of British mines, underground working, the 'miner's life', the transport and distribution of coal to, finally, its use in industry. It is a densely informational as well as a visually dynamic and noisy film (there is a prominent soundtrack of music and orchestrally produced machine noises), projecting two principal 'arguments' – the centrality of coal-mining to British industry and the hardship and dangers of the miners' life. As I shall show, the second of these involves some degree of ambiguity, or even ambivalence, of treatment. Formally, it is self-consciously experimentalist, drawing on a range of Modernist models,[1] including the work of the Soviet directors Eisenstein and Vertov. Visually extremely busy, with extensive movement within the shot as well as montage effects, one of its principal features is the partial integration of the visualisation with the musical score (Benjamin Britten) and the narration. For a short period, these elements are joined by choral extracts from W. H. Auden's 'Colliers' Chant'. There is no actuality sound at all – all machines noises are produced by an orchestra, with a consequent distortion in both tone and volume. An outline of structure will help with further analysis.

Outline of structure

Opening

(Pit, winding gear set against cloudy sky; in semi-dark; dusk or dawn.) 'There is the mine. There are the miners' (sung chorus). Narration begins: 'Coal mining is the basic industry of Britain' (music – piano, percussion, orchestral backing).

Surface sequence

(Commentary over film): 'This is the surface plant of every mine.' Winding gear, slag heaps, coal conveyance buckets and washing machinery. The by-products of coal listed (gas, coke, tar, oil, etc.).

Areas of coal production

(Map of Britain – each area identified in turn, with number of miners employed and annual tonnage produced, under drumbeat soundtrack.)

Facework

Miners with helmet torches walking down gallery to coalface (continuation of drum rhythms). Singing on soundtrack ('Colliers' Chant'). Shots of horses pulling wagons. Men stripping off to work ('temperature reaches 80 degrees'; 'the miner works in a cramped position'). The Davey safety lamp. ('The seven and a half hour shift begins') – facework by hand. Individual output figures ('22 cwt per shift'). Shots of falling coal. ('The miner stops to eat'), snatches of conversation (over-dubbed) between miners eating and drinking – close-ups here (male choral singing in background). The machinery of mining. Coal cutters in action, ripping at the seam. Accident rate ('every working day four miners are killed, and over 450 injured and maimed. Every year in Great Britain one in every five miners is injured'). Shift finishes.

End of shift

Cage goes up (montage shots of winding gear). Miners' voices – 'we're going up'. Cage arrives at surface. Female choir on soundtrack.

Miner's life

Shots of miners walking back home from the pit ('The miner's life is bound up with the pit. The miner's house is often owned by the pit. The life of the village depends on the pit.) Shots of pit houses. Shots of washing lines. Long pan left across waste land and slag heap to a held shot of a tree bent over in the wind, then across to a ruined mine building and tilt up to sky.

Transport and use

('Transport and distribution double the price of coal'.) Goods yard, rail wagons and signal box. Movement of wagons across points (editing to emphasise precision and rhythm of mechanical processes). Use of coal domestically, for electricity production, locomotives, shipping, export and industry (illustration of each with orchestrally produced noises: generators, mechanical grabbers, ships being coaled, power station).

End sequence

Shot moving along pipeline (sounds of steam), then inside locomotive cab going into tunnel in cloud of steam. Pit-head shots. Opening sentences spoken again in reverse order; camera pans to pick up miner walking down street and then moves back to pit-head.

It can be seen that some of the phases which I have identified are transitional, bridging between sequences, whereas others have an expositional function. In fact, there are two principal transitional sequences in the film, both of which show a strong 'poetic' character, though of radically different kinds, together with a relative reduction in referentiality (the commentary ceases and the images become richer in connotation). First of all, there is the montage of going up in the lift cage, which attempts to generate a visual excitement correlating with the men's spirits as they go off shift. After a brief exposition of the miner's life, there is then the lingering shot of the tree bent against the wind, a shot which precedes a tilt upwards to the sky before a transition to the busy goods yard and the first shot of the 'distribution' sequence. That this shot, accompanied by a climax in the female choral singing, has a symbolic resonance beyond its depiction of features of the landscape seems clear to most viewers. In their brief discussion of *Coalface*, Miles and Smith (1987) see it as indicative of the 'pastoralism of a "real man's world"' and as part of the film's attempted naturalisation of the human and industrial struggle which is its focus. At a more abstract, formal level, the shot provides a moment of 'rest' within the depictive flow, one to be immediately contrasted against the mechanistic urgency of the goods yard.

As I have indicated in my outline, the last sentences of the commentary reverse the ones with which the film opens. This aesthetic device provides the film with a self-conscious artefactual 'completeness' of a kind which reinforces its identity as a project of expressive transformation as much as of reportage.

Coalface: the bleak excitement of industry

Although I shall attempt to explore the particular features of its aesthetic as they variously relate to its intentions and themes, *Coalface* is very much a film of Modernist enthusiasms, so that one way of describing its overall depictive project would be in terms of a 'Modernist realism', a category which, whilst not self-contradictory, certainly suggests internal tensions. The orientation of shot-type and of editing evidences these enthusiasms clearly enough, frequently echoing the work of earlier and contemporary European cinema in this respect. Britten's score, dissonant and heavily percussive, fits perfectly with the visualisations offered. Perhaps more orginally, the commentary itself is 'scored' into the music as well as being composed to fit the pictures. It is read throughout by a strong, emphatic, male voice, using cadences which (in contrast to other documentary films of the 1930s) display no signs of the colloquial or even the sociable. It may well be that there is an attempt to achieve a kind of abstract 'voice of fact' through this stern, at times dramatically impassive, articulation, linking it to elements in contemporary poetry and reportage (including radio).[2] Its extensive and enthusiastic use of statistics would further connect it to aspects of literary Modernism. Far too frequent and dense to be assimilated by even the most engaged viewer (and often placed across striking images in a way which reduces the attention which can be given to them), the function of these statistics is as much affective/impressionistic as it is informational. That is to say, the figures contribute considerably to the overall aesthetic impact of the film as well as to its communicative 'efficiency'.

I want to look now at the way in which the film's formal and thematic elements are related, so that both the complementarity of these and also their points of tension can be identified.

Form and theme

From the perspective of the mid-1990s, a film lasting eleven minutes, which takes as its ostensible subject a major national industry, seems more than a little odd. Such a combination of extensive topic with limited expressive scope suggests that some version of 'impressionism' will necessarily provide the communicative mode. That is to say, unless the film is to focus on an *aspect* of the industry and to organise its discourse in terms of a delimited focus, its comprehensiveness of reference will tend to pull it towards taking the depictive distance of the 'sketch', the selective 'outline'. It therefore necessarily makes extensive use of the broadly indicative and of the associative (e.g. the metonymic employment of montage to suggest the magnitude of the topic) in the absence of the time to sustain detail for long or to offer a fully articulated exposition.[3] *Coalface* does, indeed, offer an 'impression' of the coal industry and I have already suggested how the organisation of this is determined as much by the possibilities for aesthetic innovation offered as by any specifically referential requirements. It is interesting, here, how 'industry' is related to 'workers'. The film celebrates the contribution of the former to national economic life in a manner fully consonant with other films of the 1930s movement, yet it also has an interest in the latter which derives from the movement's democratic, egalitarian impulses, its interest in the 'ordinary' and in the nature of 'work'.

'Necessity' is perhaps the most useful way of describing the terms upon which the coal industry is depicted. The film is a restrained celebration of the way in which the response to this necessity brings national economic development. However, at the same time as it appears to be impressed (and at points perhaps excited too) by the human and mechanical energy needed to win coal, it also registers the risk and the general hardship which this 'winning' entails. Framing its account within the (implicit) terms of necessity allows the film to countenance the status of the miners as 'victims' as well as 'heroes' (see Winston 1995 and Higson 1995), without finding it necessary to use terms of critique and reform. For necessity requires no more than recognition. I shall examine some of the implications of this perspective later, but one point where its effect is clearly apparent (and I think awkwardly so) is in the commentary noted above, where the shots show the pit village as the miners return home after their shift. What are we to make of the repetition of 'pit' and the emphasis given to this word in the following three sentences?

> The miner's life is bound up with the pit.
> The miner's house is often owned by the pit.
> The life of the village depends on the pit.

At one level, this might be regarded as simply descriptive, but its rhetorical organisation suggests a purpose additional to description. But what purpose? The centrality of 'the pit' is certainly not to be celebrated; neither the tones of the commentary nor the visualisation of 'environment' permit that reading. However, it is difficult to see the description as carrying the *critical* force it might do in another context, one in which the terms of criticism had already been established. It seems to me that the way in which 'the pit' circumscribes the miner's life, in relations of dependency and ownership, is, again, placed here within the terms of 'necessity'. The extra-descriptive resonance of the lines derives from the registered *intensities* of this limitation, this perceived (and imposed) 'unity' of mining. Despite their negative inflection, these intensities are part of the 'awe' with which the film views its subject; they are not articulated as social critique.

At many points, the depiction of the miners in *Coalface* is anthropological in its 'otherness' and distance. This is partly a consequence of the difficulty (perhaps impossibility) of using interview speech, so that the men are always presented from the 'outside', framed within, and subordinate to, the industry. The repeated use of the singular ('the miner') in describing both their working life and their community further strengthens a sense of the exotic, the fascinatingly strange. The terms in which miners are first presented in the film – the shots of the walk/march to the coal-face – establish this feeling immediately. Portrayed in flickering torchlight which casts their shadows against the walls of the gallery, they walk along to a soundtrack of drumbeat and chant. The 'primitivist' resonance of this scene, followed up in many of the subsequent shots of underground working (for instance, the semi-nakedness of the face-working; the choral cry of triumph over a shot of coal falling away from the face) sets up relations of viewing which serve emphatically to 'de-normalise' the miners and effectively, if only temporarily, to 'de-socialise' them too.

It is almost as if they become a hardy, subterranean race, locked into a daily, heroic battle for coal against natural forces and dangers.[4] The particular economic and social terms of their work are displaced by their partial figurative transformation into creatures of classical mythology. I have noted above how the terms of the commentary work to support this. Another way in which the same general effect is produced, though from within a rather different set of aesthetic codes, is through the 'mechanisation' of the miner in sequences whose composition and rhythm, together with orchestral sound accompaniment, suggest a blurring of the division between man and tool, man and machine. The choral backing, though it too unifies, generates by contrast a strongly humanistic framing, a sorrowful sense of strong feeling and expression 'at the edges' of what the film actually shows.

What is the communicative purpose of *Coalface*? Clearly, it is an exercise in realist expressive form, an exercise in the advancement of film as art. As such, its purposes are aesthetic, the production of pleasure in the audience through visual and aural excitement. Yet it also an exercise in public communication, part of that broader 1930s documentary enterprise of making social relations, including those of work, more visible and of undertaking the 'civic education' upon which the successful development of modern democracy and modern industry was seen to depend. How far are the two impulses integrated in *Coalface* and how far are they contradictory ambitions, mutually compromising each other's integrity and success?

It is difficult to assess the contemporary terms in which the particular 'art effects' of *Coalface* were interpreted, but, as I have noted, the film's articulation is a harsh, and disturbing one, even brutal at times. There is none of that lyricisation of the industrial which can be seen in earlier films, such as Flaherty's *Industrial Britain* (1931), where an attempt is made to 'see' modern industry in terms which have continuity with a calmer, rural national past. In that sense, *Coalface* is much closer to its influences in Soviet film, where the excitement of the modern is accompanied by a sense of dislocation, dissonance and the sheer power of the machine. I remarked earlier that these do not develop into the terms of social criticism (for quite obvious reasons, in the case of the Soviet films), but they generate a degree of *non-human* energy which is at once both fascinating and alienating and which stops the film simply articulating approval for what it shows. In their useful discussion of the film, Miles and Smith (1987) draw attention to the gender divisions perceivable in *Coalface* and note the contrast between the strongly masculine world of underground, with its half-naked workers, and the feminine world of the surface, with its supporting, dutiful domesticity. The gender division is certainly used as a tonal device in the film (e.g. the female choir soundtrack which starts as the cage reaches the surface), but whatever inequality is documented is unproblematically 'reflected' rather than being identified as such. Miles and Smith also note a degree of 'male narcissism' in the depiction of the bodies of the underground workers. Here I would disagree. It seems to me that the contexts, postures and depictive mode for the facework scenes minimise the erotic or even aesthetic charge which the images have. It is the less than fully human dimension of 'the miner' which is, once again, the predominant factor in this portrayal of bodies which are 'heroic', 'victimised' and emphatically 'other'.

Grierson was certainly aware of the problem of 'aesthetic displacement', the way in which artistic self-consciousness in a film could impair its integrity as a vehicle for public communication, pushing the theme itself into secondary importance.[5] However, he also approved of the way in which aesthetic design, including pleasingness of rhythm and beauty of composition, could enhance viewers' awareness of the real world and of working processes.[6] *Nightmail* was to be a great popular success largely because of this kind of reinforcement. In *Coalface*, however, the sheer scope and energy of the Modernist experiment in vision/sound combination and the affective ends to which this is put (e.g. shock, awe, excitement) place 'information' under more pressure than occurs in most other films of the 1930s movement.

Housing Problems

Whereas *Coalface* impresses with its aesthetic density, it is the 'maximum transparency' approach of *Housing Problems*, its direct and sustained address to its topic, which has caused the film to be widely referred to in the history of documentary. The essential communicative idea of *Housing Problems* is 'testimony' – the shooting of sequences in which 'slum dwellers', sitting or standing in their own houses, give an uninterrupted account, in direct address to camera, of their living conditions. These testimony sequences are organised into a 'before and after' structure, most being shot in old, condemned houses but the last two being shot in the new flats to which people have been moved. Although easy enough to produce with current lightweight camera and recording equipment, in 1936 the shots were only achieved with considerable production effort (involving the use of lights placed on scaffolding and shining into the rooms from outside: see the account of production in Sussex 1976). A 'bridging' section is provided by a sequence which looks at designs for new housing, together with the provision of newly designed cooking and heating appliances (allowing mention of the gas industry, sponsors of the film). The overall structure is that of a commentary film, with an unseen main narrator and an unseen 'specialist' narrator who is a councillor on a London housing committee. The film may be seen, in part, as a work of radical ethnography (almost a kind of early 'access' programme), giving previously marginalised or unheard voices a chance to express their grievances publicly. This is the view taken of the film by its makers, as I shall show later. However, there is no doubt that *Housing Problems* is also a work of promotion, both specifically for the gas industry and, more generally, for the work of 'enlightened civic authorities' who are seen to be effectively putting an end to the slums. The political and social terms in which 'housing problems' are addressed and 'solved' (in many ways a more accurate title for the film would be *Housing Solutions*) have been the subject of considerable debate. Again, I propose to examine some of the main terms of this debate below.

Outline of structure

Introduction

Anonymous commentary (over film of 'slum' houses): 'A great deal these days is written about the slums. This film is going to introduce you to some of the people really concerned. First, Councillor Lauder, Chairman of the Stepney Housing Committee, will tell you something of the problem of slum clearance.' (Councillor speaks in commentary over illustrative shots. Describes typical slum architecture, poor roofs, narrow alleyways, falling mortar, bulging walls. Comments on 'typical interior of a decayed house' and notes over image that 'this lavatory and sink has to do for four families'.)

Testimony of slum dwellers

Commentary: 'And now for the people who live in the slums. Here is Mr Norwood': Mr Norwood speaks (standing in his room before fireplace). Talks of bugs, mice and rats, the lack of washing facilities, cooking difficulties and loss of some of his children through poor conditions. (50 seconds)

Commentary: 'This what Mrs Hill has to say': Mrs Hill speaks (in her damp room and then on her staircase). Talks of filthy walls, vermin, crookedness of staircase and of some of the rooms 'The whole house is on the crook.' (1 minute 30 seconds)

Commentary: 'And here is Mrs Gray': Mrs Gray speaks (standing at head of bed). Tells a story of waking in the night to find a rat in her baby's cot. (50 seconds)

Commentary: 'And here is Mr Burner': Mr Burner speaks (with wife and two children, before fireplace). Talks of having one room, problems with water, food storage. Hopes council will 'liven their ideas up' and looks forward to time when 'every working man' will have a decent flat. (1 minute 10 seconds)

Councillor Lauder (voice over illustrative shots): 'The more enlightened public authorities have been applying themselves to the task of slum clearance with energy' (shots of new houses). Lauder talks of problem of where to put people 'while their hovels are being pulled down and new houses built for them'.

Designing the new

Anonymous commentary (over illustrative shots). Remarks on: designs of new flats from the British Steelworks Association and the cement industry; prominence of gas fittings for cooking and heating in these. Example of the design for the Quarry Hill estate in Leeds; importance of light, soundproofing, space and cheap household appliances; gardens in the new model estates.

Councillor Lauder (voice-over): 'When a public authority embarks on slum clearance work, it must take people as they are. It is, however, our experience that if you provide people from the slums with decent homes they quickly respond to the improved conditions and keep their homes clean and tidy' (shot of new flats and children playing. Pan across modern tenement block).

Living in the new

Commentary: 'And now let's have a word with Mrs Reddington': Mrs Reddington speaks (sitting in the corner of her new flat). Talks of the 'nice little place' she now has. All windows can be opened. (40 seconds)

Commentary: 'And now Mrs Atribe': Mrs Atribe speaks in voice-over (shots of flat). Talks of her two nice rooms, cooker and portable copper.

Commentary: 'All the same, Mrs Atribe will never forget the rats in the house she had before': Mrs Atribe (now sitting at table with her husband standing on her right). Tells story of large rat found in the room. Drama of husband chasing it and, with some difficulty and noise, killing it by jumping on it. (Total 1 minute)

Caretaker (to camera; leaning against wall in flats' courtyard): talks of his duties ('There are two caretakers on this estate'), minor repairs, the collection of litter, safety of children, good order. Lists caretaker duties through the day until midnight (including 'unstopping' of sinks, baths and lavatories). (50 seconds)

Councillor Lauder (voice over illustrative shots): 'Up to the present, only the fringes of the problem of the slums have been touched. However, there is reason to hope that within the next ten years, considerable strides will be made towards removing the worst slums.'

End montage: unidentified voices talking of bad conditions over mixed shots of old housing – alleys, children playing, woman beating carpet against wall, etc.

The basic organisation here can be seen to be relatively straightforward. The 'problem' is established visually and in commentary, then a sequence of four testimony segments instantiate it in particular experience, using cutaways to illustrate specific problems (damp walls, vermin, decayed plaster, subsidence, etc.). The 'planning' sequence looks at the architectural 'solutions' being proposed, and this leads on to the caretaker's brief account of how a new housing block is maintained and the two final testimony segments which document the improved quality of life which follows. However, the final testimony segment is split, with the second half referring back to bad times in the old housing. This leads on to a final, short section of speech and images representing 'slum' conditions. That the film ends with the 'old' rather than the 'new' is, I think, of some significance, partly modifying a basic structure which emphasises solutions and progress.

Form and theme

It is worth looking in more detail at two aspects of the film. First of all, the visualisation and speech of the testimony sequences and then at the incorporation of these within the terms of the commentary and the overall communicative design. Speech from slum dwellers, or former slum dwellers, takes up some six minutes, about a third of overall running time. To contemporary reviewers, there was no doubt but that this was the most striking aspect of the film, the one which made it memorable. In the *Spectator* for 19 October 1936, Graham Greene reviewed the film in terms which compared it to the accounts of BBC radio: 'Compare the characters in *Housing Problems* with the frightened, ironed-out personalities with censored scripts whom the BBC present as documentary.'

Although quite possibly unfair to the full range of BBC features work of the period (see Scannell 1986), this comment gives some sense of the impact which the 'testimony' method had. However, there are a number of questions surrounding how this method works and the social relationship with the viewer which it assumes. Before addressing these, an extract might be helpful in establishing the general character of the speech, even though the manner of delivery varies considerably from speaker to speaker. This is how the first 'testimony' segment begins:

> *Commentary*: And now for the people who have to live in the slum. Here is Mr Norwood.
> *Mr Norwood*: These two rooms I'm in now I have to pay ten shillings a week for and I haven't enough room to swing a cat round. I've also five other neighbours on the side of me who are in the same predicament as I'm in myself. And I'm not only overrun with bugs, I've got mice and rats as well. With the washing, my missus has to send out every little bit of washing there is, every drop of water we have to go out to the yard for, to fetch in ... And as far as cooking, we have to use the gas stove alongside the bed, where we sleep.

As in all the testimony segments, the speech is delivered directly to the camera (not slightly 'off' to a questioner) from a static position in a room. The composition of this basic shot rarely changes throughout the speaking, although there are cutaways to illustrative material. The theme in all cases is description of housing conditions and the limitations on living which they impose. Only in the case of Mr Burner does this shift, at the end, into explicit criticism of the Council and a general wish that 'every working man' will one day soon have decent, hygienic living conditions.

Perhaps the first thing to note about this mode of communica-

Housing Problems: testimonies
of deprivation

tion is its *formality*. I have noted elsewhere (Corner 1994) how it is best regarded as a form of mediated public speaking rather than an exercise in the kind of naturalistic spontaneity within whose terms a television interview today might be constructed. Although the term 'interview' has been used of these sequences in *Housing Problems*, it is altogether the wrong term for the kind of communication which results, a defining feature of which is that it does not appear as an answer to a question but as a self-authored statement to the viewer (an 'access' message, as I suggested earlier). We know that Ruby Grierson, John Grierson's sister, was involved in the encouragement and general preparation of the speakers (Sussex 1976), but it is also claimed by Anstey that there were no full rehearsals and no script whatsover (comments on this point are found in Sussex 1976 and the BBC *Arena* programme of 9 March 1982).

Modern viewers of the film sometimes register uneasiness at what they believe is the uneasiness of the speakers. Certainly, and not suprisingly, most of the participants look and sound a little awkward in their performances. But to be cued by sympathetic embarrassment of this kind into an interpretation of the speaking as somehow 'inauthentic', perhaps even the result of directorial management (thereby illegitimately 'set up'), is to be oneself a victim of the ideology of spontaneity, of modern television naturalism. Indeed, the very awkwardness of non-professional performance in *Housing Problems* can be seen as a guarantee of communicative honesty. People who have no prior experience of public speaking perform public speech acts to the camera. They employ the conventional fiction of the camera as addressee, thereby appearing to look at, and speak to, the audience. The effect is one of powerful immediacy and engagement, all the more so in the reception conditions of cinema, far better suited to occasional moments of explicit 'public' address than to those semi-private accents which have since become a feature of television's domestic register.

What of the second point then, that whatever their local power, the placing of these segments within the film's system of exposition and evaluation is such as to 'contain' them and to confine their status to the secondary?

Anstey himself has reflected on the film's making in such a way as to suggest that 'access' was a primary aim:

> We narrowed ourselves down in *Housing Problems* to a very, very simple technique, which was open to us, at that time nobody had done it, and we gave the slum dwellers a chance to make their own film. This is why we kept all the aesthetics out until the very end ... what we felt was 'this is their film not ours. We don't want any directorial intervention. Their story is strong enough by itself.' (Interview with Roger Graef, *Arena*, BBC 2, 9 March 1982)

A similar point is to be found in another interview, in which he reflects interestingly on questions of method:

The art of record

Rotha often criticised *Housing Problems* because he thought there wasn't enough directorial intervention and guidance and shaping of the material. Well, Arthur [Elton] and I talked a lot about this, and we felt that the camera must remain sort of four feet above the ground and dead on, because it wasn't our film. (Sussex 1976:62)

As several commentators have pointed out (for example Miles and Smith 1987), this disclaiming of 'ownership' points at best to a partial truth. The overall project of the film is certainly not that of the slum dwellers, even though the main commentary places their testimony as a principal component of the 'evidence' (its simple, repetitive way of introducing the speakers has an. artlessness, even an awkwardness, which gives the local embedding of the testimony a degree of discursive democracy). The main expositional project is the progess being made in slum clearance as a result of the co-operation of planners, architects and local authorities. The speakers add 'subjective experience' to 'objective conditions' on both sides of the before-and-after divide. Their selection for the film would necessarily be partly determined by the variety of the experience they offered (avoiding too much repetition), the commonality of this experience (across the variety, certain levels of deprivation are a constant) and sufficiency of numbers (4 before/2 after is perhaps close to the minimum necessary to generate a sense of the 'representative'). This principal project is articulated within a discourse of 'progressive managerialism', and is in part an exercise in reformist civic education, noticeably suspect in some of its social assumptions when Councillor Lauder speaks of the behaviour of slum dwellers and their ability to keep their homes clean once transferred to improved accommodation. The speech of the caretaker (occupying the lowest level of the 'official') indicates both the custodial character of his duties and, in its phrasing and syntax, the language of bureacratic *routine*, of 'rules and regulations' and of 'proper times'. The sponsor's message about the contribution made by the gas industry is incorporated within the managerialist account of 'improvement', though there is no sense in which the film can be regarded simply or even primarily to be a promotional vehicle for the industry, since its depictive range extends far wider. Anstey has also commented on the terms in which sponsor and topic were related:

Arthur Elton and I succeeded in persuading the gas industry, who, after all, had a liberal tradition, a nonconformist tradition, that what you could do with film was to identify a big organisation with social purpose, to the advantage of both. Perhaps this was the Grierson notion passed on by Elton and myself that, in a way, no great corporation can dissociate itself from whatever the national issues are at any given time – particularly if, like gas, you're in the field of housing, basically. You're providing a public service. Anyway, we argued with them about this and they agreed to do a film on slums and slum clearance. (Sussex 1976:62)

So the 'access' project of the film is very closely circumscribed by other discursive requirements which are, themselves, part of implicit political and social perspectives. That the film does not develop an investigation of rentpayers' action groups, for example, nor place the problem of housing within a broader context of class inequality at the time is not surprising, given its origins and the character of the 1930s documentarist movement as, essentially, a reformist group operating within the terms of a contemporary social democratic consensus.[7] This should not excuse the film from its complicities and blurrings, but it requires that some attempt be made to understand the specific circumstances of its making and the range of real options available. Andrew Higson (Higson 1995:200) comments on the way in which the viewer is kept 'at a distance from ... the working-class victims of the film' by the intervening commentary, and thereby denied the possibility of 'identifying with their emotional states'. But, framed though their speech is, the slum dwellers are not like the miners in *Coalface* – mutes whose depicted actions concern the documentarist but whose own experience goes unregistered. Although it is hazardous to speculate on class-positioned readings, particularly where such an historical distance is involved, it does seem to me that Higson's reading conflicts with at least some contemporary interpretations (see Graham Greene above) and many if not most current ones too. What Higson regards as a device of distancing (the formal framing, the mode of speech) can also be seen, as I have suggested, as the means of an integrity in self-presentation.

Unlike *Coalface*, *Housing Problems* presents the viewer with few, if any, opportunities for pleasure. The absence of music from the soundtrack is of significance here when we compare it with the major function played by music in the other film. It is a tightly referential exercise in description and exposition, with little affective intent beyond that which is generated by the manner in which the slum dwellers talk of their conditions. The Dutch film-maker Joris Ivens is quoted as regarding the film to be among those British documentaries which 'fell into the trap of exotic dirt. You could not smell these London slums' (cited in Petley 1978). But the slums of *Housing Problems* hardly offer the excitement of the 'exotic' – they are too soberly illustrated, the limitations they impose on living too graphically described, for this.

Conclusions

Coalface shows the film documentary being used a central means for the development of cinema art. Its strongly affective use of music and its editing mix suggest, if anything, a distant forebear of the television commercial, although this is not to pass a direct judgement on its treatment of the coal industry. *Housing Problems* points more directly to the development of form and function in documentary television. It raises questions about 'ordinary speech' and the terms of its visual presentation and contextualisation. The relationship of the film-maker to 'official' discourses, ones institutionally linked to production (if not always by sponsorship), can be seen to be problematic.

The social class-relations of the 'social problem' documentary, the various ways in which class distance registers itself in a depiction of 'otherness' which becomes at times anthropological, are factors in both films. In *Coalface*, 'the miner' appears within an aesthetic structure which gives priority to striking visual effect. In *Housing Problems*, the 'ordinary' breaks through directly in the form of testimony, then raising questions about its articulation with the other speech in the film.

Both films show tensions and contradictions in the documentary project which still challenge film-makers and which are variously illustrated and explored in the chapters which follow.

4

Look in On London (1956)

This chapter is both a study of the early history of television documentary in Britain and an enquiry into the forms of television talk, particularly of that most important of speech genres, the interview.[1] Despite these broader aims, however, the focus is placed on specific programmes which, as in other chapters, are made the subject of detailed analysis. These programmes are short documentaries taken from a series, *Look in on London*, which was broadcast in 1956, the first full year of 'independent' (commercial) television in Britain. Whereas in other chapters I am frequently concerned with the originality and distinctiveness of a particular documentary, here I am more concerned with what the chosen works indicate about more general shifts in the development of the medium. In that sense, the examples which I draw on stand as directly 'representative' as well as having interest in themselves. Therefore, rather than proceeding from detailed description and formal analysis through to substantive issues (my procedure in most of the other chapters), I shall organise my discussion under a number of subheadings which bring questions of form, theme and context together around transcribed examples of programme discourse.

Contexts

Essentially, I am concerned with questions of transition and development during the mid- to late 1950s – a time when the nature of broadcast provision was significantly changed by the breaking of the BBC (British Broadcasting Corporation) monopoly and when so many shifts were occurring in British political and cultural life.[2] Within that frame, I have an interest in knowing more about the ways in which the documentary output of the BBC and ITV (Independent Television) variously responded, in image and speech usage, both to the new centrality of television as a medium of reportage and to cultural and social change. More narrowly still, among those discursive developments by which broadcasters sought to make documentary competitively engaging, the emergence of the location interview as a staple form of 'dramatised exposition' seems to me to be of particular importance.

The substantive focus, then, is provided by the early phases of television 'actuality' documentary and, more particularly, by those kinds of address to the viewer, modes of enquiry and visualisations of the social developed by ITV companies in their initial bid to compete against the BBC by providing what their senior executives often chose to call 'people's television'.[3] During this period, earlier registers of authoritative, public-service commentary and emerging formats for investigative journalism are mixed with fresh attempts at exploiting the domestic, personalised and sociable dimensions of the new medium in such a way as to provide documentary with egalitarian accents (though, of course, neither the motivation nor the social substance behind these accents can be taken for granted). Older cinematic traditions of the 'filmed essay' (as explored in Chapter 3) or the public information film connect with developing styles of conducting and shooting interviews, and with forms of location reporting in which a new directness and immediacy are increasingly sought, despite the physical limitations of 35mm film-making (especially when recording synchronised sound).

In what follows, I want to concentrate on three documentary programmes made and transmitted by Associated Rediffusion. The primary emphasis is on the mix of visual and verbal registers and styles of address apparent at this stage in the development of television's documentary discourse. Despite the hazards of cultural interpretation, I am also keen to discover what this formal mix might indicate about the social assumptions framing the documentarists' relationship with, on the one hand, the chosen topics, their contexts and the people whose images and voices serve to embody them and, on the other, with the members of the audience – their knowledge, values and expectations.

First of all, it may be useful to consider more closely some of the consequences of the shift from documentary within cinema to documentary within television, from documentary *films* to documentary *programmes*. I have referred in Chapter 1 to the general significance of this shift for the history of documentary internationally. However, an examination of *Look in on London* 'exposes' the conventions of documentary at a key point of transition, with both older codes and newer ones observable. The programmes thus point backwards, to the classic work of the 1930s and wartime, as well as forward, to the recipes of documentary series' journalism which we are familiar with today.

The social address of documentary television

Quite apart from the advantages which it eventually derived from changes in camera and recording technology, documentary television was almost from the start able to exploit properties and conventions of the medium which inevitably pulled it away from cinema-based styles of exposition.[4] Paramount here was the essentially 'domestic' character of a television service, coming into the living-rooms of the nation as part of a routine, regular provision and frequently viewed either in small family groupings or alone. Two related lines of advance led from this basic fact about the character of the system.

First, it became possible to produce documentary programme material within the larger format of a *series*. Here, continuity across the changes of topic could be provided by a regular presenter or presenters who would not only serve to give the series an identity, along with such things as title sequence, theme music, etc., but by becoming familiar to the audience would thereby perhaps generate something of the trust and the pleasure in expectation and recognition which familiarity can encourage.

Secondly, presenters were able to project a more informal relationship with the audience by using to the full the advantages which television 'direct address' speech can bring to the discursive work of exposition (e.g. colloquial speech-rhythms, expressive eye contact and the use of pronouns to set up relationships of complicity and identification within the process of viewing). In television, unlike cinema, the viewing space of the audience (home) can be intimately aligned with the institutional space of television (the studio/station), promoting a sense of mutual interiority in respect of which excursions to the actualities of the 'outside world' can proceed as joint ventures. Thus an alignment of space as well as an alignment of time ('immediacy') can form the 'setting' for television address. Moreover, the fact that the majority of the presenter/narrators of television documentary output were not experts or specialists (as in 'talks' broadcasting) but were *reporters* and *interviewers*, further heightened the potential for linking presenter and audience into an 'us'.[5] Television documentary, though it developed a strong vein of impressionistic, aesthetically self-conscious and clearly 'authored' programmes (drawing both on the 1930s cinema movement and on the pre-war tradition of radio features), had an increasing tendency to favour the 'journalistic' mode. Here, the more directly informational kind of 1930s film (such as *Housing Problems* – see Chapter 3) provided a more useful precedent along with concurrent developments in radio journalistic practice. Given the typical themes of journalistic enquiry, and given the medium's potential, indicated above, for personalised, intimate discourses, it is not at all surprising that the various forms of the interview, almost entirely absent from the 1930s cinematic tradition, should become the staple form of the new medium.

The BBC documentary-maker Norman Swallow comments on an early stage in the emergence of a new kind of social address in his discussion of the innovations begun by the BBC's *Special Enquiry*, first broadcast in 1952 and considerably influenced by the success of the American CBS (Columbia Broadcasting System) programme *See It Now*:

> The professional expert was replaced by the enquiring reporter, a man whose initial knowledge is no greater than that of the viewer on whose behalf he conducts the enquiry. He never dominates the programme, for most of its length he is only a voice speaking words that are slightly more personal than those of a film commentator ... . He moves from place to place, using his film camera as a reporter might use his notebook and pencil. He asks the questions that a sensible layman would ask ... . He was the fixed point of the enquiry, the man through whose eyes and ears the viewer absorbed the story. (Swallow 1956:51)[6]

Elsewhere (Corner 1991a) I have explored in some detail the project of *Special Enquiry* as a new kind of television journalism in which the narrativised reportage of the 'man on the spot' was interspersed with the more conventional commentary-over-film and, less conventionally, with the accessed voices of 'ordinary people' in direct-to-camera testimony and opinion. By the time a year or so of competition had intensified the need to build (or to keep) audiences by devising more entertaining approaches, the note of dutiful restraint suggested in Swallow's comments was no longer generally apposite. For yet newer versions of the 'personal' within the 'social' were being constructed, within newer rhetorics of documentary story-telling.

The 'sociable eye' of *Look in on London*

In exploring the shift towards more popular styles of documentary programming after 1955, I have chosen to focus on example from this 1956 series partly because three of the fifteen programmes made (identified as 'Sewermen', 'Streetcleaners' and 'Tramps') have not only survived but can be hired from the British Film Institute.[7] Tracing the history of television's various mediations of 'the social' is beset by the problem that huge gaps exist in the archive of tele-recordings and filmed inserts available for study. Of course, many programmes were simply not recorded at all and went out live to disappear for ever, while even material shot entirely on film was not often kept for very long. This makes it only too easy for a researcher to foreshorten programming developments and to over-emphasise links or contrasts by generalising from a strictly limited and potentially unrepresentative collection of surviving programmes.

Nevertheless, I believe that many aspects of the programmes selected relate both to general changes in documentary form in response to the need to compete for the expanding television audience and, more specifically, to an attempt by the ITV companies, with their newly recruited staff, to produce kinds of actuality material which contrasted appealingly and profitably with the more conventional BBC formats. The *Look in on London* series was made during an early phase of ITV's operation, subsequently dubbed 'The Retreat from Culture'. This phase, lasting for much of 1956, followed financial crisis in a number of companies resulting from initial advertising revenue being insufficient to cover costs. 'Serious' programming was dramatically reduced and the Independent Television Authority's requirements for a 'balanced' schedule were temporarily waived. The emphasis on programmes low in cost and high in popular appeal is very clear from several sources (see, for instance, Sendall 1982: 326–9).

The programmes were fifteen to twenty minutes long and, initially, were transmitted at 10.00 p.m. on Wednesdays (just before the very popular Western series *Gun Law*), though later they were shifted to a Monday spot. The producer of the series was Caryl Doncaster, a documentarist with extensive BBC experience behind her. The programmes were directed and presented by Michael Ingrams, who had been successful in Associated Rediffusion's popular and pioneering news magazine *This Week*, also produced by Doncaster.[8] The basic idea was a weekly 'look' at an aspect of life in London, mostly organized in terms of different kinds of public-service job and daily routine. The underlying model appears to have been a straight development from the social democratic explorations of much 1930s documentary. The object is once again to reveal the essential interdependence and engaging variety of the different elements in a fundamentally consensual social order. Two central themes from the 1930s are evident: revelation of the 'hidden drama' behind essential industries and public services, and the documentation of social problems (e.g. bad housing, vagrancy, low wages) relatively independent of explicit political or economic analysis.

Yet the programmes differ in a number of respects and often sharply both from earlier cinema documentaries and from those earlier television documentaries which I have either been able to see or to locate descriptions of. For a start, each programme's construction of the 'social' involves a much tighter focus on specific individuals encountered *in situ*, as it were, during the course of the weekly expedition. As well as primarily representing a (mostly occupational) 'type', these individuals are also investigated by the interviewer in terms of their more personal and private identities – in respect of family life, hobbies, leisure, etc. In this sense, then, the series provides much more of a 'people show' than most earlier documentary formats,[9] though given the scarcity of archive material, it would probably be inaccurate to place emphasis on its distinctiveness within contemporary developments.[10] Nevertheless, the programmes also have general informational business to manage (e.g. about London's sewage system, about refuse collection and disposal, about welfare provision for vagrants), and this they do largely by reverting to a relatively conventional use of commentary film.

A second, general respect in which the programmes differ from most earlier work is in the kinds of relationship which they are able to strike up with the viewer, chiefly by being able to realise those communicational possibilities of broadcast television mentioned above and by having the strand of individualised human interest and interaction just described. The invitation to 'look in' is here not only an invitation to knowledge but to entertainment (as a 'busker'-type theme tune, prominently featuring a banjo, makes clear). The accepting viewer adventures out 'on location' with the genial reporter as guide, to be taken into circumstances and encounters which, despite their being *recorded* on film, are mediated strongly within conventions of television immediacy. These conventions were currently getting a new edge through developments in OB (Outside Broadcasting) – magically linking the comfort and security of domestic viewing with the happenstance and knowledge of 'out there' experience and activity.[11]

A broad sense of some of the more general social and presentational ideas which lay behind the devising of the programme can be found in the comments of its producer:

> In those days the image of the Beeb [BBC] was very upper class and stiff establishment. The voices, clothes and 'personas' of the interviewers were public school, and of course ITV, appealing more to the working man, changed all that.

And, again, on production intentions:

> We were also all young and believers in a classless, buoyant Britain, and a variety of accents. Above all, we wanted everything natural, and to get ratings and hold interest we pruned out ruthlessly and tried to start everything in an exciting manner. (Letter to the author[12])

I shall develop these preliminary observations by examining a selection of transcribed extracts from the programmes. This should allow points and questions around three themes in particular to receive some depth of illustration. These themes are the relations between 'the public' and 'the private' set up by the programmes, the conduct of the 'enacted encounters' of the reporter-on-location and, finally, the governing assumptions at work in the programmes' overall address.

Public and private

As in the other surviving programmes in the series, the exposition of the edition 'Streetcleaners' is chiefly organised by movement between two basic types of material. There is the 'lively', human interest of encountering different kinds of people at work – an interest grounded in the 'location interviews' upon which each week's journey of discovery is based. Then, set within this, there is the direct delivery of information through voiced-over film, involving altogether more formal and distanced viewing relationships.

These two constituents of the documentary account are constructed within differing rhetorics of the documentary 'eye'. The newer rhetoric places the viewer as the invited, close 'onlooker' in relation to the enquiring activities and social encounters of the guide/reporter, though an 'uninvited' camera often discovers subjects in their activities just prior to the official arrival of the programme in the person of the reporter. A typical sequence is from such a scene of 'discovery', into which the reporter enters, through a medium shot of reporter and subject/s, and then into an interview exchange mixing variously distanced 'two shots' with alternating close-ups of speakers plus occasional cutaways to the reporter. The limitations imposed by the equipment at this stage in the development of actuality shooting, together with the related rehearsal requirements, combine to give a static, tableau-like quality to the encounters in comparison with later conventions of mobility and continuity in the engaging and holding of the viewer as onlooker.

The sections of commentated film are strongly word-led, with the sequence of images largely confined to the directly illustrative role of depicting places and processes underneath a light descriptive account. This account is peppered with 'remarkable facts', sometimes drawing revealingly on a programme's deepest social assumptions ('Each one of us throws away in a year an equivalent amount of food to feed the average Indian for three months') and occasionally modulating into tones of sub-Dimbleby sonority ('By next year the old kipper bones, cigarette cartons, newspapers and the sweepings from street, shop and home will all have changed into rich, brown earth').

In all three programmes examined, the project of discovery/exposition gets off to a brisk start. Here is a transcription of the opening of 'Streetcleaners', following the titles which, in the programmes discussed, locate the programme name on a placard somewhere within the establishing shots.

> (CU [close-up] shots of broom sweeping gutter; speech in VO [voice-over]) Who wields this broom? Fred Robinson, Robbo to his friends. He keeps one and a half miles of Maida Vale in a state in which you'd wish to find it – which is not the state you left it in.

The programme is hereby immediately launched upon an enquiry having both a sharply personal dimension and an address to the viewer mediated via the category of 'citizen', a category in which a degree of 'taking-for-granted' of public services can be assumed and jokingly chided. 'We' do not know who Robbo is, 'we' expect clean streets but leave litter. 'We', presumably, relate to Maida Vale as the kind of area we might live in (perhaps a more problematically specific interpellation?). Notice, too, how there is offered an alternative, more intimate rendering of the cleaner's identity – an early signal of the kind of bridge which the programme, through its onlooking and overhearing practices, wishes to construct between viewers' world and subject's world.

After this opening sequence, the programme (through the presenter/reporter) moves in to *arrest* the flow of the taken-for-granted activity in order to open it up for viewer understanding; to explore its occupational and personal as well as its public and organisational aspects. This requires the expositional theatricality of the 'as-if-spontaneous' interview, seeming to be generated abruptly out of the presenter's encounter with the working routines of the chosen subjects and relayed to the viewer as part of the programme's ongoing, co-present enquiries. The first section of interview proceeds as follows. (Throughout this chapter I have used I, and R, to indicate, respectively, Interviewer and Respondent.)

> (Medium shot of street-cleaner with a handcart sweeping gutter, reporter enters L.)
> I   Good afternoon.
> R   Good afternoon.
> I   You ever get tired doing this all day long? (Cut closer)
> R   No, I don't get tired at all.
> I   Don't you?
> R   No.
> I   Don't you ... doesn't it get a bit monotonous sweeping the same gutters?
> R   No, I got so used to it now.
> I   How long have you been doing it?
> R   Seven years.
> I   Oh, what were you doing before then?
> R   I was working for the Kensington Borough Council. (CU face)
> I   As what?
> R   As a dustman.
> I   Which do you like best, street-sweeping or dustbinning? (CU reporter)
> R   Well, I'd sooner be a dustman.
> I   Would you?
> R   Yes.
> I   Don't you get a bit of lumbago with all those ... carting those heavy dustbins around?
> R   No, I got so used to it.
> I   Did you? What happens to you on this job? What sort of people do you meet?
> R   Well, I got half a cigarette here now what a gentleman give us to me the other day. (CU hands and cigarette box)
> I   Well, you've kept it?
> R   Yes, he always comes out the mansions every morning wet or fine, an,d er, takes twenty fags out, takes one out, breaks it in half, gives one half to me puts the other back in his pockets.
> I   Ha! Ha! Ha! every morning?
> R   Every morning, wet or fine.
> I   Who are these chaps? (Reporter's eyes shift to out-of-shot distance. Dustcart arrives.)

What seems immediately striking here is both the directness and, on occasion, awkward naivety of these initial questions about 'work'. This is all at some distance from the elaborately scripted (and often deeply condescending) fluency of many earlier kinds of documentary approach to working experience. Nevertheless, the terms on which this devised encounter between the representative of television and the street-cleaner takes place seem to shift uncertainly between a brisk, 'official' interrogation and the simulation of chat. No hand microphone interposes between presenter and subject and the presenter's posture is emphatically 'casual' (hands in pockets), contrasting with the other's nervous rigidity. The regular repetitions ('don't you', 'did you', etc.) and the sudden jump in level

Look in on London

to an implausibly general cue-question ('What happens to you on this job?') also suggest both an early stage in the development of this type of television interview performance and (perhaps) a relatively inexperienced interviewer. The problem may be seen as partly one of producing speech in an adequate *performance register*. This register mimics the syntax and cadence of a private exchange but, of course, it is throughout shaped by the requirements of staging a specific type of public display. For the interviewee, the tensions involved in maintaining a performance without straying out of his allocated role as a spontaneous speaker are considerable, and I shall return to this question in relation to later examples.

The 'chance' arrival of the dustcart at the end of the sequence provides two more interviewees and the start of further anecdotal explorations of working life (memories of earlier times, coping with the smell, unusual things found in the rubbish, etc.). It is when the cart pulls away, leaving Robbo and the interviewer 'alone' again, that the programme moves to a very different level of the social. As the cleaner puts his gear back on his handcart, this exchange occurs:

(Reporter to street-cleaner, cart in between)
I   Off home now, are you?
R   Yes.
I   I bet you need a good bath now after ...
R   I haven't got a bath
I   You haven't got a bath?
R   No, not where I am. It's a requisitioned house, it's condemned.
I   Condemned?
R   Yes, it's been condemned ever since 1939.
I   And you've been in it all that time?
R   Yes, and I'm still waiting to get into a council flat.
I   Ah, you're on the list, are you?
R   I'm on the list. I'm on the Kensington Borough list and the LCC [London County Council] list and I'm still waiting.
I   Oh and it's really bad is it?
R   In a very bad condition.
I   No, ...
R   It's unfit to live in.
I   Is it?
R   Yes.
I   Well ... er ...
R   There's only me and my missus and we're eating and sleeping in one room.
I   Could I come back and meet your wife?
R   Yes, you're willing [*sic*] to come back and have a look at it and see what you think of it.
I   Well, that's very kind of you, hm, tell me, while we're going along, (they walk off) what happens to all that rubbish that, er?
R   All the rubbish goes into the salvage van and goes down to Westminster to be 'chuted into the barge ...
(Fade to film sequence with reporter VO)

Here, once more, it is the apparently spontaneous route by which the information and the follow-up request are delivered that is crucial to the effect. Since the programme has not so far indicated that the question of the housing conditions of council employees will be part of its concern, this sudden turn in the direction of its attention appears quite astounding when read in the context of current documentary convention.[13] The fact that the move to this new aspect of the social is, as it were, *dramatised* as a scene of expectations confounded (leaving aside interesting questions about how it originated in the research and pre-take planning), rather than being introduced through some voiced-over link or to-camera comment, simulates precisely that sense of ongoing development (the presenter portrayed as being as surprised as the viewer) sought by the programme as a whole. Thus at the finish of the exchange, when yet another shift of focus and register leads into a sequence of commentary film on the processing of refuse (presented as a parallel phase to their conversations as they 'go along') the scene from which the fade-down is made presents the bizarre spectacle of a very urbane-looking man in a natty business suit escorting a street-cleaner (pushing his handcart) home! It is the highly personalised framings of the occupational and the social within which the programme works that permit this narratively continuous movement from the initial, *topic*-constituted typification (street-cleaning, a street-cleaner) to the more intensively individualised representation of *person* and personal circumstances. In this latter, the referenced *category* of the social becomes unclear (typical street-cleaners' circumstances? typical manual workers'? typical working-class?).

Given this re-framing, from the occupational through the personal to the domestic, the sequences in Robbo's house betray some uncertainty of address. Awkwardly 'square-on' in shot and initially stilted in their attempts at a spontaneously colloquial route through to the kind of information sought, they depict Robbo and his wife being interviewed about the condition of their home, the weekly budget, leisure-time hobbies (they have no television), and even their happiness together. The mix of questioning here blends elements of jovial inquisitiveness about the personal (though the class tones and manner of the interviewer make this role a perhaps less comfortable and certainly a less convincing one to perform) with more serious investigative goals. An anticipated move to a new flat and speculation about the 'new life' which will follow provide a way of offsetting the strongly negative portrayal of Robbo and his wife's conditions. However, the programme does not attempt to develop (in the manner of, say, *Housing Problems*) an overt theme of social improvement by which depicted deprivation is reassuringly framed.

After another brief sequence of commentary film, this time concerning the use of London's refuse in land reclamation, we are returned to the streets again for a final comment:

(Reporter's VO:CU shot of broom sweeping gutter.) And tomorrow Robbo's old broom will be busy again. This time we shall know who it is we are passing the time of day with. (Passes Robbo at work, greets him and moves close to camera for direct address.) One more of London's millions who's no longer a stranger. (Walks off with a farewell wave to Robbo.)

Here, at the end of the programme, the kind of social connections aimed for come out clearly in the suggestion of future familiarity. In the classic tradition of earlier film documentaries, but in a far more direct manner, 'we' are being put in touch with 'others' – the programme is promoting not only knowledge and vicarious social adventure but also a form of social relationship. The final line whimsically supposes some slow but steady process by which strangers are transformed into acquaintances through the programme's not only social but 'sociable' address (see Scannell 1988 on broadcasting's modes of sociability). Though, clearly, Robbo is no more a 'stranger' to his friends and workmates then 'we' are to ours, the line carries an implicit notion – linking it back to the project of the 1930s films – of the disturbing anonymity of the urban mass and of the need to strengthen connections of community. Creeping into this concluding comment there is perhaps a hint of a documentary ideal altogether more ambitious than that of disseminating popular knowledge: an ideal of ultimate parasociality, in which documentary introduces everyone (and their jobs) to everyone else. I shall discuss some implications of this idea in the context of the series as a whole, but I would like first to turn to a brief examination of the principal feature of the programmes' exposition.

Interview – encounter – enactment

The programmes use new ideas about televisual documentary form to produce actuality material which is itself able to set up new kinds of relationship with audiences through its ways of accessing the social via activity within location *mise-en-scène*, quite apart from the relationships projected verbally by commentary and presentation. Yet this rendering of the social, freed from the limitations of studio treatments and with a newly democratic/populist sense of appropriate topics and framings, now had to construct naturalisms of behaviour and speech to exploit fully the possibilities for heightened immediacy and dynamics. Shooting styles, on-camera activity and speech registers sometimes display uneasiness and inconsistency in these initial phases of extending the range of documentary discourse.

Some indications of this have already been given, but a further example can be found in another programme in the series, 'Tramps'. This attempts to explore aspects of the life of London's vagrant community and, eschewing the usual introductory address, it starts abruptly with the presenter in a lodging-house chatting to a seated group of men. One lodger's comments about a particular reception centre are soon interrupted by a shift to a filmed report ('Before you tell me about it, I want to take the viewers over to see it') in which we accompany the reporter into the centre. This leads through to a meeting with the centre's warden which develops as below:

(Centre yard, warden in conversation with man, other men in background)
Warden   ... So don't be foolish and go out ... leave the centre, stay until

you've had your vacancy allotted to you. All right, my lad?
Man   Yes sir, thank you very much, sir.
Warden   Off you go.
(Man walks off, reporter enters, they shake hands)
I   Mr Hollis?
R   Mr Ingrams, I'm very pleased to greet you at our reception centre here.
I   Thank you very much. I've had a bit of a look, bit like a barracks, isn't it?
R   Very much so. Built in 1878 as an old workhouse. Rose by any other name. Now a reception centre.
I   Now suppose I walk in here today and tell you that I'm destitute, which isn't so far from the truth, what happens to me?
R   You would be asked for particulars – for yourself, and sign a form to say you were destitute. Making a false statement would cause you to be prosecuted for making a false statement, but all things being equal you would be admitted.
I   And what then?
(Cut to warden's VO; film sequence)
You would be directed to the bathroom where your clothing would be thoroughly inspected for vermin.

A number of things are of interest here. First of all, there is the very explicit manner in which the reporting is dramatised chronologically in the form of a visit – thus projecting, for viewer involvement, the sense of ongoing enquiry, a sense further reinforced by the facetiously self-dramatising character of the initial questioning. The warden is first 'discovered' giving advice to one of the men and it is into this framing of unobserved onlooking that the reporter walks to be formally welcomed. Like a number of other occasions in the programmes when interviews with officials are featured, a problem of finding and sustaining appropriate registers of address arises. The interaction, though essentially a public act, feigns 'private' behaviour. Unlike the television professional, the subject/interviewee may find that the mixed form of speech best suited to this cannot be easily produced, even after preparation and a run-through. Thus we have the apparent awkwardness of a visually rendered one-to-one exchange in which the colloquiality of the reporter contrasts with the stiff, 'on the platform' formality of the respondent. From the start, the warden stays within the syntax and phrasings of 'official language', being perhaps reluctant to risk the loss of authority within the exchange which might follow a more personalised performance, quite apart from the difficulty of getting such a performance right. This is underlined by the move from his interview speech to his voiced-over commentary. The latter, though it continues in the basic register established in the interview, is clearly recorded at a different phase in the scheme of filming and, read from a script, it loses all semblance of conversational rhythm or spontaneity, having the itemisation of institutional procedures as its primary concern.

Both the explicit referencing of a report as 'in process' and the uncertainty of respondent register are clearly apparent again in the exchange which ends a further section of question-and-answer following the warden's commentary. Here, a strong class inflection to the reporter's vocabulary is obvious too, as the programme subordinates itself to authority, whilst representing this as the seeking of *personal goodwill*:

> (Reporter to warden in centre yard)
> I Now, I've a favour to ask of you. Will you give me a *carte blanche* to go round, look at everything and maybe talk to one or two of your ... er chaps?
> R Certainly. You're most welcome to go round to speak to who you like and see what you like. If you require further assistance I shall be at your disposal.

It would be useful to have more programmes from this and other contemporary series available in order to see how far the represented relationships with officials and managers have general difficulties with sustaining the naturalism of 'on location' disclosure and the enactments of relaxed spontaneity upon which this is based. Unlike most of the manual and skilled workers interviewed in the programmes, officials may, in varying degrees, feel that they are put at risk by the scrutiny of the visiting television team. They may therefore have too big a commitment in projecting 'correct' impressions to develop the performance both of publicly informative comment and yet also of ostensibly situation-generated chat which the presenter seeks to elicit. It is also true that whereas the workers are frequently seen to be *interrupted* by the presenter in the course of their working routines (e.g. sweeping the gutters, clearing a sewer), thus preclassifying subsequent interview exchanges with them as variations on 'casual talk' (however uneasy or interrogatively weighted these may be), officials are seen to enter the space of the programme voluntarily and with their own professional identities and terms in play from the start. To put it another way, the programme is seen to 'happen on' the workers but to involve officials by prior arrangement.

To illustrate this point and the associated discursive conventions, a sharp contrast can be drawn between the above encounter and the initial section of 'Streetcleaners' cited earlier or with this exchange from the programme 'Sewermen':

> (In sewers, two men working, shovelling silt. Reporter to second man who pauses, hand on shovel)
> I What do you feel about night work?
> R Well, it's just something you gradually get used to, like. It's like everything else: you adapt yourself to it.
> I Have you been doing this work long?
> R Well, close on four years.
> I What were you doing before?
> R Well, I was a milkman.
> I Do you prefer this to being a milkman?
> R Yes, I settled more to this than I did to the milk trade.
> I That's ... that's an astonishing thing that you should prefer sludge to milk ... . Tell me why?
> R Well, for one thing it's ... I don't know ... it's just something that you

The art of record

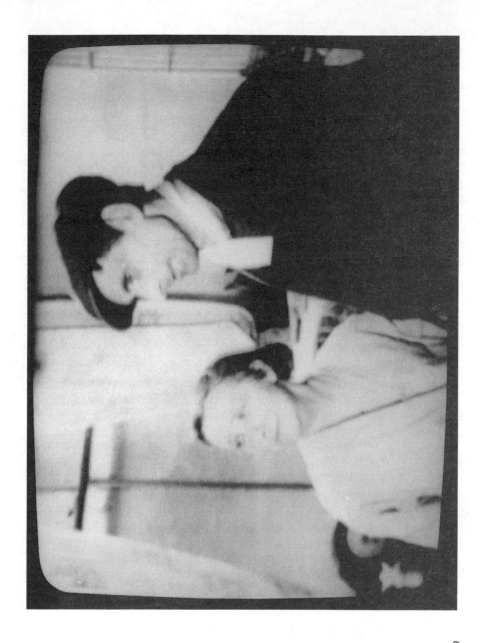

Anthropology at home: Robbo
and his wife in *Look In On London*

just can't explain I think that that ... anyway I think as a milkman you're never done. We do know when we're done here at least.

I I see, the hours are the big thing, are they? Is the pay better here than on a milk round?

R The actual flat rate, flat rate, of course the milkman gets more local commission and all that.

I Hmm, are you married?

R Yes.

I Does your wife prefer you doing these shorter hours with less money to longer hours and more money?

R This is more steady and more regular like, you know, that's her general idea.

I So, she's pleased.

R Yes, really, yes.

I Good.

(VO) Time for me to climb back to the outside world

Here, as in the 'Streetcleaners' interview, the push through to the personal is rapidly achieved through references to the nature of the job being performed and the enquiry is conducted in what certainly seems to be a disconcertingly brisk style. The interviewee has little choice but to accept his allocated role as the amiable supplier of 'particulars'. As with other interviews of this kind, an anthropological character is given to investigator/subject relationships as a result of the distance, assumed and then emphatically signified, between 'us' (here, inhabitants of the 'outside world') and the particular and strange world of work which we are bridged to by the programme's depictions.[14] At one point, the idea of strangeness is given a condescendingly jokey treatment through the suggestion that the interviewee prefers sludge to milk. This specific rendering of strangeness is located within a larger strangeness typifying the relationship between the programmes' own discourses and the whole realm of working-class jobs, speech and recreation. Part of the series' character as social adventure, as well as its agenda of enquiry, derives from this strangeness, raising questions about the class character of viewing relations and of response among its contemporary audiences.

'Looking in': terms and contexts

My initial interest in these programmes was a teaching interest. Their differences, across a thirty-year gap, from current documentary images and speech, proved useful in relativising the conventions of documentary realism and in opening up questions about the links both with changing social and political relations and the developing technical means of representation. In particular, this stage of the move towards greater immediacy, intimacy and continuity (key ingredients of 'watchability') seemed important in respect of its *performance* requirements, which move closer to those of fictional realism. A rather paradoxical gap thereby opens up between the terms of representation (spontaneous, ongoing revelation projecting co-presence with the viewer) and the determining, though largely hidden, terms of construction (organisation and preparation of the interviews, enactment of various entries, encounters, farewells, etc., editing so as to construct a condensed chronology for the account). This is clearly bound up with the idea of grounding exposition diegetically (each week's 'trip') rather than organising it explicitly through themes and topics. As other examples in this book illustrate, topic-structured programmes can employ a range of different representational forms (e.g. studio direct address, filmed report, archive compilation, studio and location interviews) without 'enactment' being demanded beyond the normative convention of supposing interviewees to be engaged primarily in interpersonal exchange.

The personalised, diegetic format of visit and encounter, capable of incorporating through its presenter both serious and light-hearted themes, must have been regarded at the time as one of the most promising ways of producing popular documentary, given technical practicality (e.g. the constraints on any vérité approach). As suggested above, the simulation of Outside Broadcast 'liveness' and the general importance attached to getting television 'out of the studio' were probably strong influencing factors on the idea of approaching social enquiry through the naturalistic representation of 'finding out' as, itself, a sequence of interactive social episodes. There is a contrast here with the use of interviewee voice-over so effectively pioneered in television documentary by Denis Mitchell.[15] In this mode, places, people and social actions are viewed within the framing given by the speech of unidentified and often unseen participants, whose apparently unsolicited recounting of anecdotes and opinions provides a rich, informational address, grounding the film in 'subject' rather than 'observer' consciousness. However, the 'inner' character of speech thus elicited and used (the term 'think-tape' was coined to describe Mitchell's innovative use of the tape recorder for speech collection independent of the camera) provides neither the concise, factual responses of the 'enactment' method nor its drama of sociability.

The specific 'social optics' by which *Look in on London*'s invitations are constructed inevitably relate to its broader cultural, as well as to its formal and technical contexts. Its (often awkward) movement between 'public information' and 'human interest' strands of enquiry stems in part from the fact that this is still the first phase of actuality-based social exploration by television. It is the sense of a largely unexplored social landscape on the one hand and a new and enthusiastic domestic audience on the other which informs the programmes' self-consciously bright and informal address and their notions of what, using the format, can engagingly be 'found out'. Within the terms of the social democratic perspective from which their expeditions into the city are mounted, there is clearly a lot of finding out to be done. The ostensible *topic* of each programme therefore only loosely governs the local organisation and treatment of the actuality material (including the interview-encounters), as is clear in the sequences from 'Streetcleaners'.

Here, it is perhaps important to note that although the manner of enquiry frequently contains echoes of a genial chat style founded precisely on hierarchic division (such as one might find, for instance, between officers and men in the forces), the programmes *do* attempt to register 'work' in a way quite different from most earlier documentary versions of the social. Elements of working experience and of working lives (e.g. hours, rates of pay, conditions, leisure opportunities), often entirely absent from documentary framing, are here located firmly within it. The clear class-resonances of the encounters between presenter and workers and the confident middle-class versions of sociability upon which the presenter's egalitarian adventures are based also interestingly point to the absence of professionalised 'classlessness' at this stage in the emerging repertoire of journalistic performance.[16] Comparison with earlier, marked inflections of the class voice in documentary (discussed in relation to *Coalface* and *Housing Problems* in Chapter 3) would, however, show the 'accommodations' of post-war social change. Just how marked or how naturalised these class factors would appear to the audiences of the time is, of course, difficult to assess. The element of class confrontation tends to be made more obvious by the style of interview depiction, using continuous question-and-answer sequences and extensive 'two-shot' framing rather than the variety of more oblique, post-shoot devices which might now be used in the development of occupational or personal themes (e.g. interview used in fragments with interviewer out of frame and perhaps with questions removed; interviewees' comments used for short sequences of voice-over).

In a very useful survey of representations of the British working class in the period 1957–64, Stuart Laing discusses the development of the 'affluence' ideology and of the idea that an increasing spread of middle-class values followed from rising standards of living. He notes that '1956 was the key year for the consolidation of this image of an affluent Britain undergoing embourgeoisement' (Laing 1986:17).

Look in on London seems placed on the edge of the buoyant, Conservative, 'New Britain' discourses which Laing documents. Some of the assumptions behind its questioning and its projected appeal appear to be partly framed by that calculatedly depoliticising perspective, with its notions of established consensus and the shift to brighter times being brought about by market expansion. In that respect, its vein of class-confident populism can be seen as part of an experiment in new forms of discursive management. Nevertheless, as I have shown, it locates and represents its subjects within the framework of real differences in working conditions and living standards, within a society where 'welfare' is still a central and necessary term of concern. In doing this, it continues and develops a dominant, earlier strand of documentary discourse, connecting a public-service style surveillance of the social with a more innovative if also uncertain investigatory interest in 'the people'.

A selection from one series is clearly no sound basis for 'reading off' a general system of social relationships or its typical modes of mediation. Much remains to be done in the history of broadcast documentary, both in primary research and in producing a more secure theoretical and analytical grasp of developments. It has been part of my argument in this chapter, linking with the analyses contained elsewhere in this book, that close scrutiny of the forms of speech as they develop distinctive conventions of performance and of projected social relationship are an important part of such enquiry.

5 *Cathy Come Home* (1966)

Cathy Come Home was written by Jeremy Sandford, produced by Tony Garnett and directed by Ken Loach. It was shown on BBC1 as a *Wednesday Play* on 16 December 1966 and was widely reviewed in the press, subsequently being seen to be instrumental in developing public awareness of the problem of homelessness. There was a short-term response in terms both of public donations to charities and the review of national and local housing provision. The emergence and public profile of the housing charity Shelter has been linked to the broadcast.[1] Some commentators, however, have attempted to correct what they see as exaggerated claims for the social consequences of the programme by pointing to the relatively short duration of the 'Cathy effect', however intense this may have been, and the continuing and increasing problem of homelessness (see Sandford himself on this latter point in Sandford 1976).

In its mixing of dramatic and documentary elements, *Cathy* has come to be seen as a representatively 'classic' piece of British television, articulating social problems through a hybrid aesthetic which moves the viewer through a number of spectator positions, variously placed in relation to on-screen action and sounds. More generally still, it is often seen as a piece of 'essential television', producing out of its combined tactics an immediacy which could not be paralleled in any other medium, even in cinema. Yet the film has also attained a strongly individual stature, for although it can be placed in relation to the broader movement of British documentarism, its specific organisation and rhetorical range are, as we shall see, quite distinctive.

Sandford had previously worked on a radio documentary, *Homeless Families*, which he had researched in London. Disappointed with the apparent lack of response to the broadcast, he set about writing a film treatment, drawing on a large number of newspaper clippings, audiotape transcripts and notes (Sandford 1973, extracted in Goodwin *et al.* (eds) 1983: 18). Initially, Sandford had great difficulty in getting the script of *Cathy* accepted for television, and re-worked it as a book, but Tony Garnett eventually took it up for the BBC and Ken Loach was made director. Shot on 16mm film and on location, the production, though a television play, was able to benefit from the 'realist film' aesthetic which had already been established in British cinema.[2] This aesthetic had developed the portrayal of working-class storylines within contemporary or near-contemporary settings, catching at the reorganising of relations of class and gender, of work and leisure and yet the continuation, within a dominant national climate of aspiration and increased prosperity, of radical inequalities. The location-film format provided the basis for the kinds of documentarist address which give the play much of its power. Though the specific conventions of dramatic and documentary style which *Cathy* uses are very much of their period, the particular energy of their combination ensures that the film has both a continuing dramatic impact and a documentary resonance with audiences.

The following discussion will seek to highlight the particular features which resulted in *Cathy* attracting critical controversy in a manner which prefigures the debate around more recent 'drama documentary' productions. I discussed in Chapter 2 the way in which the use of this term, and others like it, such as 'docudrama', often hides important differences in the conception and execution of works. Close study of *Cathy* suggests some of these differences and my later analysis will illustrate them further. However, it is worth noting here how Sandford himself saw the advantages of applying the dramatic method to what is in many respects a documentary intent. He notes what are effectively three immediate advantages:

> Most people find it hard to be themselves in front of a tape-recorder or movie camera. And there are many places to which these cannot get without destroying the very thing they come to show. But the researcher–writer can get into most of these places and talk to those who have been there, and can then script an objectively accurate re-creation of what really happens and what people are really like when they are not posturing for the cameras. Also the camera can only interview particular people about their particular view of some event. The dramatized documentary writer can quintessentialize the wider implications. (Sandford 1973, extracted in Goodwin *et al.* (eds) 1983:16)

So the drama-documentary can avoid the problems of nervousness or posturing encountered in working with ordinary people. It can overcome the problems of 'access' which might thwart a conventional documentary approach and it can construct a very particular account in a way which is informed by more general circumstances.

Of course, all these three 'advantages' might equally as well be considered as liabilities. Working with actors rather than ordinary people might be seen to risk evasion of the public responsibilities of television, in respect both of veracity and of representational democracy, particularly if it became a general procedure. The ability of writers to produce an 'objectively accurate re-creation' may seriously and justly be doubted and, indeed, a defence of dramatised documentary which places emphasis on this is likely to become vulnerable quite quickly, as opposed to one which highlights the problems of achieving 'objectivity' in *any* form of television. Finally, 'quintessentialisation', whereby social themes not made explicit or subject to examination become decisive in the formation of character and action, hides begged questions about what the 'wider implications' actually *are*. Again, the play of inferences upon depiction is not a 'problem' unique to this form, but Sandford's claims seem over-confident in the context of the more sceptical climate which now surrounds the medium's relationship to 'truth'.

Description

Cathy Come Home is a narrative about a young woman, her marriage and her various experiences of homelessness as a mother, culminating in the enforced removal of her children by officers of the Social Services. Its episodic structure begins with a scene of Cathy hitch-hiking into London, having run away from home, and follows her through the next five years or so, ending with her sitting on a bench, alone and distraught, at a London railway station. A key principle of its organisation is the regular provision of first-person, past-tense narration by Cathy herself. As I shall suggest below, this reflective voice, commenting on 'then' from 'now', serves to feed both the dramatic and the documentary dimensions of the film. It is crucial both in regulating the relationship of the viewer to what they see and hear and in connecting between scenes (sometimes involving considerable jumps in location and time). *Cathy* develops both as 'story' and as 'report', the latter being produced through the use of images and speech which generate a documentary referentiality around the main line of narrative action, thereby connecting this to contemporary reality in a way which differs from conventional drama.

The main storyline can briefly be indicated as three sections of development.

1. Cathy runs away from home. In the city she meets Reg. They fall in love and marry. Their first flat is expensive to rent but they learn from a building society about the problems of buying a house. Cathy becomes pregnant, but Reg has an accident at work for which he receives no compensation since his employer is not working within union terms. The couple look for cheaper lodgings.

2. Cathy and Reg move in with Reg's mother in a tenement block but disagreements soon push them out into old, low-rent terraced housing. Their landlady dies and they are evicted by the new owners following a court order. They seek a place on the council-house list and take a caravan outside town. The camp is the focus of local discontent and violence and the caravan is set on fire and destroyed, killing two of the children. The couple move to a 'squat' in abandoned terraces and then to a tent. Finally Cathy is taken into emergency hostel accommodation with the children, but Reg

The art of record

is not allowed to join her there (though he secretly enters her room on the first night).

3. The accommodation is shown to have a mixture of women, with varying backgrounds. Reg visits Cathy. In desperation, Cathy asks Reg's mother to take care of her eldest son temporarily because of the effect on him of hostel life. At an assessment board, Cathy hears that she is not at the top of the list for a home on the new estate. She attacks board members for their attitude towards her. The decision is made to put her into inferior, 'Part 3' accommodation. She enters the accommodation, based on dormitories rather than private rooms. Reg visits her here but reports that there is no improvement in his own position. Cathy has a confrontation with a nurse over the death of a baby in the hostel. The nurse accuses Cathy and other assembled mothers of a lack of cleanliness. Cathy attacks the nurse and appears before the hostel director. He mentions not only this incident but also the case of a young woman fitting her description who has spoken to journalists about conditions in the hostel. It is suggested that Reg has ceased to pay the fees; one of the board members queries whether she is really married. Cathy is evicted from the Part 3 hostel. Finding no room to rent, she ends up at a railway station. Officers from the Social Services arrive and take the children from the fighting, screaming Cathy. She is left sitting alone on the station. In a final shot, over which the captions and the credits are run, she is seen in mid-close-up with traffic noises on the soundtrack, suggesting that, as in the opening shot, she is on the road again, looking for a lift.

This division of the narrative into three sections is not formally marked, nor would I want to claim that it is superior to other ways of seeing *Cathy*'s organisation. But the viewing experience seems to me to be one which it is useful to reflect upon in terms of this division. First of all, the social establishing of Cathy, Reg and family; secondly, the cumulative misfortunes and steady 'descent' of accommodation levels; finally, institutionalisation and the removal of Cathy's children.

Analysis

A critical appreciation of *Cathy* can best start with an attempt at identifying the way in which its dramatic and documentary aspects interrelate and complement each another. I shall consider first how the film is organised as drama, and then look at its 'extension' into documentary, though I am well aware that these terms do not indicate clear-cut categories.

Cathy as story: dramatic form

By being principally about one person, whose chronologically organised activities form the basis of almost all the scenes, *Cathy* develops the character-continuity of conventional drama. This continuity is regulated, as I noted above, by the extensive use of Cathy's voice as commentary over scenes and as 'bridges' between them. Derek Paget has observed how this overlaying of 'then' action with 'now' voice, begun right at the start of the film in the sequence of hitch-hiking into London, provides a classic framing for the story, setting up expectations about a tale of personal experience and becoming (Paget 1990:95). The tone, confiding and often ruminative, is in many respects a 'speech' version of first-person novelistic narration. However, a key difference is that whereas in written fiction using such a device the action itself is most often *described* by the narrator, in *Cathy* the commentary relates to what is *being seen and heard* by the viewer on the plane of dramatic action. 'Then' is constructed by discourses independent of the placing voice of Cathy, which, as well as adding extra information, opens up powerfully on the motivations, feelings and 'inner significance' of events. There is also a further twist to this alignment of voice-over and depiction, in that the recollective voice appears to be organised in response to the *depiction* of past events rather than to those events themselves. That is to say, the discursive alignment is not dissimilar from someone talking about the images in a photograph album, the pages of which are being turned by another person. Rather than the depictions 'illustrating' what is said, they appear to prompt what is said, stimulating memory and occasionally producing the accents of spontaneous recall.[3] The viewer is not meant to deconstruct the overall effect to the point where a 'now' Cathy is consciously perceived as the discrete source of commentary: 'then' and 'now' merge to the point where Cathy's comments are often read *within* the dramatic frame, sometimes with the force of *present consciousness*. But the organisation of Cathy's commentary in relation to the dramatic diegesis is important, central to the kind of documentary space which the film wishes to develop around its central action, and I shall return to it at points below.

The fact that Cathy's is the only head which we are allowed inside throughout the entire play carries the implications which first-person narrative does in written fiction. That is to say, it serves to align us empathetically with her account and to see the behaviour of others in relation to her experience. Whilst this strong projection of subjectivity does not preclude the possibility of viewers finding fault with her and 'objectifying' her in their viewing as a focus of criticism (perhaps finding sympathy for some of those with whom she is in conflict), the use of one privileged subjectivity clearly has consequences for the 'route' taken by a viewer, particularly on a first viewing. This mode of *unseen* direct address to the viewer compares interestingly with a moment in the film which a number of critics have judged to constitute 'seen direct address'. This occurs in the fraught interview with the hostel board, where Cathy temporarily loses control and angrily accuses the board members of not caring about what happens to her. Filmed from an angle which aligns the viewer with Cathy's address to the officials, her outburst 'Ain't you room in your houses, ain't you got one single room?' seems to seek a 'secondary addressee' in the audience itself, although the terms in which this is registered by viewers *as accusation* will depend on their own personal circumstances. Later on, I want to examine the presentation of officialdom in the film, and the management of viewer responses to it, in more detail.

Another feature of the action which connects it firmly to the conventions of dramatic fiction is the extent to which the narrative space, and therefore the space of character portrayal, is a 'private' rather than a 'public' one. Reg and Cathy are placed in both kinds of space, but the depiction routinely closes in around intimate moments, projecting facial expressions, dialogue exchange and local action in a way which only dramatic performance can achieve. When, for instance, Reg visits Cathy in her first night at the hostel, the intensity of emotions is registered by close-ups and shot-reverse-shot composition which, quite apart from the fact that the setting is her bedroom, generate a very different kind of depictive effect from that which any conventional documentary could achieve, even by extensive and intrusive use of 'fly-on-the-wall' methods. So the performative dimensions and directorial controls of realist drama are fully employed in *Cathy*, even though they are the core of a larger discursive project. The brief scene, early on, in which Reg's grandfather is about to be taken from the family home and into care, shows this well. Though briefly achieved, the scene is thematically important since the primary reason for his daughter requesting his move into care is the lack of space in the house for others of the family without accommodation of their own. The action is played out with the grandfather seated between his daughter and a female social worker who has come to assess the situation. Her talking *about* him rather than to him, her tones of condescension ('you'll be allright, Grandad') and the cold, bureaucratic character of her demeanour and speech, indicate themes general to the whole play. In one sense, this is a documentary moment, illustrative of a bad and sad side to 'social care'. But it is also powerfully a dramatic one too, anchored in performance. As the decision to place him in a home is made, the camera closes up on the old man's face, shaking into tears. This is not primarily a moment of characterisation (we have seen very little of the grandfather before and we do not see him again): it is a moment in which a general problem is particularised and registered as personal tragedy. The performance is, like others in the play, projected interrogatively ('why is this happening?') and the audience is meant not only to be moved but to be discomforted by it.

However, like many realist plays, *Cathy* also develops a level beyond that of naturalistic depiction, a level at which indications are offered of more general symbolic import. Two examples, one verbal, can be taken from the earlier part of the film. When Cathy and Reg first discuss marriage and their future, Reg talks of his fantasy of having a Jaguar car with no brakes. This comment is clearly designed less to serve any direct narrative requirements than to sound a warning note to the audience about the risks that lie ahead. It seems to me that this kind of overlay of symbolism carries some risks for the integrity of the film, not only because it is in danger of being too explicit, but because it rather heavily marks out the fecklessness of Reg in a way which can become awkward in responding to the subsequent plight of Cathy and its causes. I shall return to this point.

Another use of symbolic discourse occurs in a scene which shows the couple embracing in the sunshine by a stream, partly shaded by trees and with a lyrically fulsome popular song of the period on the soundtrack. As the camera angle shifts, the stream is seen to be partly polluted with detergent foam. Here, as in the first example, the ostensible narrative development towards happiness is being under-cut – first, by the ironic use of contemporary romantic cliché, and secondly, by the inclusion of a marker of pollution. So, at these points at least, the viewer is put into a position of knowledge outside the terms provided by Cathy herself, as these terms follow from the disclosures of dramatic action or from her narration of her story.

A contrasting use of dramatic discourse, pulling it further in the direction of documentary and away from artifice, occurs in the scenes in which Cathy discusses her predicament with friendly but, for her, finally unhelpful housing officials. This involves the use of a kind of 'leaky dialogue', familiar from British wartime films and a feature even of current drama-documentary work, in which apparently naturalistic exchange is used as a means to give information to the viewer. There is often a tension between the requirement to hold this information-giving within parameters of the dramatically plausible and the requirement to get certain facts (and often figures) across to the viewer without resorting to graphics or commentary. In *Cathy*, the limited use of this device together with the wide range of other methods used to 'document' the context of the story means that narrative development suffers no real impediment or disruptive shift as a result.

The documentary requirement to depict Reg and Cathy in a number of different circumstances of housing necessitates a much more rapid shifting of scenes and settings than is conventional for a realist play. It also works against the possibility of any other characters developing much beyond their function as 'scene' players. This episodic and at times almost tableau-like aspect of the film (the squat, the houseboat inquiry, the tent, etc.) requires both a good onward drive of incident and emotion to carry across the 'cuts' and 'jumps' and that containing coherence which is provided by Cathy's commentary.[4]

Cathy as report: documentarism

In discussing the documentary aspects of the film, I am here concerned only with the way in which it appears on screen as images and sounds. There is another aspect of its documentarism, the extent to which the script was based on research on actual cases of homelessness over a period of time. This provides a 'basis' in actuality for what is depicted, but a number of realist-inclined novels, plays and films could claim a similar grounding. The effect of documentary truth, so central to the impact of *Cathy* upon public consciousness and to the film's controversiality, is largely a matter of its looks and sounds.

I noted above how, at certain points in the narrative either 'to the side' of the main action or opening out 'around' it, the physical and social setting is explored with a degree of detail and for a length of time which extends beyond the conventions of the realist play's concern for contextualisation. There are often two elements which mark such passages out as 'non-dramatic' in mode. First of all, the soundtrack contains a sequence of voices, often heard only for a sentence or less, speaking about their lives and circumstances. The speech is anonymous, the speakers might or might not be the people briefly portrayed on camera going about their business. Clearly, the voices stand for a 'common experience' in which Cathy's story is rooted and within which it is shaped. This speech montage over film is very much the method of one kind of documentary, projecting out into the openess of public space rather than into the constructed, private closures of drama. Secondly, the visuals provide an imaging of this public space through a grammar which replicates the 'public eye' of documentary, complementary to the soundtrack. Shots of mundane life are edited together into a representation of a peopled environment in which space and place are observed by the camera as *significant* independently of any narrative line which is being threaded through them. Indeed, at points like this, it is as if the narrative is temporarily halted to allow a brief ethnographic trip around its current location.

One such scene occurs early on in the film at the point when Cathy and Reg have to give up their first, well-appointed, flat and move in with Reg's mother, into a large, multi-storey tenement block. The scene opens with the mother making her way slowly up the iron staircase outside the tenement to the top-floor balcony. As she laboriously progresses, a sequence of the voices of other residents is heard, telling of life there in conversational snatches. The sequence moves fully back into drama with the next shot, of Cathy stirring a saucepan in the cramped kitchen of the flat, listening to her mother-in-law. A toilet flushes, and then from right behind Cathy a door opens and a young man pushes past her at the stove. The camera shifts back to the tenement courtyard and the lines of washing as, once again, voices are heard describing the conditions, telling stories, arguing. The movement into and out of 'story' is shown here particularly well, and the way in which the broader discourse of place is, as it were, initially 'wound around' a thin outlying strand of 'story' – the mother's ascent of the stairs – seems a fine piece of pacing and integration. Although located within the narrative dis-

Cathy Come Home: barricading
the house against eviction

course, the 'surprise' sequence of the toilet, an environmental fact documented by dramatic action, uses a device found elsewhere in the film. In the scene in the terraced squat, for instance, a sense of 'homeliness' and family routine is established by the camera's view of Cathy and her children in a front room, only to be broken as a voice calls Cathy off to the left and we see a 'neighbour' standing outside, fully visible through the huge hole in the wall where a window used to be. 'Inside' becomes 'outside'.

I noted how sequences of concentrated documentarism occur 'off story', as it were, just to the side of the main narrative development. Another mode of documentary depiction is occasionally employed to give the main narrative action something of the feeling of actuality footage. Here, the parallel is either with news film or with extended observationalism of the kind employed in vérité. When Cathy and Reg are evicted from the terraced house following the death of the landlady, the sequence is shot with some of the stylistic markers of action-led camera. That is to say, stability of frame and composure of *mise-en-scène* give way to a visualisation appearing to have caught a real incident and filmed it within the limitations which such filming entails in respect of camera positions, steadiness of composition, the following of action, a soundtrack containing 'incidental' sounds, and so on. Together with the intensity of the event itself, reinforced by the gathering of neighbours jeering the bailiffs as they force their way into the house and remove the couple and their possessions, such filmic 'limitations' draw on the language of factual reportage. They put viewers more directly and resonantly in the position of *witnesses* than a more dramatically articulated treatment might do. The projection of positions of vicarious witness is a key element in the overall communicative design of the film. This projection complements the closer, more empathetic relationships with the viewer primarily developed through the portrayal and speech of Cathy.

Although I want to discuss the question of 'deception' in this kind of production more fully later, developing my general comments in Chapter 2, it is worth pointing out here that scenes of the kind just described above do not require that viewers believe, even temporarily, that what they are seeing is a record of real events. The effect is gained without any fraud as to the referentiality of the image being perpetrated. Given their embedding in dramatic structure, such scenes work as simulations ('as if' devices) so, whatever arguments one might want to conduct as to their aesthetic and social propriety, to regard them as mechanisms which mislead viewers as to the status of what they are watching is to make a considerable jump of speculation and to ignore entirely the question of the interpretative frames used by viewers 'following' this sort of mixed material.

Perhaps the sequences most typical of *Cathy*'s distinctiveness are those which, like some of those mentioned above, move between 'story' and 'report', weaving an interface between the two which exploits to the full the representational force of different modes. One of the strongest of these sequences involving Cathy directly comes towards the end of the film, when she is placed in Part 3 accommodation. She is seen wheeling her pram along outside the stone cloisers of an institutional building. The next shot shows her from inside, opening the door and registering, in close-up, shock and dismay at what she sees. From this moment of dramatic reaction the camera shifts into its more expansive, documentary mode, slowly panning around a noisy, crowded dormitory in which a number of families are trying to get on with their business. Cathy and her children gradually walk through the dormitory to an empty bed. The camera observes their 'journey' but then moves on to complete its surveillance. What we see in this documentation of the dormitory is what Cathy sees herself and what causes her reaction on entry. But this is only partly true, for the exploration of the interior is not properly a point-of-view shot. Its measured pan is not aligned with Cathy's direct and dismayed gaze and it quickly shifts to a high-angle position so as to 'sweep' the room and register its overcrowdedness the more effectively.

Such developments out from the story into the observation of context and environment would seem slightly jarring were in not for the fact that running alongside the voice of Cathy there is, throughout the film, a thread of unidentified voices commenting on the housing problem, and on its social and political origins and consequences. As Cathy's voice connects and merges with dramatised action, so the non-continuous stand of voices connects and merges with the sequences of documentarist expansion. It provides the film with a reportorial dynamic running alongside the narrative and at times framing it. I have discussed the commentary voice of Cathy in terms of its likeness to first-person novelistic narration. But one of the characteristics of *Cathy* is not only its 'code mixing' but also the way in which certain depictive elements in it become inflected in different directions, towards different communicative modalities, according to the overall discursive context. At times, Cathy's voice becomes less like that of a guiding narrator and more like that of a documentary interviewee, registering not linkage and development so much as localised personal experience, a testimony of frustration and despair.

I have explored the formal organisation of the play in terms of its dramatic/documentary mix, attempting to identify how the conventions are employed and combined. I now want to take a different tack, and consider some of the themes and implicit propositions which it generates. This does not mean leaving behind questions of communicative form but readdressing them from a different angle.

Themes and propositions

'Officialdom'

In constructing his account of Cathy's 'descent', Sandford necessarily has to bring her into contact with officials of various kinds –

local housing officers, hostel management boards, care assistants. In most cases these are represented in personally unsympathetic terms. Their attitude to Cathy, displayed both in what they say to her and, sometimes, in what they say about her, is largely ungenerous and critical. In the case of the higher officials, the tones of class-complacency and class prejudice appear. This is particularly true of the upper middle-class woman who sits on the hostel's management and review board and whose remarks are the immediate cause of Cathy's outburst of anger.

At one level, what is presented is the mismatch between Cathy's experience of deprivation and the bureaucratic language of 'official care', with its way of regarding victims as potentially if not actually 'deviant'. This comes through in the exchange between board members following Cathy's accusations and after she has left the room:

Mrs Green   What's your opinion, Warden?
Warden   She's not an easy person by a long chalk. Keeps
her children quite tidy but – well, as you see, she's not too co-operative.

At another level, however, the officials are marked in a more deeply personal way as unsympathetic. This is more a matter of facial expression and of speech tone.

Since it is Sandford's basic position that there is a *systemic* problem in national housing provision and that this is the primary cause of Cathy's misfortunes, it does not follow that all those charged with implementing the inadequacies of present arrangements have to be seen as unkind personalities. However, there are two possible reasons for this as a writer's and director's tactic. The first is to 'close down' the characterisation of officials in line with Cathy's likely perception of them. Thus the subjectivity (and potential 'bias') of portrayal here is linked to the subjectivity of the main character. This would work best in a narrative extensively using point-of-view sequences. But, as we have seen, *Cathy* mixes modes extensively and quite often portrays the interaction between Cathy and officials in an observationalist style. It seems most likely that we are meant to 'read' the officials here directly as they are projected to us, not somehow 'route' them through the displacing mechanisms of Cathy's own feelings and anxieties. We observe *both* Cathy and officials, and the camera alignment is often one which places us behind the officials, sharing their view of Cathy. That there can be a mismatch between Cathy's view of what is going on and what is really going on seems to be made explicit in the 'outburst' scene when Cathy finally erupts with the charge: 'Runts! I saw you laughing there. Wipe that smile off your face!' Whatever level of institutional condescension and class prejudice might be interpreted as being behind the board's treatment of Cathy, it is clear to the viewer that 'laughing' and 'smiling' are not going on. In that sense, Cathy's attitude towards the board is revealed by the dramatic exposition to be at least partly grounded in misperception. Of course, her reaction is seen to be understandable at this stage, given what has happened to her.

If the idea of 'point-of-view' depiction seems an unsatisfactory way of explaining the character tonings used for the officials, then it may be that Sandford and Loach simply found it necessary to personalise the systemic problem in this way in order to get the message across with sufficient force. A more 'balanced' set of characterisations here would simply have risked having 'badness' located at too high a level of generality and would not have provided the film with the local contrasts and conflicts which it needs. Such a stereotyping strategy brings advantages, but one of the problems it courts, apart from risking reduced plausibility among viewers detecting exaggeration, is that it is very likely to preclude a sympathetic response to the film from many of those professionally working in the area. This may, or may not, be a price worth paying.

Children and growth

Throughout the film, there is an emphasis on child-rearing and the difficulties of doing this in cramped, unhygienic environments. That Cathy continues to have children despite the couple's continuing misfortunes has been noted by some viewers as an element which contributes to her problems. Sandford clearly recognised this as a (prejudiced) line of interpretation, because he gives Cathy a voice-over comment which directly addresses the issue:

> Now I was pregnant again. Some would say it was wrong to have another kiddy when you're overcrowded as it is, but I don't think so. I think kiddies are God's gift; you don't do right to deprive anyone of the chance of life. Love's what's important in a child's life. Love is more important to a child than what they call nice surroundings. I know 'cos I live in what they call a respectable home and I didn't have it. (Sandford 1976:52).

The terms of this justification are interesting in the context of the film as a whole. Just how far the 'God's gift' argument will work with viewers inclined to be critical of Cathy's family-building is largely a matter of personal disposition, although as a general argument against family planning it might be considered both (deliberately?) weak and socially irresponsible. But how do we read Cathy's statement that love is more important than ('what they call') nice surroundings in a film which is continually documenting the adverse effect of bad surroundings on her life? And what of her use of her own childhood as a basis for this claim? It seems that either Cathy or the script itself are here conflating a decent environment with a middle-class level of 'niceness' and 'respectability'. Real conditions and class inflections are brought together in a way which finally serves to confuse. We can perhaps read this statement, like others above, as serving to indicate tensions in Cathy's own consciousness, as an attempt at 'justifying' the way her children are being brought up by contrasting this with her own childhood. Despite its experiential force, it is a contrast which is evasive of what the film sees as the main issue.

Certainly, the play-off of confinement against space, light against dark, nature against city, is worked extensively throughout the play (Fiske and Hartley 1978:55–8 brings this out well). The opening shot of hitch-hiking is set in the sunny and breezy countryside, while the last narrative sequence, showing Cathy huddled alone on the station seat, externalises Cathy's consciousness in its darkness, enclosure and alienation. When the family have moved out of Reg's mother's house and into the old terrace, emphasis is placed on the relative freedom of the yard and the children's delight in the pigeons which fly from the coop there. When they have moved out into the relative limitations of the caravan, including the dirtiness of the site area, Cathy can still reflect on the advantages which such a style of living can bring:

> And the kids liked the life here, they wandered round in the Shillington woods with the other children, it was quite a good playground really, they were for always finding things that fascinated them among the trees. I got to like it here. Dunno why. It was squalid, but it was easy going. (Sandford 1976:82)

This is, again, a speech very much in the spirit of rationalisation, of making the best of necessity. Cathy does not overstate the benefits of the life, but registers a contentment with its relaxed rurality. This is also part of a documentarist aim. In these scenes an extension outwards from the narrative is made which, instead of depicting the larger context of city housing shortages and the human consequences, connects briefly and sympathetically with the gypsy lifestyle and with its stereotyping and frequent persecution. Of course, Cathy and her family quickly become victims of this prejudice themselves. Throughout, the film is sensitive to the differences between ways of 'ordinary living', but here it goes beyond snapshot level into a concise rendering of a marginalised group whose attitudes are placed positively against dominant aspects of the 'new modern Britain'.

Causes

That the main cause of what befalls Cathy is the inadequacy of national housing policy is a point reinforced several times in the film by speakers, both in and out of shot. The inadequacy of local authorities to cope with the consequences follows from this, though their existing rules and procedures are not exonerated on that score. At the end of the play, the following captions appear:

> All the events in this film happened in Britain in the last eighteen months.
> Four thousand children each year are separated from their
> parents because they are homeless.
> West Germany has built twice as many houses as we have since the war.

I have noted how other, potentially causal, factors are brought into the narrative. The steady increase in family size and Reg's apparent fecklessness are two of these, although even if taken as causal these would do more than displace *some* of the emphasis given to the larger problem. Similarly with the portrayal of the officials. Although I have suggested that the almost comprehensively negative typing of these is not without its problems, it would take an odd reading indeed to attribute Cathy's troubles directly to uncharitable personalities.

The position of Reg at the end of the story remains uncertain and, in my experience of screening the film to student groups, there are variations in how his relationship to Cathy is finally interpreted. There is no doubt whatsover that the policy of separating husbands from wives is projected by the film as likely to cause the 'distancing' which can be observed in the couple's relationship (Cathy says: 'I feel he's drifting away') and which increasingly comes out as tension in their exchanges during Reg's visits. Some of this tension is over the amount of money which Reg can spare towards maintenance. Near the end, a comment from a member of the hostel board indicates that Reg has stopped paying the fees and there is little doubt that the viewer is meant to take this information as fact. An interpretation which picks up strongly on the idea of a 'bad system' will see Reg's drifting away as primarily a consequence of the separation. But the couple are much more than social ciphers and the 'character space' they occupy is big enough to allow for an element of character criticism in a viewer's overall response.

Conclusions: *Cathy* and the drama-documentary debate

In Chapter 2, I discussed in general terms how drama-documentary frequently faces a charge of fraud. Hostile critics claim that it is likely to mislead by claiming a 'truth value' which it simply does not have. The viewers are therefore seen to be the victims of a kind of generic trick, responding to a portrayal as if it were 'fact' when it is really 'fiction'. It is interesting that even Sandford himself appears to entertain the argument that the method could 'be dangerous in the wrong hands' (Sandford 1973, extracted in Goodwin *et al.* (eds) 1983:16), presumably with a crude kind of propagandistic function in mind.

The general wisdom on offer from those who object to the mix seems to be keep the two genres apart, however much this kind of crisp categorisation flies in the face both of sceptical intelligence and, very differently, of calculation about what can pull a good audience and get it talking the next day. In my earlier discussions, I distinguished between those productions which extend dramatically outwards from a documentary base, necessarily exercising some creative licence in their depictions, and those which attempt to achieve a documentarist effect from the basis of a fictional playscript, by using reportage modes or by extending the social context within which the action is set or (as in *Cathy*) by doing both. This distinction and its terms are by no means watertight and some theoretically anxious critics would prefer not to use them at all, but my own judgement is that, despite their whiff of naivety, they aid differentiation in an area notorious for muddle. It would seem likely that the former kind of programme, documentaries which have been 'dramatised', would be more vulnerable to criticism than the latter kind – plays or films which attempt, in part or in whole, a documentary effect. After all, such documentaries are usually attempts to reconstruct specific events and actions. They have a tightly referential, journalistic core and their dramatic character, in so far as it departs from what can be confidently warranted by investigation, might quickly be seen as dubious. In fact, the British history of drama-documentary on television shows clearly that it is the other kind of production, issuing from a playwright, which has attracted the most critical attention. The reason for this is quite clear – these productions have been much more likely to criticise official policy and to articulate critical and radical political views than work issuing from documentary departments. On the whole, documentary-based dramatisation has been respectful (sometimes too respectful) of the conventions and proprieties of 'balanced' public depiction which have become established in non-fiction television. So the area of work with the lesser chance of confusing the viewer as to the status of what they are watching (productions labelled 'plays', with well-known actors, and carrying writer credits) comes in for the most criticism because of its oppositional social ideas (see Petley 1996 on this point).

What about the use of documentary-style footage in *Cathy*, though? Doesn't this constitute a risk to integrity? I think not, since it is the main narrative line rather than the scenes opening up 'at the side' which provided the main focus of critical attention and the enhancement of immediacy and realism here was unlikely, I have suggested, to be transformed into a misreading of the general status of the material. A degree of *viewer disorientation* is certainly an intended effect of the film, as it moves in and out of modes and rapidly and often noisily shifts from scene to scene and place to place, but to feel this representational effect is not to be the victim of depictive fraud. It is true that, until the final titles, some viewers might have thought they were watching a play based on the reconstruction of one person's experiences rather than a play based on a compilation of experiences, but this does not lend itself to the polemic about 'deception' in anything like the way that opposing 'fiction' to 'fact' does.

Having earlier drawn on the idea of there being two rather different kinds of drama-documentary production, I have to say that, nevertheless, the question of which category to place *Cathy* in seems to be quite a difficult one. This is for two reasons. First of all, though doing extensive research before writing fictions is not at all unusual, the fact that *Cathy* actually grew out of an earlier radio documentary and was based on research at the level of taped interview gives the project a stronger referential base than most plays. Moreover, unlike many dramas adopting documentarist modes, *Cathy* does not use these simply to convey the main narrative events but, as we have seen, employs them in those short sequences which open up documentary space around the storyline. Finally, the construction of a fictitious character and the arrangement of fictitious incidents in a sequence would appear to put the production into the camp of documentary-drama rather than dramatised documentary. But such a judgement is more a notional one than one which classifies the 'truth' or 'falsity' of the film in the categoric manner which some critics at the time sought to do.

Rarely have writers and directors achieved the interpenetration of modes which *Cathy*, in its complementariness of story space and report space, develops. An extra edge and vibrancy is given to the mixed aesthetic by the fact that this fusion is achieved at a time when both the codes of documentary (moving towards more extensive actuality sequences filmed with 16mm cameras) and television drama (developing a tradition of writing and direction with 'social problem' themes located in working-class, realist settings) were re-forming.

Irene Shubik, a distinguished television producer who worked with Sandford on a later 'social problem' drama, *Edna the Inebriate Woman*, discusses the contemporary response to *Cathy* in a way which connects with a number of points made above:

> The authorities have not always been well disposed to his work. After *Cathy Come Home* was screened, there were many protests about the inaccuracy of its statistics about the homeless and its portrait of the authorities. On its second showing, two million council members and officials were asked to watch and see how many mistakes they could find in it. Mr Laurence Evens of the Local Government Office said, 'This play is full of blunders and omissions'. Another official complained of factual inaccuracies and another of the deliberate misrepresentation of officers of a public authority as 'gangsters', especially in the scene where the children are wrenched from Cathy on a station platform. *On its second showing, most of the background comments giving statistics were, in fact, omitted because of doubt about accuracy* [*my italics*]. There is no doubt, however, that *Cathy* would have had much less impact had a more evenly balanced picture been painted. (Shubik 1975:126)

As a 'knowledge device', then, *Cathy* was controversial in a number of ways. Whilst the imaginative freedom of the dramatist could be claimed for the general social knowledge generated by its narrative-in-context, its use of voiced-over data inevitably carried it into the more narrowly contentious arena of controversial current-affairs broadcasting.

Cathy raises questions about the kinds of relation between emotion and argument which are thought proper in making broadcast interventions in public debate,[5] although the delivering of depictive shocks and the disorienting of the viewer are harder to achieve in the late 1990s. Its capacity to 're-particularise' a perception of a general indequacy and to render that particularisation in an imaginative exploration of both 'private' (subjectified) and 'public' (objectified) space perhaps goes to the heart of the whole issue of drama-documentary, underlying the often specious criticisms of fraudulent practice. Transmitted within the limited three-channel options of British television in the mid-1960s and conceived within the refashioned 'realisms' of 1960s drama and reportage, *Cathy* deserves its status both as an extraordinary individual achievement of writing and direction and as a representative instance of British television's socialised aesthetics.

6   *Living On the Edge* (1986)

Living On the Edge (henceforth LOTE) was directed by Michael Grigsby for Central Television. It was transmitted at prime time on the ITV network in the winter of 1987 (in three segments divided by advertising breaks) and distributed for cinema exhibition by the British Film Institute. With a running time of eighty-six minutes, the documentary offers both a wide-ranging and intentionally fragmented view of contemporary Britain, using a number of different documentary modes. Grounded in forms of observationalism, it also makes limited use of group interviews and draws extensively on a richly symbolic visualisation to interconnect the parts and to relate present circumstances to the past. To this end, archive sound is frequently used against contemporary images.

The film is both an investigation of, and a response to, the character of Britain (England, Wales and Scotland are all represented) under 'Thatcherism', the economic and social ideas pursued by the Conservative Thatcher governments during the 1980s. A sense of the current inequalities, open divisiveness and neglect caused by Conservative policies is set off against the social democratic optimism to emerge from the Second World War. A sense of decline, of affliction, is registered at the national level and, through observationalist methods, at the personal level as well. The title carries the apocalyptic implication that many, if not all, the people of Britain are 'living on the edge' of a profound political and social crisis, whether they know it (some in the film clearly do) or not. Although deeply grounded in its particular 'moment' (particularly the consequences of the early 1980s economic recession), the film's political and social project has a resonance which catches at much broader elements in British post-war history. Moreover, its particular principles and methods of construction make it one of the most original documentaries to be shown on British national television during the 1980s.

Grigsby's previous work provides a necessary context for understanding both the structure and the local depictions of LOTE. Many of his earlier films are about relations of work, about hardship and about the under-represented (as the titles suggest: for instance, *Working the Land, Deckie Learner, A Life Underground*). These films often follow the strategy of 'giving a voice' to those infrequently heard, if heard at all, in public communication, whilst at the same time they visualise work with a marked concern for spatial relations, and the processes of physical activity. There is also an interest in the continuing and often contradictory presence of historical legacy (as in the treatment of colonialism and pre-colonialism in Grigsby's earlier *Before the Monsoon* and the later, controversial *Letter from Ireland*). Such interests combine to relate Grigsby's work back to the 1930s film-makers with more directness than that of most other documentarists currently working in television. As I shall note below, in LOTE this connection is explicitly acknowledged at times, through particular acts of 'scene quoting'.

Description

The basic form taken by the film is that of a sequenced movement across developments in the lives of four groups of people. Selection of the right 'focal subjects' was clearly a major aspect of pre-production. In an interview, the producer, John Furse, noted: 'we "cast" it very carefully and went through hundreds of possible "characters"' (Petley 1987b:169). The groups are:

(a)   A farming family in Devon, who have been made bankrupt largely as a result of the crisis in agricultural policy affecting prices and creating over-production.

(b)   An extended family on a housing estate in Birkenhead, whose circumstances involve a young mother whose husband is in prison.

(c)   Two families from a South Wales mining community, shaken by the experience of the coal dispute of 1984/85 and concerned about the future of the coal industry.

(d)   A group of unemployed youths from Glasgow, who take the night coach to London to look for work.

Group (b) has two 'extensions', in the form of a group of elderly residents of Birkenhead (whose memories of the war and its aftermath are pivotal) and a scene involving a young 'rap' composer and performer living on the estate.

Around these four focal groups, the first two developing principally in the form of segmented, observationalist narrative, the second two working as discussion groups, a range of interconnecting images and motifs is constructed. These include general shots of setting (the Devon countryside, the Welsh valleys, the City of London, and so on) and a large number of images serving to connect and amplify both the 'national' and 'personal' dimensions of the documentary as a whole. Amplification of the 'national' is achieved partly by the use of archive sound recordings of post-war political leaders speaking about the national economy and national prospects. Grigsby has observed in interview that 'the film is in the form of a collage, and the structure is quite impressionistic'(Petley 1987b:169).

Of the four strands, only the 'Devon' story has a strong resolution of some kind at the end of the film. This involves the leaving of the farm by the family; their driving away from it for the last time. Throughout, the 'Devon' story has more projection than the other narratives, and it is not surprising that it is used to conclude the film. Other narratives culminate with varying degrees of closing significance; the Birkenhead mother visits the father, in the local prison, with her new baby; the Scottish youths make their coach trip to London; the Welsh mining community is left via a shot of a shift's trip to the pit-head and an elegaic sequence mixing shots of the valleys and villages with archive voices from the 1984/85 coal dispute. It is significant that there is a theme of journeying, of travel, involved in the broad movement of these narratives, a theme given expansion in the non-narrative sequences. I shall discuss this further below.

Given the complexity of the film, it would not be helpful to block out all its contents in a manner which would be of value with a single-narrative or single-exposition structure. However, in order to convey something of the overall organisation, before moving to more specific, selective analysis, I indicate below the shifts of the first and then the last ten minutes. This indication is not given at shot level, but in terms of the broader unit of depictive sequence.

Opening

1   Sequence of shots of enclosed escalators in the Lloyd's building, London (City finance centre); people in motion on them. An eerie musical soundtrack mixed with scraps of broadcast news.

2   Music strengthens to rock beat. Slow rising shot, aligned with outside wall of Lloyd's Building, revealing a London panorama; buildings both ancient and very modern.

3   A rural landscape with farmhouse. Bird sounds. Cut to kitchen sink: mother with daughter singing verses of 'Old Macdonald's Farm'. News on economic downturn in farming. Cut to shots of farmer looking out of french windows. Shots of deserted farm sheds and pens. Shot of farmer at window from outside. Solicitor's voice, cut to solicitor's office. Farmer and wife present. Details of loss of farm, talk of 'court order'.

4   Urban estate, traffic. Cut to baby being fed by middle-aged woman, young woman in front of mirror prepares to go out. Intercut television commercial for clothes shop ('Can't Wait' refrain). Cut to young woman and man walking on pavement in conversation. Aerial shot of estate. Inside of pub; conversation about 'life today'. Cut to one of the conversationalists in his flat singing his own song, 'Smack City'. Estate street.

5   A field; farmer and daughter walking and talking. A gate; both stop and talk further about loss of farm and what it means. Long shot of farm in setting of fields.

6   Short sequence from 1930s film *Victoria the Great* in which the

achievements of nineteenth-century empire are celebrated in a speech to the Queen by one of her ministers.

7   Shots of the sea, waves, docks, tugs; leading to shots of pub conversation between elderly men about the 1930s.

Although this opening section shows a less rapid movement of shots than occurs at other points in the film, it does indicate the kind of 'associative' manner in which, both visually and aurally, themes are developed and intertwined. Often, the soundtrack is 'carried over' from one shot to the next, either by a time-lag or an anticipation in respect of what is shown.

Ending

1   After baptism of baby (Birkenhead), mother and two daughters talk in the front room about changes in ways of living over the years of their experience.

2   Daughter with baby catches train and then walks alongside prison wall to enter main gate of prison.

3   Coach-station scenes intercut with comments from Glasgow youth about job opportunities. Shots of coach on motorway at night – inside and outside. Glasgow youths depicted sleeping in seats. Dawn and arrival of coach at Victoria Station.

4   Farm. External shots. Inside, family at table for tea. A poem written about the loss of the farm by the son is read out by the daughter. All are upset by it.

5   Possessions being removed from farmhouse. Furniture and television set (a shot of this is held) lie out in garden. A trailer van (horsebox) is packed with household possessions.

6   Birkenhead estate. External shot. Inside, mother and daughter at kitchen sink. Radio broadcast of Budget-day speech by Chancellor (Lawson) ... 'This is a budget for success.'

7   Bare room inside farmhouse. Outside, dusk; car and trailer pull away from house and move along winding lane, up hill towards horizon. Quietness except for natural sounds, then music on soundtrack. Voice-over (miner's wife): 'If we give in, our kids go down the river. Our kids have got to believe, they've got to keep fighting and keep going.'

Once again, the associative system of the film can be seen at work here, in the culmination of its themes.

Analysis

Having looked at the broad organisation of the film with a descriptive emphasis, I now want to move in closer in order to analyse its formal operations and the local (sometimes 'micro') relations these have with thematic development. In order to do this, I have selected two brief 'slices' from the film where it seems to me the nature of the depictions and the transitions between them illuminate the film's more general originality of project and method. In each case, I shall list and describe the shots within the section and then develop a brief critical commentary around these.

Example 1: country/city/war

This example is approximately six minutes long and occurs about a third of the way through the film (in the network television version it started 'Part 2', following a commercial break).

1 Farmhouse wall shot from outside at night. Lit window in the left upper part of frame. The farmer's wife is seen ironing. Sound of wind combined with (low-level) sound of *The Archers* on the radio.

2 Farmhouse in landscape of fields. Lights in windows. Wind noises. Loud sound of 'pips'.

3 CU of daughter in public telephone box, shot from outside enclosed booth. She places change in slot and talks about her father's health.

4 Lit telephone box in a medium shot which depicts its shape against the night sky. Conversation continues.

5 Return to CU of speaker.

6 Trees silhouetted against moonlit sky, with wind-blown clouds behind. Shot held; wind noises and then archive soundtrack of Neville Chamberlain making radio declaration of the commencement of war against Germany, 1939.

7 Children playing on urban street at night; street lighting.

8 Police-car siren. Police car with flashing lights drives past.

9 Birkenhead waterfront, lit pub seen from outside. Across the Mersey, the lights of Liverpool pierhead. Group singing ('We'll Meet Again').

10 Pub interior. Large group, mostly elderly, drinking and singing to piano and guitar.

11 Conversational group of three men observed at bar from medium distance.

12 Closer shot of men, one talking, two listening. Talker describes the politicising effect of being in the forces during the war and the 'surge of feeling', the recognition of the need for change, which followed its ending. He uses the phrase, with some irony, 'a land fit for heroes'.

13 Projector beam in cinema

14 Sequence from 1941 propaganda feature-film *Dawn Guard* in which two soldiers on sentry duty discuss what things will be like after the war. This concludes with comment 'We've all got to pull together. We've found out in this war how we're all neighbours and we mustn't forget it.'

15 Return to Birkenhead pub. CU of pianist and guitarist. Man at microphone leads singing of 'We'll Meet Again'.

16 Singing continues. Shot of Devon countryside at night, a cemetery on a hill.

This segment of the film displays a number of those different modes which I referred to earlier. There is the observationalism of the telephone call and the pub conversation, the diacritical tensions introduced by the use of archive film, the symbolic theming achieved in the contrastive continuities of light and darkness, inside and outside, then and now.

The segment starts with domestic activity viewed from outside at night, marking precisely the idea of home as the place of identity and of light and warmth. This is ironically inflected in the use of *The Archers*, 'fictional' farm life playing into the space of real farm life. That the family are under imminent threat of losing both their home and their livelihood is the context for understanding the significance of this image. The shot of the farmhouse in its setting serves to place these immediately personal problems in a broader portrayal of the rural, with its traditional connotations as a key component of national identity. Here, the link is with the sequence in Humphrey Jennings's *Listen to Britain* (1943), in which a farmhouse is shown in a similar night-time setting just before the 'pips' of the BBC's nine o'clock radio news are heard, with all that means within the routine of national wartime life. In LOTE, the sound is that of the telephone box 'pips', the shot shifting to the telephone booth and the concerned daughter's call. Glowing in the dark, the telephone box is rendered in a way which connects with the dark exterior/bright interior of the previous shot and with the sense of security, identity and connectedness which is generated from this. Even the emphasis given to the 'pips' themselves, as they occur twice in the sequence, sets up a degree of opposition, of minor hindrance (here part mechanical, part commercial) to the smooth flow of conversation, making its personal tones and the sense of potential (and imminent) isolation more marked.

The cut to silhouetted trees against moonlight is a further indicator of setting, but also a plane upon which an historical transition can be worked. With the voice of Chamberlain, this shot itself becomes inflected into the past, as the British countryside on the eve of war as well as the surrounding countryside in which farm and telephone box are set. Once again, a personal narrative and a national, historical one are being interwoven.

With the cut to the urban street, new themes are set in play though the continuities of night and lights remain. The passing police car reinforces these continuities – the siren carries the theme of the outbreak of war through into a new, contemporary setting. As so often in this film, continuities and contrasts are played off against one another.

The Birkenhead pub is established in terms which fully develop the symbolic pattern. The lights of a major wartime seaport are seen in the background, whilst in the foreground there are the lights of the pub itself, combining with the sound of singing to project the strongest sense of interior warmth and group identity, of an 'inside' sharply defined against 'outside'. Moreover, the kind of singing and the song itself seem almost like a re-enactment of wartime life, the expression of a structure of feeling generated in that moment and all the more bizarre and powerful as an object of contemporary observation. This singing is a project of group memory and also of a kind of group nostalgia, so that the depiction carries with it a pathetic dimension, of something lost and of an act of partial retrieval.

The conversation of the group at the bar is 'found' and overheard in this setting. The connotations of the past, the mood of past against present, are anchored and developed in a specific personal account which represents a generational experience and a generational (though also class-inflected) disappointment.

A move out of contemporary actuality is indicated in the shot of the projector's beam which precedes the wartime film extract. This is not necessary in order for the viewer to be able to interpret the material as archive, but it gives the use of the footage a clearer articulation and framing as it further amplifies what has gone before. The wartime fiction speaks to present reality, the irony of the co-operative hope against the privatisation and division.

Cutting back to the pub singing again, our interpretation of the singing and the song becomes responsive to the meanings which we have collected from the wartime scene. What was once merely signalled has now being instantiated, concisely put before us as raw 'then'.

The accumulated meanings are carried over into the shot of the quiet countryside and the cemetery, as the singing is too, prior to further development of the rural strand of the film.

I want to comment more generally on the strategies involved here after looking at both of the selected extracts, but I am interested in the 'associative' method and the routes which it allows the film-maker to take through widely varying materials. The method is rooted in a high degree of localised referentiality (the film is, as I have noted, primarily grounded in local instances, closely observed) but is able to generate sufficient symbolic force from the depiction of this both to 'bridge' between sequences and to interconnect and amplify themes. Although there are, throughout the film, short scenes whose function is self-evidently to advance a connotative thematics, the strength of the film (and the depth of its relationship to the work of Humphrey Jennings, is in the way the referential and symbolic functions are organised 'vertically' (within the sound/vision combinations of any one shot) as well as 'horizontally' (in the development of the film as multi-narrative exposition and argument.[1] I shall come back to these terms of analysis.

Example 2: two transitional sequences

I have indicated that part of the strength of LOTE lies in the way in which the movement from scene to scene maintains an overall impetus whilst being being able to register, and be expressive of, the specificities of place. It is a balance between the intensive rendering of 'identity' and the extensive rendering of relationship and connection. This latter project is in part a directly referential one, mapping the changing character of that set of interconnections which constitute a changing Britain as a substantive topic of concern, and partly a symbolic one, working 'above' the primary referentiality to advance a more abstract set of themes.

In this next example, I want to take two short sequences of transition, both realist and symbolic, which develop a little further my exploration of what is going on. My first example above had a strong transitional character, so there is some continuity in discussion. But

Visual metaphor in *Living On The Edge*: the dereliction of Britain

there the effect was grounded in observationalism, whereas the two sequences I am concerned with here work with a different depictive balance.

Sequence (a): 'nation/community'

This short sequence occurs about halfway through the film.

1   Cut from Birkenhead family talking in front room to long panning shot of Mersey estuary. Camera pans from R to L, picking up residential areas and docks on both banks. Soundtrack is 1960s pop classic 'I'm into Something Good'. Halfway through pan, soundtrack is overlaid with archive speech of Apollo 8 astronaut reading brief passage from Genesis ('In the beginning' to 'let there be light'). Pop classic continues underneath and after.

2   Pan dissolves into another L to R pan shot, of a Welsh valley, its pit buildings and village. This shot pulls back and down, coming closer to the rooftops with their clusters of aerials. Soundtrack moves from pop song into medley of theme tunes from three classic broadcasting series of the 1950s and 1960s, radio's *Housewives' Choice* and BBC television's *Tonight* and *Juke Box Jury*. The shot continues across and above the roofs until it is directly over a main street. Dusk is falling; house, shop and car lights are on. Voices are then heard on the soundtrack, discussing the present difficulties of life in the mining valleys.

3   A group of miners and their wives in a domestic room, talking.

Whilst shot 1 has some of the elements present at many stages in the film, an ironic (but also thoughtful, not simply assertive) combination of archive sound, music and image, shot 2 is more distinctive. It is a way of taking us into the world of experience of the miners' families, of entering the specificity of this particular community. The melding into shot 1 achieved by 'continuing' the long pan preserves the relaxed gaze of the former shot, a view offered to the viewer for *contemplation*. The slow revealing of the physical identity of this community, tracking in from its limits to its 'centre', registers its actuality with a high degree of referential respect. However, specificity and identity are connected back up into 'nationhood', and into past constructions of this, through the use of the popular television themes and the idea of coming in over the roofs and aerials, the key sites of entry for the messages of 'mediated community' and, in this case, perhaps of 'mediated disunity' as well. At one and the same time, then, the community is rendered both as specific and as a version of 'ordinary Britain'. It is worth noting how, once again, the film brings evening and its darkness/light combinations into both its formal aesthetic and its social thematics.

Sequence (b): 'money'

This sequence occurs some ten minutes after the one described above.

1   A shot of the Lloyd's building in London. The shot moves up the side of the building from ground level to the top, picking up in the process a gradually widening and lengthening view of the capital. It is dusk, lights

are on in the foreground offices (within which people are seen to be at work) and in the buildings out to the horizon. Soundtrack is the 1960s hit 'Something in the Air' which sings of a 'revolution' coming.

2   Westminster Bridge with Tower Bridge behind. Commuters crossing in medium shot, silhouetted against dusk sky.
3   Commuters in tube passageways and stairways, a sequence of shots of faces and bodies.
4   Inside the Lloyd's building. Desks, computers, offices. Staff at work. Music continues but is overlaid with financial news reports.
5   Slow descent shot down shopping-mall stairways (resemblance to building in previous shot), halting at ground floor, where a clothes shop's automatic doors swing open.
6   Tracking shot down central avenue of shopping mall or precinct, passing the long line of shops, shoppers and the palm-planted seating areas. The soundtrack is made up of brief extracts from broadcast news (talking of house prices and rising crime) and from financial commercials (talking of the benefits of credit-card schemes, the availability of shares in British Airways and British Gas). Underneath the music continues, increasing in tempo.
7   Cut to a Birkenhead street, a group of donkey-jacketed street-cleaners walking past shops with brooms and a bin.

It will be evident that this sequence shares some features with the one which opens the film and which I described briefly earlier. There is the concentration on London as the capital city of Britain, connecting many of its meanings together, and on the new buildings of finance capital as central to the 'new' Britain. Once again, the mode of shooting produces images both for referential engagement and a more abstract reflection. Here is a city with a currently powerful building seen in relation to those buildings (of the church, of government) which have previously symbolised the defining power. The fast but smooth elevation of the camera from street level to a 'commanding' view carries the sense of an ascendant force, a new dominant. Here are the people of the city caught up, distracted, in the everyday business of getting to and from work. The 'revolution' of the soundtrack song appears in relation to the images to be a 'financial revolution' and a 'retail revolution'. There is busyness, there is development, there is progress, there is opportunity. This is offset against not only the irony of the depiction but of the more negative elements placed within it, like the rising crime figures. Then, in a sharp juxtaposition, we jump to another part of the film's 'Britain' and return to closed shops, shabby streets and ill-paid jobs.

These two extracts exemplify key features of the film's documentary approach. The 'ethnographic' concern with specific experience as revealed primarily through speech is never very far away, but a higher level of discourse of implicit exposition and argument serves to interconnect this and to transpose it into more general terms.

Before moving on to comment more generally on the themes and propositions of LOTE, I would like to look at two more instances from it. These are not mixed-mode 'sequences' but 'scenes', keeping a unity of space and time and being projected largely if not entirely in one mode.

The first of these scenes occurs about mid-way through the film and is the first point at which the Glasgow youths (all male) are introduced. They are established through shots which, in a self-consciously stylised way, depict two youths standing either side of an opening in a wall and then two more standing either side of the entrance to a block of flats. A cut is made to a room where the youths sit around, some on the floor, discussing the 'second-classness' which has been imposed upon them in their failure to find a job ('just a job – not a lot to ask for'). The main mode in which the discussion is shot is observationalist, trading on the documentarist fiction that the speech events are occurring without the intervention of the production team. At times, however, an inflection towards the interventionist, interview mode is indicated. Statements by the youths about the predicament they are experiencing become too explicitly informational to be readable as addressed to others in the room. They are offered (once or twice quite explictly) out of frame, to the production team which has assembled them for the purpose. This method works, but it only just holds back the exchanges from developing a tension between real and ostensible addressees of a kind which would risk generating a sense of the 'artificial' and the 'contrived'. The fact that the observationalism places the boys as participants in a *discussion*, rather than in *casual conversation*, helps this containment, whilst the cramped terms of setting and *mise-en-scène* work to give 'discussion' here a degree of spatial and social naturalism.

Perhaps the most powerful observational moment in the film occurs towards its end, as part of the story of the farm. In this scene, the farmer and his wife and daughter are shown seated at a kitchen table following a meal. The shot is taken 'side-on' to the table, with the wife and the daughter on the left of the image and the farmer on the right. The mode is directly observationalist and its focus is the reading-out by the daughter of a poem composed by Alan, the absent son, and sent in a letter. The poem, which asks 'where have all the farmers gone?', is both read and listened to as a 'first hearing' and towards the end it causes the mother to break into tears and the daughter to finish her reading only with difficulty. After gathering themselves, the family comment on the truthfulness of the poem, on its accurate assessment of the new selfishness in the country at large ('who cares?').

This is an intense scene because it involves the witnessing of personal distress. It can also involve viewers in the profound discomfort of embarrassment at the witness role they are made to assume. A private act unfolds, in relationship to which any onlooking is posed as dubious. Yet our observation is meant to be instructive; we are being directed to contemplate the meaning of the loss of the farm as it shows itself precisely at the private centre of family life. But if one response is to feel the authentic pain of this loss, whilst perhaps also registering an awkwardness in the observationalism through which it is mediated, another response is towards questioning the integrity of tl   pro-filmic itself. This radically different interpretative tack may be prompted by the extent to which the scenes' personal drama pushes so far into 'the dramatic' as to raise questions about its spontaneity. How far have the family 'rehearsed themselves' for this scene, how far are they 'acting' their distress at the reading and their exchanges of indignation afterwards? These questions may seem either mean-minded or beside the point, given the established truth of the family circumstances. However, my view is that without going so far as to undermine the scene, these interpretative options trap it between what, in relation to its specific content, are the improprieties of intrusion and the improprieties of performance.

Themes and propositions

Having looked at a selection of the formal principles and devices employed in LOTE, I want briefly to examine the expositional and argumentational ends which they serve. As I have indicated, the film operates an 'indirect' mode of description and commentary. However, there is no doubt that its informing perspective is carried through into its portrayals with sustained emphasis. We can, I think, usefully identify three broad themes at work.

The 'unravelling' of Britain

Important here is the film's attempt to connect contemporary circumstances to different points in the movement from the social democratic settlement of the immediate post-war years. The potential inherent in 'Wartime Britain' is picked up explicitly in personal reminiscence, old film, and in the echoing in several shots of that contemplative/celebratory style by which wartime film-makers such as Humphrey Jennings depicted the 'meanings' of Britishness. It is offset against the deprivation, inequality and industrial and social neglect which the film documents in its primary sequences. The historical gap between the two moments is selectively explored by the use of the archive sound of Harold Wilson, Harold Macmillan and so on, speaking both of economic problems and possibilities. A recurring associative theme in the film is that of neglect and abandonment (in the farm, in the pit valleys, on the huge urban estates). This is frequently triggered by shots which linger, without music or speech, on spaces and places. In contrast to these are the highly mobile, musically strong sequences showing the London Lloyd's building and city shops, where the confidence of a new kind of ascendant national power comes across. Throughout the film, music drawn from popular hits is used not only ironically, in relation to their lyrics, but also (like the archive speech) as a way of generating historical connections, various 'thens' to place against 'now'.

It is an important factor in the kind of view and argument which LOTE offers that both urban and rural Britain are portrayed. The intercutting between the plight of the Devon farming family and hardship on the Birkenhead estate gives a scope to 'Britain' which, among other things, allows a much more resonant relationship to be established with the past. The film develops its own, critically edged, sense of 'heritage'. This helps to connect the broader, established meanings of British historical identity with the moment of the Second World War (again, Jennings provides an important precedent here) and sets off both against contemporary decline. The inclusion of the rural is therefore strategic as well as being a significant element in a sense of 'comprehensiveness' (to which the inclusion of the Welsh and Scottish sequences also clearly contributes).

Elements of resistance

The film's tone is, then, a markedly pessimistic one. It is an onlooking and a overhearing of individual disadvantage and decline set within the context of national, political neglect. But the registering of this is partly offset by the registering, too, of qualities of resistance. These are both individual qualities, manifest in personal rejections of the 'New Britain' and also group qualities, still seen to be constitutive of the community of the Welsh mining valleys, to be there in the solidarity of the 'March for Jobs' and even to be partially present in the collective identity of the Glasgow youths.

Depiction of 'resistance' in both fiction and non-fiction productions having a broadly socialist perspective has a troubled history. The omissions or under-recognition of social forces and dispositions running counter to those of dominant socioeconomic groups risk too negative a portrayal, implicitly indicating the futility of 'marginal' struggles. On the other hand, too much emphasis on counter-tendencies risks underestimating the extent to which the established order is economically secured and politically legitimated. It risks misjudging the existing potential for change, in the process perhaps romanticising (and homogenising) 'ordinary people' and failing to recognise the partial, pragmatic and compromised terms within which much political progress is achieved. It is this kind of emphasis which LOTE seems to me to veer most often towards, particularly in the way it routinely overhears only politicised, anti-Government conversation. In the case of the Devon farming family, this is essentially a moral critique: among the Glasgow youths, it edges towards the revolutionary. That it should find such views is not, of course, implausible, but it is worth noting how the registration of any kind of pro-government opinion from sections of the working class would severely jeopardise the film's project. This kind of documentation, which would raise no greater problems of selectivity than the kind of material which *does* find its place in the film, would interfere with its rhetorical shape and impede the terms of its implicit closure around power/resistance. That closure is 'sealed' with the words of the miner's wife in the final shot: 'Our kids have got to believe, they've got to keep fighting and keep going.' In the context of what is seen to be happening in Britain, there is a 'pathetic' quality to this statement (that is to say, it has a sad, gestural force) but it is clearly also meant to have propositional force, making a significant (no matter if marginal) level of anger and opposition into an imperative for the next generation. When I have discussed the film with students, there are often differences in the interpretation of this factor and in the extent to which the comment is seen to strengthen or to weaken overall credibility and persuasiveness (both that 'things are this bad' and that 'there is also a significant struggle being continued').

The 'commercial' society

As I have illustrated above, the film's focus is on the experience of 'ordinary' people under 1980s Conservatism, where this latter politics is seen as one more stage in the steady shift away from the post-1945 social democratic vision. The film implicitly, and sometimes openly, counterposes the 'co-operative' ideal against the 'market individualism' of the 1980s. The intercut use of material from television commercials is used to this effect, and the key scene in establishing this as a central theme is the one in which the move is made from the Lloyd's building into a long tracking shot in a shopping mall, with a montage soundtrack of 'siren voices' promising instant satisfaction on credit. It is important that the film sees the rise of the 'new order' as essentially based on the seductive power of commodities rather than on coercion, although that is a factor, too, in the bleak deprivation of the estates and, more directly, in the policing of industrial disputes. Again, as with the question of 'resistance', the level of achieved success which an individualistic, commodity culture has enjoyed and the extent to which changes in the nature of the 'popular' have been welcomed by ordinary people are issues marginalised in the account. The film wants to place market values at the centre of its pathology of Britain, but it cannot easily tackle the question of popular attitudes towards these values without risking attributing gullibility, and perhaps even blame, to 'ordinary people' themselves.

Conclusions

In a number of ways, LOTE is a highly original documentary and its screening on national network television at peak time indicates an element of British broadcasting policy which may not survive the increased marketisation of the mid-1990s. In attempting to engage with its representational distinctiveness, I have also indicated some of the problems which its approach raises. These are not to be seen solely as possible limitations in the programme itself, they

also point towards more general difficulties for films and programmes which attempt to 're-imagine' the documentary project
and to articulate a politically questioning attitude to large audiences. There are three issues which I would like to identify here as
having this kind of wider significance.

Dispersal and repetition

The discursive economy of the programme turns on the relationship
between the grounded instances of deprivation and misfortune on
the one hand, and the more generalised historical/political account
carried by images and sounds on the other. Such an economy has
to come to terms with problems of dispersal, repetition and development. Grigsby's method is one in which *duration*, a steady
engagement with situated instances, is a necessary factor in the
knowledge which the film seeks to impart and a necessary balance
to the more concise 'editorial' commentary carried in the montage
sequences. The observational mode, used particularly in the Devon
and Birkenhead scenes, runs some of the same risks as television
vérité (see Chapter 2) in that its real-time durations may seem to
exceed its informational throughput. This is particularly a problem
where observational narrative is regularly interrupted by the move
'across' to other settings or 'up' to a more general level of discourse.

There is also the possibility of a repetitive element occurring as
a result of the situated instances being insufficiently differentiated
from each other, in their general implications, to sustain a yield of
'new knowledge'. This is a familiar problem in documentary construction. Of course, an element of repetition may well be part of
directorial intentions, serving to reinforce the themes, to add weight
of evidence to the case and offset any suspicion of generalisations
being developed from the 'isolated instance'. LOTE, with its running
time of approximately one and a half hours, rather radically extends
the duration over which a television audience is to be engaged by
an *in*direct, non-fictional address. Some viewers who I have spoken
to about the film, even though they have been in sympathy with its
basic political perspective, have found both the pace of development
of the observational sequences too slow and the element of thematic
repetition too pronounced. For others, the relaxed, contemplative
mode of the film, the space it provides for associations to form and
thematic 'echoes' to be found, is a major feature of its appeal.
Clearly, the generic expectations set up by other kinds of television
programme become critical here, as a director variously chooses to
respect, extend or subvert them. In a period when these conventions are undergoing rapid change, the documentarist seeking both
an originality of depiction and a large audience is faced with a
strategic challenge, often amounting to a dilemma (more will be
said about this in Chapter 11).

Visual pleasure

LOTE's intensity of imaging, its regular concern with presenting the viewer with a beautiful picture, gives it a strong aesthetic projection, all the more so for these sequences being set off against its observationalist passages, where the visualisation is inevitably more 'muted'. Elsewhere (Corner 1995a) I have discussed the emergence of a bolder image aesthetic in television documentary, tracing its connections with tendencies in cinema and in advertising. For some of the sequences in LOTE, the notion of 'hallucinatory realism' seems appropriate. Here, the referential force of the depiction is certainly deployed (the Lloyd's building, a shopping mall, a Birkenhead pub, and so on), but the mode of depiction displaces this into a heightened intensity, defamiliarising what is shown and making it available for the less directly referential (associative/symbolic) dimension of the account. There are several short scenes in LOTE, for instance, a shot of a huge US Air Force transport plane taking off, whose potency at this displaced level is largely a function of the sheer beauty of the image and the amount of time in which the viewer is allowed to take pleasure in it. The pull of the music here, offering a groundtone of mood or (in the case of the 1960s hits) a whole range of affective intensities and modalities of 'attitude', is often vital.

The introduction of such an aesthetic in a film of this kind raises questions not dissimilar to those raised about the 'poetic realism' of 1930s documentary and some of the wartime films of the British documentary movement. The extent to which a concern with formal attractiveness 'displaces' the referential such as to make the subject itself secondary to its formal appropriation has been a frequent topic of dispute. As we have seen in other chapters, the question of self-conscious stylisation is only one manifestation of a central and inescapable tension in all documentary projects, that between their status as discourse and their status as record. The very explicitness of Grigsby's visual aesthetic in LOTE, its emphatic non-naturalism, makes it difficult if not impossible to accuse him of an attempt at a covertly *enhanced* realism, whilst the counterbalancing pull of his observationalist moments constantly works to connect his associative pattern to the local, the immediate and the concrete.

Directorial 'voice'

LOTE is a documentary with a quite clear, if nearly always implied, assessment of 1980s Britain. The ideas behind this were expressed in an interview with Grigsby shortly after the film was completed:

> Right from the start, I wanted to make a film about the betrayal of the post-war dream. For all its impressionistic structure, there is a sense in which *Living on the Edge* is more direct than some of my other films, and perhaps that is because I personally feel a very deep sense of betrayal ... Right through the class structure, there is a deep sense of unease, cyn-

icism, isolation and betrayal – betrayal of the ideals of the compassion-
ate, caring society that was promised in 1945 when everyone dreamed
of a real change and a new era. (Petley 1987b:169)

In this interview, Grigsby also notes the 'arrogance' of a film-
maker trying to 'impose solutions' and rejects any suggestion that
the film might be open to a charge of defeatism. Yet I remarked earlier that there are possible problems with the particular mix of
despair and resistance projected in and by its account. This is not
only a matter of an internal tension between two interpretative
positions but of the way in which 'ordinary people' are posed variously within the film as victims of the system, happy dupes to its
consumerism and politicised opponents of its values. An awkward
mix of vanguardist and populist ideas about the popular, working
its way variously through into particular aspects of the depictive
strategy, seems to be the main source of this uncertainty. Again,
this points towards a more general problem in British political film-
making at the present time. In his discussion of the options and pitfalls for the 'critical documentary', Bill Nichols (1983) focuses on
the issues surrounding two different kinds of format. As I have
noted in Chapter 2, the vérité/observationalist approach he sees to
be guilty of effacing directorial 'voice' through its very naturalism
of portrayal, amounting to an act of bad faith towards the audience.
What he terms the 'string-of-interview' film risks a circular, self-
confirmatory structure, in which testimony is used to support a
given political and social position, and where the argumentative
and persuasive force of the film for those not already sympathetic
to this position is often marginal. LOTE is neither vérité nor 'string-
of-interview' in structure, although its overheard speech often has
a self-consciously testimonial quality, at the edges of naturalistic
veracity. I have suggested that its own 'argument' is perhaps most
powerfully carried in its visualisations, where affective power and
implicit proposition are combined. Whatever its problems in realis-
ing all the elements and levels of its project, LOTE is an outstanding attempt at engaging with contemporary reality through a
documentary language which draws deeply on the work of the past
as well as pressing forward to new connections and combinations.

The Life and Times of Rosie the Riveter (1980)

7

Connie Field's *Rosie* was made by Clarity Productions in 1980 for independent distribution. It has been shown on television both in the United States and Britain. *Rosie* is an exercise in popular historiography, telling the story of women workers in industry during the Second World War by following the personal accounts of five women, three of whom are black. 'Rosie the Riveter' was the popular typification of such workers, initiated by the artist Norman Rockwell in a cover for the *Saturday Evening Post* in May 1943 (the cover showed a muscular but still 'feminine' riveter at her lunchbreak, 'posing' with an air-driven riveting hammer across her knees and with the word 'Rosie' on her lunchbox). An upbeat song carried the typification further into popular culture.

The interview accounts first establish a pre-war biography for each participant and then follow a three-phase structure of wartime recruitment into industry, experience of wartime industrial work, and post-war 'demobilisation'. The women's testimony has elements both of critique and celebration and these elements are very effectively combined. The different levels of discrimination and prejudice, ranging from the subtle to the gross, are documented through anecdote, but there is also a strong expression of achievement and satisfaction in trade skill. In the post-war phase, this expression forms part of a critical perspective, as well as an articulation of deeply personal denial and regret, when the women are 'returned' to the domestic sphere and/or to service industries. Throughout the film, the accounts of the women are intercut with official US propaganda footage about women and 'war work'. This ranges from films designed to encourage women into the factories to the material designed to rationalise their displacement by men returning from the war. The mixing of the two kinds of material, and the use of contemporary songs on the soundtrack, give the film a high degree of pace and watchability. Formally, the film can be seen to be original in two principal ways. First, it is innovative in the use it makes of its women 'interviewees', who become central characters in an act of combined remembering and reflection and are in no way placed as secondary to another discourse (the film is without commentary). Secondly, its counterpointing of personal testimony with archive propaganda provides the film with a critically comic dimension and carries its critique beyond its primary historical topic. It becomes a film which is also about 'official' information and women's lives. Analysis of it provides the opportunity to engage with some questions concerning the nature and development of film propaganda (and, pertinently, its relationship with the development of documentary). Connie Field has discussed at some length her ideas about the film and her methods of selection and construction. In my own critical commentary, I shall introduce points from her account to support and expand the analysis where it seems appropriate. First of all, an outline of the structure of *Rosie* provides a useful base upon which to proceed.

Outline of structure

Opening

Titles: contemporary images (cartoons, magazine covers) and song 'Rosie the Riveter'.
　　Introduction to the interviewees:
　　Lola Weixel
　　Margaret Wright
　　Lyn Childs
　　Gladys Belcher
　　Wanita Allen
　　(ten seconds each, seated in interview setting, looking at camera and then freeze-framed with captions of name and where they are from).
More contemporary images.

Establishing biography

Caption: 'The late 1930s.'
Margaret,Wanita, Gladys (pre-war lives and work).
Wanita (story of hearing outbreak of war declared on radio after Pearl Harbor raid, intercut with newsreel footage).

Mobilisation and recruitment

(Troop ships on newsreels, war-effort publicity films.)
Gladys, Mary, Lola, ·Lyn, Lola, Gladys (stories of going into industrial work).
(Further film of women entering factories, propaganda
accounts of their speedy conversion from the 'home'.)
Margaret, Wanita, Lola (stories of initial prejudice of male workers).
(Propaganda footage including women employees in 'interview' sequences.)
Wanita, Lyn (further stories of prejudice and discrimination).

Wartime working life

(Music, newsreels of women industrial workers.)
Gladys, Wanita, Lola (work anecdotes).
(Film footage involving supervisor of women employees talking of abili-

ties of women workers.)
Margaret, Gladys (further work anecdotes).
Lola, Wanita, Margaret (pay discrimination; union organisation).
(Film footage with supervisor's account continued.)
Wanita (story about women not being allowed to use showers).

Domestic life and working life

(Newsreel montage, songs.)
Lola, Lyn, Wanita, Margaret, Lola, Margaret, Wanita (need to keep working when at home; husband's expectations of 'housewife/mother' role. Interview testimony intercut with film of day nurseries).

'Problems' with the women workers

(Newsreel on falling-off of production, 'failures' of effort; propaganda urgings to fight this.)
Margaret, Lyn (story of her confrontation with bosses over discrimination against a fellow-worker).
(Film of shipyard launching.)
Lyn (story of attending launches).
Lola (story of solidarity amongst workgroup).

War's ending

(Archive film sequence – 'Peace' headlines in newspapers, celebration in streets. Returning troops, problems of 're- employment'. Women workers to become 'wives and mothers' again.)
Lyn, Lola, Gladys, Margaret, Lola (stories of being laid- off).
Wanita, Gladys, Lyn, Lola (stories of being out of work, of being refused jobs).

A role resumed

(Film propaganda on disruption of marriage and neglect of children caused by women working. Woman psychologist reports on threat to family of economic independence of women and dangers of 'frustration', de-feminisation, etc.).
Lola, Gladys, Margaret, Lyn, Wanita (other kinds of work found, mostly menial).
Lola (her dream of making wrought-iron gates, never realised).
(Film sequence – new families, babies, houses.)

Lola (on the baby boom).
Margaret (the new emphasis on cooking tips and child-rearing advice).
Lola (women workers just a 'joke', society prepares women psychologically for given roles; the denial and loss entailed).

Ending

Music ('Rosie' song).
Lola (last remarks on the spirit of solidarity, then freeze-frame).
Final credits are intercut with shots of all five women in action of some kind before being freeze-framed (Lyn walks up ship's companionway; Gladys parks her truck; Wanita and Margaret are at a back-garden barbecue; Lola is walking down a street).

The above outline is rather lacking in detail when compared with the initial sketches of content which I have been able to provide in other chapters. What I have wanted to do here primarily is to call attention to three things. First of all the chronological/historical organisation of the film (which my analytic division brings out as a sequence of phases, although of course the film itself is organised as a continuous flow with the archive film newsreel announcements acting as the principal marker of development). Secondly, the regularity of the movement between testimony and archive footage, a regularity which provides the film with its distinctive dynamism. Thirdly, the extent to which the film uses its interviews in 'slices', returning to its five witnesses repeatedly in the advancing of the account. We can see from this outline, for example, that Lola makes some seventeen separate 'appearances' in the film, opening it and closing it. I shall discuss below the way in which she quite frequently performs a function closer to that of on-screen narrator than interviewee, in the extent to which she articulates a more general perspective as well as describing her own experiences.

I want to proceed by looking first of all at some further characteristics of the two modes most prominent in *Rosie* – the mode of interview testimony and the mode or modes of official propaganda.

Interviewee as 'character'

Rosie integrates its interviewees into the film as part characters, part presenters. That is to say the stories of the five women have an intensive, subjective dimension and a more objective expositional function through which they become indicative of a general process. Unlike conventional documentary practice, however, in which interview testimony becomes necessarily subordinate to an expository discourse sustained by other means (e.g. commentary; presentation), the interviewees in *Rosie* constitute the principal discursive element. This places the women themselves as the articulators of the film, rather than as recruits to its project (although, as we shall see later, the shaping influence of the film-maker in selecting and constituting the terms of this articulation is still considerable). The fact that they are all seen in the title sequence, freeze-framed and identified by caption, establishes this role right from the start, which is then further strengthened by the concise biographical sketches (subject voice-over and photographs) through which their narratives are begun. The conduct of the interviews themselves (very few questions on soundtrack, interviewer never in shot, different and 'appropriate' settings for each interviewee and, in general, a gaze-line just offset from direct address) supports this more prominent status. Field has commented interestingly on her approach to interview *mise-en-scène*:

> Two of the women were filmed where they used to work, Lyn on an old victory ship that was built in the Second World War, and Lola in front of a factory where she used to work, with the New York skyline in the background. I flew Margaret from Los Angeles to my offices in the Bay Area because I couldn't afford to fly my crew down. I then created a

clinic-type atmosphere for her in one of our offices because she then worked in a clinic, and I wanted her surroundings to say something about her life now. With Juanita [Wanita in film captions -JC], I rented a Winnebago and drove her out to the Ford River Rouge plant so we could see the factory in the background with the smoke rising out the window, because, in my mind, that image says Detroit. And Gladys was filmed inside her house because it rained. We were going to shoot it outside her house, but it still works for her because the house is decorated in a way that is characteristic of homes in the southern mountains, which is where she grew up. (Zheutlin 1988:229)

In this way, then, the setting of the testimony is organised to be significant and to be both biographically and thematically supportive.

Perhaps, too, the frequency of appearance of the five women is instrumental to their personal salience and to viewer empathy. One can imagine the film with fewer interviewees, but the problem here would become the familiar one of the *representativeness* of recounted experience (I discuss this further below, once again drawing on Field's own comments about her practice). One can also easily imagine it with more interviewees, but then the problem quite soon becomes not only a dispersal of affective viewing relations but the generation of too much specific information, too many instances, than can be usefully carried forward in the historical shifts which form a primary axis of the film. There is also the problem of repetition – of how many specific (locally various) versions of a more general truth about circumstances a viewer will accept before judging the provision of testimony to be in excess of requirement.

Interview 'character' and interview speech are mutually reinforcing for the women of *Rosie* because their speech primarily concerns acts of reflective memory in the first instance and only then a commentary (implicit or otherwise) on an objectifiable 'topic'. There is a most imaginative piece of editing at the beginning of the 'mobilisation and recruitment' segment (identified above) in which Wanita tells of how, as a domestic servant, she first heard of the news of Pearl Harbor, by being invited into a room to listen to the radio. The film moves smoothly from her account into an an archive recording of President Truman's Pearl Harbor broadcast and declaration of war. Under this is arranged a short sequence of images of people listening to the broadcast (some of these images are drawn from fictional footage, some from actuality material). With the Presidential speech continuing, the film then shows each of the five women for a few seconds, in their interview location, apparently listening to the broadcast, before shifting to visual footage of the President speaking. Through this device a number of things are brought about. The women are further grouped together into a solidarity of witness without thereby losing their individual identity. The sense of them 'reliving' the hearing of the historic pronouncement upon which the course of their lives was to change is one which wonderfully manages both to combine, and yet also to place into a relationship of distance, 'then' and 'now'. This sense precisely of the operations of memory (involving both distance and proximity) enriches overall awareness of the film's project and provides it with a powerfully, if nicely understated, exemplification. Finally, in the shifting relationships between testimony and image, the sequence achieves a moment of fusion.

It is one of the strengths of *Rosie*, and of a number of other films produced by feminist film-makers, that it provides each of the women with the time to develop reflection, and the anecdotal basis for this, rather than hurrying them to the point at which they most obviously 'contribute' to thematic development.[1] In his suggestive article, 'The Voice of Documentary' (1983), Bill Nichols has remarked on the problems with what he calls the 'string-of-interview' format (a classification within which he does not place *Rosie*, whilst nevertheless noting resemblances). One of these problems is the danger of a self-confirmatory circle in which interviewees are shown lending experiential support to an emerging, general version of the truth which they have been precisely chosen to underwrite. I shall discuss Nichols's assessment of *Rosie* more fully below, but it is clear that one of the ways in which the film attempts to avoid this charge is not only by the counterpointing of testimony with 'official' archive film but by the degree of personal 'space' which its participants occupy. This space gives an integrity to the testimony which renders it less appropriable by external intentions than might be the case with a more urgent treatment of the issue. Moreover, 'depth' is given to the women by the placing of 'then' within the terms of 'now' and by the consequent sense of personal development and expanded awareness. By contrast, the archive footage remains vulnerably caught within the rhetorical expediencies of its time.

Although the women vary in their way of speaking and, throughout the film, talk about topics which relate variously to the 'personal', some idea of the modality of testimony speech in *Rosie* can be gleaned from this transcribed extract. It is Lyn, talking about how she was taken on as a welder:

(spoken against shipyard background, Lyn seated)
We went to Moore's shipyard to get signed in because they called that they needed four fitters. And when we got there the superintendent took the three white persons that was with me and left me sitting outside and came back in about forty-five minutes and said 'No, we don't have any openings.' I said 'what do you mean? I was told at the school you had five openings and I was sent over as the person in charge of all the other people. Where are they?' 'Oh' he said, 'we've found places for them.' It was clear they didn't want a black woman in the elite trade of shipfitting.

Oh, I was so mad. I got up and I said 'Is there anything else open?' And they said, yes, they had welders' and burners' jobs. And the superintendent says, 'Well, you'll have to go back to school to learn to burn.' And I said, 'no, why don't you just give me a test and see if I can burn?' I got to the instructor who had all this equipment and he says, 'well, here's a nice thick piece of steel – Beverley – and I said OK and so knowing that I would tell the burner to make sure it was good and hot before he started cutting it, I started to get it hot. And he said, 'never mind, never mind, I see you know your business' and then he gave me a piece

Politicising the personal:
Lola in *Rosie the Riveter*

to cut out neat with a lot of designs on it and I got myself down like I'd seen the burners do getting ready to start to cut, and he said 'never mind', he says, 'you'll do. I'll send you in as a first-stage burner' and I said 'OK'. He said 'you'll be making one dollar five cents an hour'. If I had gone in as a shipfitter's helper, I would have only been making eighty-five so I was delighted. You know, I was making more money in five minutes than all the rest of them was making when they went in as helpers. So. That's how I got into the shipyard. And I became the only woman ever to make Shellburner at Moore's shipyard.

This is a story both of prejudice and of achievement, told with a justified pride. Its anecdotal pacing allows the viewer to share Lyn's obvious relish in recounting how she suprised the instructor with her competence and how, eventually, she ended up on a higher rate of pay than that for the job for which she had initially applied.

Although the five women are all presented in the same general mode and allowed similar types of speaking opportunity, Lola – a Jewish New Yorker who was a union organiser – seems to have more of a 'presenter' function than the others. This is partly structural – I have noted earlier how her comments both open and close the film. It is also a question of depiction, in that Lola is the only interviewee to be standing in all the shots, some of which present her in close-up whilst some pull back to a mid-shot position, portraying all or most of her standing figure. Finally, it is discursive too, since Lola not only speaks with particular clarity and emphasis, she also, more often than the others, takes on the role of spokesperson for women *like* her (talking in terms of 'we' quite frequently), moving towards a more general evaluation of what happened during the war and then afterwards. It is not necessary for *Rosie* to have a figure in it of this kind and, indeed, too salient and explicit a performance would risk putting the whole account out of balance. But there is no doubt that the regular appearance of Lola's narrational episodes gives the film a firmer and more strongly projected development. It also strengthens the positive mood of the film, since Lola, though severely critical of many aspects of what she underwent, is very much a genial person, smiling and reflecting on the past with a strong sense of wry humour as well as of regret.

Official images

The primary rhetorical use made of archive footage in *Rosie* is as a contrast to the testimony of the women. In this function, drawing on sequences of publicity and propaganda, it is a radically questioned discourse. However, newsreel sequences are also used more descriptively and positively as a way of giving a visual realisation to many of the circumstances which the interviewees describe. So, for instance, there are scenes of women workers in action on various industrial sites and, to provide broader context, shots indicative of various stages of the war. Generally, interviewee voice-over is used over such 'descriptive' sequences, serving to meld accounts with images, whereas the propaganda items need to be presented with their own soundtracks intact since much of their manipulative design is carried by their speech. This also marks them off as being from a different, and highly suspect, discursive realm, something which the viewer soons learns to recognise and to anticipate. Although viewers will vary considerably in their previous knowledge of, and disposition towards, the circumstances to which *Rosie* addresses itself, most viewers are likely to find two things remarkable about the propaganda material. First of all, they are likely to be suprised by the emphatic tones of condenscension and of prejudice disguised as tolerance conveyed by the male commentary accompanying most of the footage. This is 'discrimination' on a level far more explicit than most current public discourse. So strident are these tones that they develop a marked degree of comic force (of the outrageous, of the almost-beyond-parody), without thereby reducing the critical effectiveness of their use within the film. Secondly, as the film develops, the contrast between the terms in which the material encourages women to enter industry and the terms in which it then persuades them to return to the home becomes a marked inconsistency in the 'official' discourse. As an indicator of discursive opportunism in the service of strategically revised economic priorities, this also has a strong critical purpose. But, compressed within the film's terms, the 'sudden' reversal also has a farcical dimension, a comedy of absurd self-contradiction. Again, although the material which is drawn on varies considerably in format and tone, an example might be useful to indicate something of the communicative character of the 'official' version of events. These extracts come close together in the earlier part of the film, as part of the depiction of women's recruitment into industry:

Extract 1

(Shots of women working in an aircraft factory)
(Male VO) In the sprawling aircraft factories of the West Coast, teams of women flush the rivets that hold together the aluminum skin on the wing of a B24.
(Shot change to woman on drilling machine)
This is like punching holes in a tin of scouring powder.
(Shot change to woman on cutting machine)
Instead of cutting out dresses, this woman stamps out the pattern of aeroplane parts.
(Shot change to woman welding)
They are taking to welding as though the welding rod were a needle and the metal a length of cloth to be sewn.
(Music)
(Shot change to woman operating a steel press)
After a short apprenticeship, a woman can operate this press as easily as a juice extractor in her own kitchen. And a lathe (change of shot) will hold no more terrors for her than an electric washing machine.
(Music).

Just a minute or so later there comes

Extract 2

(Over newsreel shots of troops boarding ships and women entering factory gates, then graphs and mixed shots of women workers.)
(Male VO)
The need for women grew desperate and thousands of women answered the call. The hidden army drew fresh recruits (graph showing increased recruitment), its ranks grew to nearly eighteen million. Many of the women came from walks of life not previously considered – the mother, the young, the aged. When we asked why they had joined the ranks of the hidden army, these women gave a variety of reasons.
(Woman on ammunition production line)
My husband is a prisoner of the Japs in the Philippines. If he'd had a few more of these shells out in Bataan, maybe he would still be fighting.
(Women at factory bench)
I'm an old maid and I didn't have anyone until I took this defence job. Now I have a family of ten million to look after.
(Young woman welding, lifts up visor)
Why did I take a defence job? That's a funny question. I never thought of that before. Do you have to have a reason? We're in a jam, aren't we? I'm sorry but you'll have to excuse me, I'm too busy to answer damn-fool questions like that.
(Male VO)
Somehow that answer pleased us. No sudden emotional urge sent this young woman into war work. No loss of a loved one. No temporary economic embarrassment. No mere yearning for excitement or novelty. There are millions like her. There will have to be.

In both extracts, the form of address implies a male audience as the most significant, if not the exclusive, audience. In extract 1, the parallel between factory and kitchen is pointed out *for* the amusement of the male viewer. Like much of the promotional material drawn on in *Rosie*, its terms of praise involve high levels of condescension. In these shots, women workers are intensively objectified as 'other' – as the subject of approval which nevertheless retains the fascination of oddity, of the exotic, of the remarkable. In extract 2, the form of pseudo-testimony extends this discourse from commentary to self-description. Rather than being in any sense ethnographically oriented, the women's answers are imposed from the script requirements of national propaganda and the various stereotypes which this sees fit to employ. Both the plucky realism about ammunition shown by the soldier's wife and the new family spirit felt by the self-described old maid clearly come from this script. The rude independence of the last speaker is a slightly more innovative creation, although it is her 'manly' bluntness and disdain for small talk which is most marked. This is clear from the patronising nature of the commentary's subsequent remarks with its list of the reasons which one might *expect* women to have for going into war work. No consideration of this extract, however brief, could be concluded without noting, too, the extraordinary comment in the introduction: 'many of the women came from walks of life not previously considered – the mother, the young, the aged'. Not considered by *whom* within terms of *what* criteria? is the question emphatically posed here. Although the utterance appears to be a compression of 'not previously considered to be trainable as industrial workers', its wider resonances are illuminating and not entirely coincidental.

Like much else in the archive material drawn on in Rosie, both examples not only operate as praise-within-prejudice, they also work primarily as prescriptive models for behaviour whilst presenting themselves as descriptive documentation of it.

The argument of *Rosie*

I now want to focus on how the 'argument' of *Rosie* develops. In particular I want to ask three questions of this argument. First of all, what is the specific nature of its critique of the past?. Secondly, how does the particular selection of these five women serve to shape that critique? Thirdly, how does the critique relate to the circumstances of 1980?

In my earlier discussion I have already gone some way towards addressing the first question. The conditions of employment and of pay under which the women worked are established to be discriminatory. Although the film has many things to say about the positive experiences, the emancipatory aspects, of being a woman worker, these are framed by the pressures of economic, social and cultural marginalisation. Experientially documented, such pressures relate 'upwards' both to the national policy towards women workers (with its manipulative inconsistency) and to the form and content of the propaganda (with its stereotyping and patriarchal condescension).

The 'problem' is therefore not only, or indeed chiefly, to be located at the level of individual industries and their male managers and work-force. It is a problem which finally even transcends questions of 'bad government' to become a perceived shortcoming of the economic system itself. The same might be said of racism, the issue which runs alongside sexism for much of the testimony in *Rosie*, as earlier quotations indicate. Connie Field has said that, despite the high degree of selectivity involved in the choice of interviewees, the question of race did not enter the film with quite such marked intention as some viewers have supposed:

> Another interesting thing that happened with the film is that I didn't consciously set out to have two white women and three black women. It was a matter of just having certain issues and certain stories covered, and these five women were the ones to do it, and three of them happened to be black. Though I'm immensely pleased with the effect because all too many times blacks are used in films just to elicit the black experience, and therefore become tokens, and I think the the effect of the film is the opposite. (Zheutlin 1988:237)

Clearly, race was among the 'certain issues' which required coverage, even if not through any specific ratio of selection. The effect, whatever the intentions, is to give questions of gender and of race a roughly equal prominence (although the archive footage itself pertains most explicity to questions of gender its exclusive 'white-ness' indirectly supports the engagement with the racial issue).

Both the sexism and the racism identified by *Rosie* at different levels within American society are, then, finally registered as *systemic* deficiencies. However, the film is not explicitly an anti-capitalist film and I will suggest below that, although its popularity with audiences may rest in part on it not pursuing a line of economic radicalism, this factor has the effect of introducing a measure of uncertainty not only into the matter of 'causes' but also into that of possible 'cures'.

On the second question, Field's selection of interviewees (700 'candidates' down to five interviewees in the film) seems to have been made in terms of personal qualities and of ability to tell stories convincingly on camera as much as in terms of specific, pre-planned sub-themes, once a requirement to have 'stories and job histories which were typical of the times' was satisfied. She has noted: 'I wanted to find people who could express themselves emo-tionally as well as intellectually' (Zheutlin 1988:229). Questioned on the relationship of the views of those finally selected to the views of the film-maker, Field remarks:

> Many of the women do express our point of view. But some of that came as a suprise when filming ... one thing I did seek out consciously was a couple of women who were conscious of what happened to them in the larger historical framework. To that end, I chose someone like Margaret, who talked about the propaganda and the media after the war. (Zheut-lin 1988:237)

That the interviewees tell stories and make evaluations which are the 'truth of the matter' is something which viewers are likely very quickly to believe. The counterpointing with archive footage is not an attempt to problematise knowledge of history by inviting the viewer to choose between competing versions. This method *has* been used by radical film-makers but in Rosie the archive footage is for the most part projected as self-evidently untrue (it demonstrably belongs to the genre of deliberate untruth) because its epistemolog-ical function is to reinforce the veracity of witness and to reduce the likelihood of a viewer becoming sceptical about 'typicality' here. There are problems, anyway, in imagining women of similar expe-rience who would offer explicit evaluations of a kind *contradicting* what we have from the selected five. For instance, the acted responses to camera of 'workers' in the propaganda films become, in the wider context of *Rosie*, hopelessly inadequate and implanted accounts, lacking any referential validity. That many women recruited to industry were, *at the time*, unaware of the degree of sys-temic discrimination they were working under is certainly proba-ble. However, the interviewees' own acts of memory depict a *process* of reflection-as-self-awareness, and it is this process which the film asks its viewers imaginatively to follow.[2] This becomes its main 'line of knowledge', the means by the 'personal is made political'. In this sense, the women do not have a 'viewpoint' which is potentially in contrast to that of other women; they have access to certain truths through experience. The consensuality and security of this position is only troubled when assessments move to the very highest levels of generality, as they do for instance in some of Lola's remarks about the way in which society 'prepares women' for certain roles. Here, as I remarked earlier, the question of 'causes' becomes implicitly one about patriarchal capitalism. The film judiciously holds back from making explicit this level of critique (one which has implications for a reading of the 'rightness' of the whole war effort), preferring instead to trouble official myth with a powerful and self-aware 'history from below' which is not at too much risk of having its main, interrogative project falling victim to the political predisposition of audiences. Similarly, to have introduced interviews with those involved in the policy and administration of female war work would have weakened the force of the contrast between footage and testimony, even allowing for the potentially unconvincing nature of any attempted 'justifications'.

My third question, about the relationship between the historical critique and 'now', is clearly a related one. The film reveals a 'true' history which lies beneath the national myth of women wartime workers.[3] Through oral testimony, it documents this history to be one of systematic discrimination against women in general and against black women in particular. The cynicism of official policy on the recruitment and post-war disbandment of the female labour 'army' is exposed and the nature of its publicity appeals shown to be fraudalent, sometimes comically so. How does such an examination of the past relate to the present? For this is certainly not a film which (like some television series) looks back at a 'bad' past from the perspective of an 'improved' future. I have noted how, towards the end of the film, when Lola begins to talk of the way in which women are 'prepared psychologically' for certain roles, the critique opens out well beyond the historical, but the extension remains implicit. A degree of uncertainty about how the present can be 'read' in the context of the past is clearly a corollary of that uncertainty, discussed above, about the level at which questions of 'cause' are finally to be addressed. What is to be 'carried over' from the historical analysis into the present, both in relation to the specific issues of women and 'work' and of the official use of *mis*information and also in relation to the general issues of an economic system apparently grounded in gender inequality?[4]

The film's strategy here seems to be that of provoking a question in the viewer rather than addressing this question directly. That is to say, those in the audience for *Rosie* who do not already hold the opinion that gender discrimination constitutes a major inequality in many modern societies (including the USA), are given good cause to ask, 'how much has really *changed?*' Of course, for those already persuaded of current inequities, the film acts as a revealing insight into aspects of its historical presence at an earlier (and cruder) phase of articulation.

As we have seen in other chapters, the matter of how explicitly, and in what form, a documentary film chooses to provide its audience with evaluations is of great significance, particularly so where such evaluations are directly political in character. Sometimes, as here, the provocation of the viewer, by sharp contrasts and intensities of recorded experience, towards the thinking (and feeling) which will lead to politicisation of an issue and, if it is historical, to its placing in relation to the present, is more effective than an explicit treatment. It is also more prudent as a way of engaging with viewer expectations of the 'political' which may work against an open response to documentation and testimony (but see White 1995 for a more strongly critical judgement on the relations between the historical and the political established by the film).

Conclusions

Rosie is an important film both in the development of the documentary exploration of oral history and the use of archive footage to support and also, more significantly, to counterpoint (and thereby strengthen by contrast) what is said. By variously establishing its five respondents as 'characters', it gives them a status beyond that of the conventional interviewee and generates a strongly affective viewing relationship as well as a cognitive one. Its use of official publicity films is at the same time comic and critical. Throughout most of the film, the movement across testimony and footage provides a strong dynamic. Only in the last quarter of the film does this give way to a slightly more static structure, as the chronological narrative slows down and more time is given to reflection on different aspects of the post-war phase, with its abandoned hopes and re-entry into a realm of restricted social and occupational opportunity. In relation to its historical subject and to the bearing this subject has for an understanding of the present, the film is implicit in its evaluations, working in the final section towards an encouragement of reflection in viewers rather than their agreement with any specific propositions. Although it is a film which sets up a 'play' of discourses by its use of testimony against archive materials, its approach is finally a realist one – the truth of the woman is established against the lies of the official propaganda. In other chapters of this book, I have discussed how such an option is not always available to the film-maker, or even always desirable.

When The Dog Bites (1988)

8

When the Dog Bites (henceforth *WTDB*) was shown on British Channel Four Television in 1988. It was made and distributed by Trade Films Ltd of Gateshead, a leading and innovative independent film and video production company. Directed by Penny Woolcock, it takes as its theme the town of Consett, in County Durham, and offers a sequence of reports and explorations into how the town and its inhabitants have fared in the years following the closure of its main industry, the steelworks, in the early 1980s. Attempts at small-scale reindustrialisation within new 'industrial estates' have been made by international companies, but the closure has changed the character of the town and the way of life of Consett people in often quite radical ways, with reduced incomes, various kinds of frustration and nostalgia and a range of individual attempts at alternative forms of employment, some of which have been spectacularly successful, others of which have failed.

The general theme of a community under process of change, essentially a change which is a part of a larger industrial restructuring, is one which has been tackled by a number of recent filmmakers (including Michael Moore, whose *Roger and Me* is discussed in Chapter 9) but rarely if ever has it been tackled by such a bravura use of different documentary styles as evidenced in *WTDB*.

That the film was also a controversial one in the community which forms its subject, provoking a number of highly critical responses, also serves to indicate how the older and familiar problems of 'typicality', 'balance' and implicit editorial perspective underlie its distinctively energetic and innovative approach. The enigmatic title is drawn from the song 'Favourite Things' from *The Sound of Music*, the lyrics of which relate ironically to the dominant mood of the film. Such a self-conscious 'puzzle' phrasing also fits in with the general aesthetic of the whole project, as I shall show.

Description

The explorations of *WTDB* involve the mixing of what can be seen as three distinct, if often closely related, documentary discourses. These are:

1 A sequence of interviews with people variously implicated in the 'story of Consett'. These people are ex-workers, ex-managers, unemployed youths and also those active in the 'new' economy of Consett; for instance, a development officer, the manager of a new factory, individual entrepreneurs. The *mise-en-scène* of these interviews is often strikingly non-conventional. One interview takes place in the local swimming-bath, with the interviewee swimming into shot and providing interview comment whilst standing with water at chest height, the lower half of his body visible under the surface. A recurring sequence of ex-workers' comments is depicted in black and white, as is the interview with the factory manager.

2 Various sequences of observational footage, shot on the streets of Consett; in a club where a drag act is being performed; in a home where a young man is practising escapology, in a well-appointed home where china figurines are being shown and sold to a group of women. Some of these sequences of observation, notably the escapology scenes, take on a clear symbolic as well as naturalistic force in the context of the film's main themes.

3 A strand of dramatisation involving the characters Rose and Bill, with Rose, much younger than her (married) male partner, frustrated by her boring job at the crisp factory, and Bill, made redundant by the closure, constantly dreaming up implausible ways in which he can make money and achieve success. The incorporation of this strand within the documentary is undoubtedly one of its most innovative and controversial features.

The basic model, then, is that of a 'string of interviews' documentary, incorporating within it some striking settings and forms of depiction – to which has been added not only a degree of observationalist portrayal but also scenes from an acted narrative which is played for comic as well as serious effect. The three strands are woven together into a cumulative development. In order to address their inter-organisation more closely, it would be useful to look first of all at the opening five minutes of the programme, during which a number of themes are initiated and ways of looking established.

Opening sequences

1 Opening high-angle shot of a town street at night. Lights, people and a firework exploding as a cluster of sparks in the sky. Shot descends slowly to pick up large clock-face, illuminated, on tower. Further slow camera descent down side of clock-tower, to street level, where young people are walking and mingling. The camera picks up a young woman in a leopard-skin fancy-dress outfit as she crosses the road to the side on which a number of people are noisily walking. Having followed the woman across the road, the camera then shifts direction to track alongside the youths, who are singing, shouting and grinning at the camera. Many of them enter a pub, the camera follows, exploring the activities

happening either side of the 'route' taken through the crowd, swinging left and right to observe drinking, talk and dancing. Throughout, a jazz song, 'When the Dog Bites', is sung on the soundtrack. The whole of this sequence is contained within one shot.

2   Outside the pub door. A woman pushes through. Immediately she is met by a man who walks beside her and sets up an argument with her about what she should be doing to make more money. The camera focuses on them in mid-close-up and presents them frontally as they walk down the street. They continue to argue, the woman scorning the ideas of the man about becoming a foreign correspondent and a writer once he gets a word-processor. The nature of the dialogue, in script and acting, is that of situation comedy (the timing, the character of the exaggerated ambitions, the emphases of speech).

3   A swimming-bath, daytime. Sunshine reflected on the surface of the water. A young man is swimming. He stops, stands up and comments on the employment situation in Consett and his own experience of the difficulty of getting a job. No titles indicate his identity.

4   A brief return to the night-time street scene and the group of young revellers.

5   A group of workers gathered around a table in a room (in the bus station, where they work) talk of life in the days of the steelworks. (Black and white)

6   The living-room of a house. A young man is tied into a strait-jacket and faces the camera impassively. He calls 'one, two, three' and then thrashes around in an attempt to release himself.

Analysis

Enough is indicated above to show the strongly non-conventional nature of the programme's structure and treatment, despite it drawing on a number of mainstream conventions. Although I want to engage with the aesthetic and referential project of the programme in more general terms later, it is useful to note straight away some of the salient features of this opening which would surely not escape notice by any viewer, although it is likely they would be subject to a number of different readings. We can perhaps get some initial purchase on these by itemisation:

Hallucinatory realism and the exotic

Consett is established as 'exotic' and 'strange' in the opening sequence through the use of a number of devices. First of all, the visualisation is one which draws extensively on fictional and cinematic modes in its scene-setting. The illuminated clock against the night sky, the fireworks, the leopard-skin girl, the hectic revellers, produce a sharply non-naturalistic account, working both against naturalism of mode (how we see things) and content (what we see). In fact, this opening shot draws on the opening shot of Orson Welles's *Touch of Evil* (1958), a shot designed precisely to set up connotations of exotic menace and 'risk' in a small town on the US/Mexican border.[1] Even the sequence of the crowd on the pavement is displaced from conventional vérité as a result not only of the sheer intensity of behaviour and self-consciousness of the subjects but of the camera's seemingly obsessive interest in pursuing the action wherever it leads, an interest quickly developing parodic (and thereby comic) connotations.

Multi-strand development and juxtaposition

Eschewing authoritative voice-over completely, *WTDB*'s expositional work is done primarily by the interview sequences, whilst its observationalism cuts into the town's life at several different levels. The movement, which the opening section illustrates, between a rendering of Consett's outer physical realities and 'public' activities and the various individualised 'life spaces' of the interviewees, is continued throughout the programme. Rather than the shifts between various locations of interview/testimony being used to develop an explicit thematics, they are combined with the observationalist material to build up a multi-levelled account of the town, an account which is not only various in its aspects and implicit in its assessments but which also contains conflicting elements. Once the key 'spaces' of the programme have been established, they are regularly returned to, so that the viewing\knowing experience becomes steadily more incremental and less subject to 'jarring'.

Opening up from naturalism: forms of the symbolic

I have pointed out how the opening sequence of the programme works to produce an 'exotic' Consett, whilst grounding this in a version of documentary naturalism (at times, a bizarre version of street-vérité). This enrichment and partial displacement of the naturalistic image occurs without any substantial de-referentialising of the account. As I noted in Chapter 1, a documentary which attempted to marginalise or subvert its referential axis would, beyond a certain point (different for different viewers), risk a crisis of credibility. Whilst this might not be a problem for non-broadcast 'independent' work, which could present itself as working with a chronically problematised 'real' and aim for viewer appeal in relation both to the conceptual suggestiveness of its problematisation and its own 'artfulness' in depicting this, for broadcast material seeking a popular audience, the dangers are evident. Indeed, too emphatic a shift into associational modes (in *mise-en-scène*, in form of shot, in editing and sound/vision mix) risks two difficulties. First of all, it risks 'losing' the viewer by employing cultural codes not widely accessible. Secondly, as indicated, it risks stressing the authorial over the evidential to the point where 'documentary' status is not attributed by viewers.

As I shall suggest later, part of the problems *WTDB* had with local viewers derived from these formal issues. However, there is some care taken to retain a level of accessibility in the programme, both in terms of knowledge and pleasure. The use of the escapologist, for instance, provides a metaphor on the 'problem of Consett' which is so obvious as to become self-parodic (the programme's capacity to provide cues for the ironising of certain of its elements which can also quite productively be taken as non-ironic is a further feature which points to a degree of postmodern reflexivity).

A special case of 'enhanced naturalism' occurs with the swimming-bath interview. This both disrupts expectations about the normative settings for such events as well as offering the viewer an engaging and pleasurable visualisation (Hockney-like in its use of light, reflection and the creative distortions of water refraction). How does the use of such a visualisation support or threaten the status of the speaker and the spoken within the discourse of the programme? This is a question I shall contextualise and address later, but certainly the anonymity of the speaker risks a higher degree of speaker appropriation than would be likely with a conventionally identified respondent. Part of the programme's project is clearly to work 'beyond' the individualism of the named respondent, so fetishised in contemporary journalism, but such a move raises important questions about the communicative relationships obtaining both between director and subject and subject and audience.

Getting to 'inner Consett': drama as knowledge

I suggested that one of the most innovative features of the programme is the use thoughout of a dramatic strand featuring Rose and Bill. These two not only appear in their own dramatic 'space' (sometimes rendered in black and white), but they are also to be found in the programme's observational space (so, for instance, the camera picks them up and overhears their talk as part of the audience for the club cabaret) and in its interview space (in one sequence, they are in the swimming-bath where the young, unemployed man is interviewed). This sense of a surprising overlap between narrative and evidential spaces is used by the film both as part of its project of 'de-familiarising' documentary form and as a principle of integration.

The story of Rose and Bill provides the film-maker with the opportunity to foreground tensions and frustrations only partially articulated in the interview testimony. The use of a comic format gives a conventional generic justification for the exaggerated nature of Bill's 'plans' at the same time as it offers the means for getting a strong expression of discontent into the programme, one which then becomes intertextually active with other, more qualified and muted, accounts.

Having looked at how the opening establishes a number of key themes as well as providing some central indications as to the manner in which depiction will subsequently be undertaken, I want to consider some of 'spaces' across which the film operates. These are 'spaces' in the strict sense that they are separate places in Consett, but they are also spaces in the discursive sense, in so far, as I have already illustrated, they open up on different aspects of Consett and develop by different modes of exploration. There are five such spaces which I feel it would be useful to deal with here – cabaret, the 'new' Consett, Rose and Bill, the site of the works and the porcelain seller. Certainly, other footage than this is introduced and there is a steady punctuation in the regular return to the (eventually successful) amateur escapologist and the several intercuttings of swimming, boxing and weight-training scenes in which the unemployed young man identified in the opening sequence appears. But these five spaces seem to me to have particular significance for the project of *WTDB*, inflecting it in different directions.

The Spaces of Consett

Cabaret

In several ways, *WTDB* seeks to introduce a provocative strangeness into its rendering of Consett. This is largely a matter of the forms and devices employed. However, the programme's explorations reveal that the reality of the town itself can produce what might seem some striking points of 'oddity'. The most notable of these, returned to at several points in the programme, is the club cabaret, featuring a high-intensity male drag act, using a variety of outrageous costumes (see illustration). Observational scenes of this act create both a strong sense of a community at leisure (the camera picks up the responses of the mixed audience), and a 'space' upon which certain parodic forms both of masculinity and national identity can be projected (part of the act involves the singing of 'There's Always Been An England', led by the artiste, who wears a vast Union Jack skirt which at one point springs up like a peacock's feathers). These are essentially, if not exclusively, referential functions but the cabaret scenes also possess a strong and disruptive aesthetic character, an energy of the *grotesque* which the film is able to juxtapose with the more conventional (if nevertheless variously displaced) naturalisms it uses elsewhere.

The 'new' Consett

Post-steelworks Consett is not only variously a place of thwartings and limitations (the round of job centres and weight-training), with a complementary febrility and intensity about its recreations (the cabaret, the crowded disco-pub, the opening street scene), it is also a place of hollow affirmations. These affirmations come principally from the manager of a new (nappy) factory and the local spokesman for industrial development. Contributions from both these sources are subject to considerable transformative work, both in shooting and editing. For instance, representations of both men include sequences in black and white in which they are shot from a very low-angle moving camera, kept just in front of them as they

Subversion and style in *When the Dog Bites*: the drag act

walk. This is particularly striking in one of the scenes featuring the factory manager, who is filmed entering the building, walking down the corridor into his office, all the time keeping up a commentary to the camera (although one clearly aimed at the director standing behind it, as his initial remarks, 'Hello Penny!', indicate). Both men are encouraged to become *performers* for the film, rather than simply to play the part of observed subjects or interviewees. Working within this relatively tight framework of directorial organisation, presumably unaware of the possible negative implications this may carry for their presentation, they develop cliché-ridden testimonies to the 'enterprise promise' of the community in terms which have the ring of condescension as well as a certain banality (loyalty of work-force, distinctiveness of region, etc.). Both of them are edited in ways which project their willingness to present a positive account of the community as of doubtful sincerity and as 'comic' when viewed in the overall framework of the film (indefinite though this may finally be).

Rose and Bill

Rose and Bill constitute a kind of sitcom strand in the film, one which takes the themes of the actuality sequences and develops them into an exaggerated dramatisation of 'inner' tensions. Bill the wild dreamer and Rose the frustrated factory worker, linked together in a fraught and (given the age difference between them) improbable romantic relationship, articulate a pathetic drama clearly designed to modify the context in which we respond to the interview testimony of Consett's real inhabitants. Each of the ten or so scenes involving them is a variation on the central theme – the mismatch between Bill's daydreaming optimism and Rose's sour, realist pessimism. There is no significant narrative development – each scene has the independence of a separate sketch – although the final one appears to bring to a head Rose's discontent with Bill, as she rejects the invitation to leave Consett with him and walks off. There are a number of questions posed by this innovative dramatisation, concerning not only the manner of its connection with other parts of the documentary as perceived by viewers, but also the ways in which its character-typing and stylised comedy work to provide the viewer with knowledge. Since this part of WTDB proved to be highly controversial with many viewers in the Consett area after the television screening, I shall deal with these questions later, alongside other general issues of address and function which are raised by the film.

The site of the works

In a documentary which is essentially about an absence, the site of the steelworks is imaginatively used to provide a setting both for interview accounts and for a scene in the 'Rose and Bill' strand.

Some parts of derelict industrial structure remain, 'ruins' alongside which various interviewees offer their testimony. However, the main site itself has almost entirely disappeared and the land has been 're-greened' into fields. The placing of memories of 'then' against a startlingly different image of 'now' has considerable force, which in one scene the camera develops by a slow panning which allows the full resonance of the contrast to be absorbed by viewers. The point is further reinforced by a scene in which one of the unemployed youths is observed taking a town guide down from a public library shelf and reading what he says is one of his 'favourite passages' from it. This is a description of Consett which talks of the steelworks being visible from many miles away.The camera cuts to a present-day panorama of the town, once again bringing out the contrast and working to amplify the mood of nostalgia introduced by the reading-out of the description. But an irony is at work here too (not untypically for this film), insofar as the nostalgia is for an industrial landscape, for the noise and flames of steel production, against the semi-rurality of the present site. Once again, *WTDB* catches, if only by allusion, at some of the deeper tensions and contradictions of post-industrial society.

The porcelain seller

I have noted how the film regularly offers glimpses of different ways of living and of working (or of aspiring to work). One of these, caught observationally in two or three short sequences and without participant commentary, involves a middle-aged woman selling porcelain figures to a group gathered in what is clearly her own house. The amount of time given to this (across these separate scenes) is no more than that given to certain other settings (for instance, the Boys' Brigade meeting, the amateur escapologist), but I have chosen to comment on it here because its implications for the particular construction of Consett which the programme offers seem distinctive and important. As the woman removes items from the table where they are displayed, we overhear her sales pitch, her praise for the craftsmanship and beauty of the figures and their high desirability as presents. What is projected by these scenes is 'refinement' and, as in the affirmations of the 'new Consett' sequences, this comes across within the terms of the film's overall movement as both illuminating and comic. Other visualisations and testimony subject this performance of the genteel and the polite to a critical displacement in which what is going on is readable as somehow a symptomatic (and, indeed, partly pathological) indicator of how Consett *is* in relation to how Consett *was*. Once again, this was a point of controversy for many viewers.

It is across these five primary spaces that the film constructs its account, and I observed that they are not brought to any marked conclusion. The last few minutes of the film include the scene, described above, of the old town-guide description being read out across the new panoramic view and the scene of what appears to be a decisive break-up in the Bill and Rose narrative. The amateur escapologist makes a last, heavily symbolic appearance, breaking free from his constraining straps and padlocked bag. In a final, brief shot from the swimming-bath, the young man who we saw right at the start of the film comments on the need for revolution, whilst also noting the unlikeliness of this happening. The film closes with a mix of shots of work in the nappy factory which typifies Consett's new *light* industry, the signs and hoardings on the new industrial estate and the assembly in a church meeting-hall of the Boys' Brigade group run by a (previously interviewed) ex-steelworker. The soundtrack carries the prayers and then the hymn-singing of the boys, over which the titles roll.

Some problems of theme and form

Because of its radicalism of form and structure, WDTB raises questions which are sometimes new variants on the old documentary tensions of form and purpose and, sometimes, quite new questions altogether. There seem to me to be two broad issues around which problems are raised, the issue of 'aesthetic displacement' and the issue of mode-mixing and scene-switching on the scale which the film attempts.

Aesthetic displacement

In other chapters I have commented on the way in which a regular point of critical debate about documentaries which aspire to aesthetic appreciation as well as to a recognition of their reportorial and expositional qualities (their clarity, accuracy and truth) turns on the 'balance' they achieve between these two aspects of portrayal. To the extent that a film's aesthetic system (committed to producing versions of the 'the pleasing') is discerned as *not* directly contributing to the documentation of realities, this system may be seen as 'diversionary' or 'displacing' of the reportorial project. I have observed earlier in the book how such a splitting-off of ('legitimate') literalist–naturalist modes from the ('illegitimate') use of marked stylisation was a feature of debates within the 1930s documentary film movement itself. This was in the context of a general common interest in fusing the practice of social reporting with the development of film as a creative medium, an interest which rarely chose to hide behind the idea of the 'transparency' of documentary modes and which consequently focused its differences on the question of where precisely the 'line' should be drawn between proper and improper creativity. Whilst they were therefore not naive naturalists (see the discussion on this point in Chapter 1), there seems to have been a degree of consensus amongst Grierson's group about the degree of self-effacement of the artist before the theme. To the extent that a film's use of vision and sound appeared to draw attention to its own constructed character and *away from* referent and topic, it was often regarded as falling short of documentary responsibilities. This, of course, leaves the possibility that attention might be drawn to aesthetic construction in such a way as to *enhance* a viewers' engagement with the subject, though in many cases of such critical appreciation it is not clear just *how self-consciously* the viewer is supposed to register the construction of the effect itself. With the reshaping of documentary aesthetics by the practices of television journalism (see Chapter 4 here), a much sharper sense of the division between a 'good report' and the unacceptably 'arty' developed, with, once again, the distinction between referential and artefactual emphases being critical.

Questions about the degree and kind of aestheticisation used in the production of the documentary image are not only questions about the theme/form relations of documentary organisation, they are often questions about the address and accessibility of the programme and about the social relationships of its communication. In the case of *WTDB*, the accessibility of many of the conventions used to exoticise Consett and to render unfamiliar and enigmatic the (frequently discordant) aspects of its post-industrial identity, is rather limited. They draw on and develop a discourse of aesthetic play, including a deconstructive\subversive tendency, which has had little development as a constituent of popular television and might well be read as reductive of documentary integrity. This would be partly a problem of incomprehension and partly one of rejection. Moreover, and this appears to have been a factor in the local controversiality of the film, the extent to which participants in the film are subjected to self-conscious directorial stylisation (the Hockneyesque swimming-bath interview, the extensive use of the drag act, the various displacements of the scenes involving the new managers and the ex-workers) may be seen to be an indicator of 'bad faith' and perhaps even condenscension towards them, thus breaking the perceived rules of television documentary 'fairness'. Within the terms of the relationships thus set up, it may be seen that viewers are invited to take pleasure in the distortive work performed upon others in a way quite close to the mode of the 'propagandistic'. When these 'others' include people whom the viewer might normally be expected to empathise with, as, for instance, various representatives of the materially disadvantaged, such a practice can look like a breach of the responsibilities which documentary-makers have towards the 'ordinary' human subjects of their films as well as to their viewers. Whatever the judgement here, there is certainly a degree of uncertainty of address in *WTDB* which leaves parts of it aesthetically integrated but socially 'suspended' somewhere between the actualities of Consett and the predispositions of the viewer, working clearly neither as reportorial evidence nor as directorial 'voice'. Even the way in which a viewer chooses to read the Rose and Bill strand as a dramatic exaggeration, a fiction which nevertheless references real frustrations, poses problems of authorial adequacy of a novel kind in documentary, framed as this strand is by the film's more evidentiary modes. *WTDB*'s rich sense of the possibilities for documentary 'playfulness' bring it up sharply against some of those limitations of address which can be found in other avant-garde forms. However, with so declaredly 'public' a mode as documentary they are of more fundamental consequence.

Mode-switching

The rapid shifting between setting and mode of depiction – between scenes of interview, observationalism and dramatisation – is not simply a device for conveying *different* aspects of Consett life, it is a device for conveying a sense of complexity and even an instability of identity. When combined with the lack of voiced-over commentary, it presents viewers with a puzzle to work on – the puzzle of figuring out general truths about Consett from various, and sometimes conflicting, particularisations. The enigmatic character of the account is reinforced by the way, discussed above, in which many of the modes are themselves put under pressure as communicative conventions (the composed narrative space modulating into manic vérité sequence, the 'oddnesses' of interview *mise-en-scène*, the intermittent use of black and white, etc.). The film's relative lack of interest in resolving its multiple realities places the responsibility for achieving coherence firmly on to the viewer. This can seem an irresponsible retreat from 'voice' on the part of the film-maker, even a retreat from the proper recognition of the ethical space which their own practices have created (see Nichols 1991: 76-103).

Although in recent years the conventions of documentary language have come under increasing pressure from film- and programme-makers, attempting to re-imagine both the look, sound and sometimes the function of non-fiction material, few films have experimented so vigorously as *WTDB*. As the interview material cited below shows, this experimentation was fully intended. In large part, the relative freedom of the commission from the constraints of mainstream broadcasting (the film was shown in the late-night *Eleventh Hour* slot on Channel Four, specifically designed for new approaches and attracting an audience willing to engage with them) allowed the film-maker reduced problems of accessibility and address. However, since the film was also a regional/local cinematic product, thereby attracting strong local interest (and perhaps generating expectations of it being in some way 'promotional' and 'supportive'), such problems did arise for its status as regional representation.

WTDB is a wonderfully energetic and suprising piece of film-making whose adventurous mix sometimes involves a degree of irresponsibility towards its subject. However, it retains sufficient hold on its central theme, and is so inventive in articulating those questions about identity which it finds this theme to raise, as to warrant continued attention and appraisal both by students of documentary film and aspirant film-makers.

Appendix: an interview with Penny Woolcock[2]

I wanted to ask you first whether the different kinds of formal experiments going on in WTDB *were part of your idea from the start?*
That was very much a part of it because Trade Films, where I was working at the time, was a Channel Four Workshop with a remit which gave complete freedom. It was a unique agreement which has now been scrapped but I felt all of us really, with the exception of the Black Workshops, didn't take advantage of it, especially formally, and there seemed to be this aping of current affairs – much of the work was not playful and radical in form at all. It was like every film had to say everything that hadn't been said on television before, so every film had a tendency towards a didactic socialist programme presented in this rather boring way. I think the Black Workshops were a very honourable exception to this and actually did both – presented a black perspective and played around with the ways of saying things, the whole documentary vocabulary.

I'd been working on 'Northern Newsreel', a current affairs series, and felt quite imprisoned really by having to have a 'message' to everything and this message having to be told in a very constrained way. I suggested that I wanted to do a film about Consett and when I put the idea forward initially I said the opening shot was going to be from Welles's *Touch of Evil*. And I got extra money, not part of Trade's budget, on the understanding that it was going to play around with the form. There was a desire to copy people who I had admired and also an interest in introducing an element of fantasy and desire, a more dreamy quality.

How did that relate specifically to Consett?
Well, many people had given up completely as a result of what had happened to them, but there were others who had endless schemes to make money, and so the little fictionalised sequences were drawn from the kinds of things which people had said – the mad idea about a Disneyland theme park, you know, was actually seen as a viable proposition. My approach wasn't very coherent, actually – I wanted to try a bit of drama, that seemed a good way of getting across the dreamy side of it ...

Which you wouldnt get from an interviewee directly?
No, certainly not in that very condensed way. The Bill character is a bit of an icon for all those men who had their little secret dreams which would somehow lift them out of this despair.

Where did the title come from? Is that from the song?
Yes, 'My Favourite Things' from *The Sound of Music*, 'When the dog bites, when the bee stings', you know. On a visit to Madrid, I heard it sung as a jazz song with the words just spat out and the whole thing deeply ironic. And I thought: 'When the Dog Bites', that's it. Connecting with all these things which people were doing to enter-

tain themselves and get by.

What about the opening shot, the Touch of Evil ripoff?

Well … on Friday nights in Consett people come not only from the town but from the villages around and there was this big gathering of all these young people having a whale of a time. And there is this incredible energy around. So it was partly to show something of that, to get that festival feel across. We had someone let off fireworks and introduced the girl in leopard-skin fancy-dress, who was a secretary at Trade films and not from Consett – people did feel quite offended by that, as it turns out. Word had got around that we were filming and many more people turned up, everyone piling down the street and shouting their heads off.

Could you talk a bit more about the way your initial ideas worked themselves out, or not, in the rest of the film?

Well, as I said, I didn't want to make a film which was another kind of moaning, depressing film about people ground down by circumstances – it was going to be more positive than that. Watching it again it struck me that it's underpinned by an incredible sadness and from that point of view it wasn't successful. There was a kind of manic quality to the exuberance in a way, which does come across.

Some people have complained about the lack of ordinary people's perspectives in the film, rather in the way that critics have picked up on the absence of ordinary perspectives in Roger and Me. *What about that?*

The film is trying to say something and the people you choose are to some extent chosen within that idea. I was born in Argentina, in the middle-class Anglo-Argentinian community, and it struck me that one of ways in which I related to Consett was that there was a crumbling of identity in my own background – it was about being part of a community that was in a place but which had no reason for being there any more. In that sense it was like the postwar British community in Argentina, when all the real economic influence had moved away from them. The invention of new identity then becomes important.

As your use of the drag act suggests, perhaps?

Yes. The drag act is something to do with that kind of identity crisis really. Men wearing women's dresses, singing 'Land of Hope and Glory'. It really disrupted a lot of expectations. I think that part of the reason for the way it works is to do with the fact that the gender codes are so rigid there that it is almost like the drag act is a carnival space.

Let me turn to the interview scenes. Why did you go for anonymity?

I think that was really, again, not wanting it to be current affairs-ish. We didn't name anyone. I just felt aesthetically that having names all over the place would not have been in tune with the film.

Black and white is used a lot. Any reason?

No. I just felt I had spent three years learning a straightforward craft in a very conventional way and I was intensely frustrated by it. So really I was like a bottle that had been shaken up and the stopper came out and I just went psssshhhhhhhh – I just tried everything. So black and white – it was just a feeling that it would work, that it would work emotionally. It wasn't really thoughtful, more wanting to have a kaleidoscope effect.

The presentation of the officials, the managers, is deliberately unsympathetic, of course?

Well, everyone was perhaps doing their best. But the language is pretty chilling. People are talking about a loyal work-force, a skilled, cheap labour force. But there is something really offensive about that. A sense that they are just waiting to be scooped up at a rate of pay much less than they had before. I was still very angry when I watched it again.

Was there any discussion about the film's overall politics?

No, not really. Even at the editing stage, I was unsure how to put it together and certainly how to finish it.

What about the use you make of the site of the works? Is there an attempt to bring out some of the resonances around memory there – you know, once 'industry', now 'nature'?

Well it was a very potent absence. I had never actually seen the works. And actually nothing was growing on the fields either, it was just huge ploughed fields where something had been and nothing had come to replace it. The sense of loss was palpable. And of course, it directly related to the whole issue of identity.

The film has some very engaging short scenes of 'observation'. There's the scene with the lady selling figurines. Clearly, you are doing things there at a more general level, about different values and aspirations?

Yes, but those *were* the kind of jobs which were available. It was never my intention that people should laugh at the people in the film. Anything you do other than a talking head has that potential to make people look ridiculous. I think I am now much more thoughtful about that problem.

Can we come back to the ending again. Why do people object to it?

Well, I think that was partly deliberate. Many of the films being made on the Left at that time ended with 'everything's really terrible, it isn't going to get better *but* we will fight on'. And I didn't really know what *was* going to happen – it did seem in some ways quite a hopeless situation economically. It was really leaving it open, and actually it ends on a prayer, with the Boys' Brigade group you know.

What about the response to the film initially?

Well, when we finished the film we had a viewing straight away to which we invited everybody who was in the film and all the local council people and the businessmen. I wasn't apprehensive at all. I sat outside during the screening and walked into the film theatre just after it ended and, as I came in and walked down the aisle, somebody shouted out 'Shoot her!' and someone else went 'Bang!' And I stood at the front and this woman, who I think was a councillor, sprang to her feet, absolutely apoplectic with rage, and shouted: 'Why don't you just go back to the gutter where you belong?', and people cheered. Then the people who felt that the Government were doing something useful in Consett said I had deliberately set up the left-wingers to look glorious as they wandered around the empty site, but the left-wingers felt that they hadn't been treated in a serious way. The escapologist was annoyed that his act had been cut up so it looked as though he hadn't really done his escapes as quickly as he can actually do them. People really felt offended. I was very upset. But when it came out on television, a short time later, the response was very different in that we got tons of mail – a very high response – and a lot of it was from people in the South who said what a kind film it was and how it made you really like the people in it, whereas on the whole people in the North were offended on behalf of Consett. I never dared go back. It was so hostile. Some of the youth workers that I had got on with very well, they hadn't liked it and they said to me that the word on the streets was bad. I think people thought they were being ridiculed, and apart from the escapologist – I mean it is quite funny someone doing that in his sitting-room – that was *not* the intention.

Are there any lessons learnt?

There is this problem of who's watching who, but there is always fallout at the end of a film and people, some people, always feel betrayed in some way. That's however careful you are, but I became much more careful after that film. It's a thorny problem and it was the first time I had encountered it. Though in some ways it was quite exciting that I had made something which had a response and had subverted some expectations. If you don't do that – if you tell something very simple and straightforward and don't have any questioning in the film either by the way you frame it or the sort of things you cut it against, then the people filmed will probably be happy but, you know, is that the main point ... ?

Roger and me (1989)

9

Roger and Me (1989) was written, produced and directed by Michael Moore for the independent film company Dog Eat Dog. After the initial success of screenings at film festivals, it was distributed by Warner. *Roger and Me* has attracted a large amount of critical commentary which deserves separate consideration at the end of this chapter, although I shall also drawn on it selectively in my earlier discussion. One reason for the scale of this review literature is the high level of public visibility which *Roger* achieved as a result of being handled by a major distributor. Another reason is the degree of controversy surrounding the film, both on account of its polemical and populist style and the accusations of 'bad practice' which have been made regarding its handling of chronology and its occasional adjustment of facts to suit narrative shape and pace. A third reason, less often commented on than the others, is the way in which the film engages, often hilariously, with the sheer bad faith of the 'official' justifications and hollow remedies of contemporary corporate and governmental discourse. This finds a resonance much broader than the Flint story itself, illuminating and central though this is.

Roger and Me is the story of the decline of a 'company town' in the 1980s. The town is Flint, Michigan, and the company is General Motors, whose then chairman, Roger Smith, is involved in a policy of gradual closures as the company shifts more of its operations to Mexico. The basic 'plot' of the documentary is the attempt by Moore to question Smith and to invite him down to Flint to confront those workers whose jobs he has cut and to see for himself the state of the town. As many reviewers have pointed out, this is simply a plot device. For although at the end, Moore succeeds in putting a number of brief questions to Smith at the General Motors headquarters Christmas party, it is the investigative adventures which lie in the way of, and to the side of, this quest which constitute the main business of the film. These adventures offer, in sum, a comic/ironic but none the less polemically sustained critique of General Motors policy, with the connotations surrounding the elusive 'Roger' (corporate power, luxurious dining-clubs, a retinue of PR men) providing an almost continuous point of play-off against the decline and hardship suffered by the ordinary people of Flint. The single most striking feature of the film is, however, the role which Moore allots himself within it. For the film, albeit with tongue in cheek, opens as an autobiographical piece (complete with home-movie footage) about its director, projecting his status as a 'son of Flint' whose family worked for GM (Chevrolet). When Moore's story is then connected to the larger story of the town's misfortunes, he consistently stays 'in the frame' (both literally and figuratively) as investigator, interviewer and presenter. This is much more than the fulfilling of a 'feature reporter' function, as might occur, for instance, in a current affairs programme. For with his home-town credentials firmly established, Moore's on-camera persona and commentary style continually play with the idea of the resolutely *non*-professional project, the personal grudge, the 'small guy' hitting back. This combination of factors – anti-corporate polemic, comedy, autobiographical essay, exercise in 'amateurism' and ongoing saga of investigative reporting – produces an extraordinary film which is likely to be regarded as a major landmark in contemporary documentary, whatever the individual judgements as to its attractiveness, effectiveness or ethics.

Once again, it may prove useful to look in some detail at how the film is organised, before proceeding to the selective consideration of what might be involved in making a critical assessment of it.

Structure and organisation

Unlike some of the other contemporary documentaries discussed in this book (for instance, *Living On the Edge* and *When the Dog Bites*), *Roger and Me* adopts a directly chronological narrative as its structure (although as we shall see, this turns out to be more problematic than it appears). So whilst there is a return to certain settings and interviews, there is little if any movement between scenes that is not essentially controlled by an expositional development which is also a narrative, a connected event sequence – 'what happened to Flint'. This development is regulated by Moore's *commentary* and it is a mode of organisation which privileges naturalism, making little use either of directly symbolic camerawork, associative editing or extended sequences of observationalism (in the manner for instance, that both *Living on the Edge* (Chapter 6) and *When the Dog Bites* (Chapter 8), in their different ways, clearly do).

With this in mind, a blocking-out of the main phases of the film, with some indication of the key scenes within these phases, seems both to be useful and possible without too much analytic presumption.

Establishing Moore and Flint

Family home movies; archive film of Flint Chevrolet events; formation of Union of Automobile Workers after factory occupation of 1937; Moore's wish to leave Flint after ten years as editor of the magazine *Michigan Voice*; the trip to San Francisco to work in journalism there; criticism of San Francisco lifestyles; return to Flint.

The GM plant and Roger Smith

Focus on Smith and the GM reinvestment plan; plant scenes; the production of the last truck on plant assembly line (Moore's team pose as 'TV crew from Toledo'); interviews with workers; interview with GM spokesperson (Tom Kay); visit to GM headquarters, interception by security and PR staff, requirement to make appointment; CBS and local news report more closures; interview with auto-worker who had nervous breakdown; mixing of Beach Boys' 'Wouldn't it be Nice' with shots of closed shops, derelict homes; Reagan visit ('just when things looked bleak') to take a group of laid-off auto-workers out to lunch; Flint *Great Gatsby* society garden party with 1920s theme – interviews with wealthy locals; Fred Ross, Sheriff's Deputy, undertakes eviction of tenants (observationalism, interview and voice-over); Moore traces Smith to high-class yacht club but he is not found.

Celebrities of Flint

Comedian Bob Eubank returns to Flint for annual carnival – 'Newly-Wed' TV game-show scene and interviews; the Flint parade and interview with Governor and with Miss Michigan about plight of auto-workers; insert footage of Miss Michigan later being crowned as Miss America; Ross attempts to evict female tenant; Moore visits Detroit Athletic Club in search of Smith and is escorted out; Robert Schuller, the television evangelist, visits Flint to 'purge it of unemployment' (Moore); the GM-funded Star Theatre and its provision of entertainment for laid-off workers; interview with artistic director; interview with singer Anita Bryant (she gives 'attitude' advice to the laid-off). Pat Boone visits ('Moore notes that he 'arrived just when we needed him'), old car commercials featuring Boone intermixed with interview; scene and interview with Amway 'Colour Consultant' who gives advice on matching personality to clothes but then discovers that she herself has been 'mismatched'; scene in fast-food shop where ex-auto-workers have been employed; Tom Kay interview sequence – recent local industrial successes after GM closures include 'lint roller' production (its removal of fluff from suiting is demonstrated).

A worsening situation

'Pets or Meat' rabbit farm, interview with woman who runs it; 'money for blood' transfusion sequence; crime increase (news footage); gun-range scene; gun-shop scene; prisoner officer-training scene; ladies' golf club scene (views about unemployed invited); more Ross evictions; mail-office scene and interview (forwarding mail to people who have left Flint); truck-hire interview (no self-drive trucks left due to flight from Flint); further pursuit of Smith (second attempt at GM headquarters – turned back by security guards and PR staff).

Flint as tourist centre

('Just ... one last idea.')
News sequence about development of tourism in Flint; interview with

tourism manager; new Hyatt Hotel sequence; public-relations training film sequence; Water Street Building sequence (new shopping mall); Autoworld theme-park opening, shots inside; closure of above, decline of the tourist idea; interview with city planner about 'what went wrong'.

Further worsening

GM spokesman again – GM's policies and the question of loyalty to the town; Ross carries out more evictions (interviews here); rabbit woman again (recent regulations she has had to comply with) – shown killing and skinning rabbit; *Money* magazine proclaims Flint least attractive town in USA; local protest, speeches and interviews; *Nightline* attempts to cover factory closure live but their equipment truck is stolen; a rise in crime; shootings; the building of a new jail; overnight party in jail at $100 a head for Flint socialites – interviews; GM annual shareholders' meeting – Moore attempts to address Smith from floor microphone but is cut off; overheard exchanges between Smith and staff.

Christmas

Further plant closures; confrontation between woman GM manager and Moore's team outside plant; news footage about job losses. Christmas Eve – Smith gives annual GM Christmas address (talks about Dickens and spirit of Christmas) – intercut with shots of Ross carrying out further evictions. Intercutting continues – Christmas carols and eviction footage; Moore finally gets to ask Smith questions in press huddle after Christmas address (what does he think about plight of ex-workers, about evictions, will he come to Flint? – receives evasive answers); Fred Ross interviewed (what will Christmas mean to him?).

Ending

Commentary with heavy irony ('Dawn of new era') over shot of abandoned factory; end titles intercut with interview snippets which return to: Kay (GM spokesperson) – now laid off himself; tourism manager; city planner – now moved to Tel Aviv just in time for civil disturbance in Israel; Bob Eubank (who tells a sex joke); rabbit woman; theatre manager; Pat Boone (who sings 'Happy Birthday Dear Michigan') and female singer/celebrity ('If you decide to go for it, you'll make it').
End music 'I'm Proud to be an American'.

Formal and thematic issues

I have remarked on the innovative and controversial character of *Roger* and the wide recognition of this. I think we can explore this character best by looking at the film under five related headings – 'director as star', 'investigative vérité', 'terms of critique', 'ordinary people', and 'promotional speaking'. Not all the factors contributing to the film's originality and interest can be addressed within these categories, but most of them can, and later I shall comment briefly on the more important of those which cannot.

Director as star

Moore projects a distinctive persona for his 'role' in *Roger*. Whilst this shares some features with the role of 'on-camera' investigative reporter, it differs from this in so far as it is Moore's *non-professional* relationship to the topic, his *affiliation* with Flint and his *personal* disposition towards the questioning of Roger, which are foregrounded. Such factors have a bearing on the kind of relationship which several of the interviewees have with him, treating the presence of his crew as an opportunity for self-expression and for candour. The role also differs from conventional journalistic discourse (although it is not without precedent) in so far as Moore is extensively 'on stage' throughout the film, with his own investigative adventures providing it with diegetic continuity. Whilst in a film primarily concerned with the *results* of such investigation such procedural detail would be irrelevant, and any false leads simply registered as 'downtime' not to be represented in the finished account, Moore's efforts have a primary importance for *Roger*. They serve as a near-continuous marker of the *difficulty* of getting access and information in a society dominated by corporate power. They also allow strong lines of identification to be established between Moore and his audience, an identification augmented by the apparently ingenuous and often haphazard way in which Moore attempts to achieve his goal. The representation of General Motors by its chairman, identified routinely by his first name, further strengthens this *strategic personalisation* of the issues, as well as adding to the parodic, ironic resonances (we know that the two are emphatically not on 'first-name terms'). Some critics have regarded Moore's personalising strategy as distortive of the film's ostensible project, directing away from enquiry and towards self-display. But Moore has shown himself to be acutely aware of the difficulties of holding a popular audience without a strong narrative device, and such a firm placing of himself in the frame is central to his idea of maintaining a comic, indeed black-farcical, impetus to the story of Flint.

Investigative vérité

Investigative vérité differs from the established conventions of television documentary observationalism in so far as its pro-filmic events are the *activities of enquiry themselves*, shot as ongoing action. The structure of *Roger* regularly returns to a diegesis of investigative vérité from its more conventional passages of interview and of commentary placed over library film showing events in Flint's recent history. Far from maintaining a separation between an observed world and the viewing position, a separation which 'objectifies' what is seen for viewer surveillance, the mode is one which aligns itself with an active participant/enquirer and 'follows' him in his present-tense enquiries. Such an approach mixes the high levels of evidential immediacy achieved by observationalist footage with the marked interventionism of the 'reportorial quest' formula, though normally this formula uses to-camera address and interview as its main devices and, except for brief continuity scenes (car trips, the entering of buildings, etc.), does *not* project itself as ongoing action. Clearly, the expectation of such action being *thwarted* (e.g. admission to buildings refused, confrontations with various officials) considerably enhances the interest potential of such a mode, giving it the status of *entertainment* in addition to its contribution to the production of knowledge within the film.[1] A continuous level of 'enabling fiction' remains, of course – the investigator is placed within the diegetic frame, but there is no attempt reflexively to depict the accompanying film crew itself.

Terms of critique

Roger is a film which works with a very clear idea about the source of the bad things which have happened to Flint. This source is the perceived irresponsibility of GM management towards the quality of life of its work-force. A quite direct critique is offered of Roger Smith's policies towards the local plants. A more indirect but no less strong critique is offered of the various ways in which this basic 'truth' about the fate of Flint is denied or attemptedly covered over by political bad faith, PR, civic promotionalism, folksy individualism and the continuing 'good times' of Flint's wealthier citizens. But there is a certain naivety (assumed or not) about this critique in so far as it appears surprised by the way in which the logic of corporate profit overrides any obligation which the company might feel towards the city. For in what framework of analysis might it be assumed that this would *not* happen in any circumstance where there was a tension between the two 'allegiances'? That the film does not offer any indication of *alternative* economic arrangements to those of corporate capitalism does not reduce the potential force of the ethical critique which it does offer. But the extent to which this critique relies upon viewers being shocked by behaviour which is, in fact, perfectly consistent with existing economic logic, limits its analytic penetration at the same time, perhaps, as it extends its appeal well beyond the radical audience.

Contextualising this 'primary critique' of capitalist corporate policy, there is the 'secondary critique' offered by the juxtaposition, throughout *Roger*, of scenes of deprivation with scenes in which the activities of Flint 'society' are depicted. These latter scenes include sequences at a garden party, at a ladies' golf club and, perhaps most memorably, at the all-night party held to commemorate the opening of the new jail. At the jail party, the basic themes of the indifference and facetiousness of the well-to-do in the face of Flint's problems – their glib offerings of the 'positive' view – are joined by the irony of showing partygoers at their play – enjoying the pretence of being prisoners and jailers (in one scene they excitedly don riot-control gear and grab batons; in another they have their fingerprints taken). How does this older, more familiar division of the rich and the poor relate to the overall project of the film? Although some critics have questioned its force in relation to the more specific accusations made in *Roger*, I think that it effectively puts a very

The art of record

large question mark against the idea of Flint as a 'community', against the idea of a neat relationship between topography and identity. Such a relationship is, as I will illustrate below, a key component of the *promotional* view of Flint's future.

Ordinary people

A number of 'ordinary people' appear in *Roger*, where they are variously portrayed as living their lives at least partly within the terms dictated by the shifts in Flint's fortunes following the GM pull-out. Some are more obviously 'victims' than others. For instance, those people who we see being evicted from their homes by Deputy Ross are suffering in the most direct way from the downturn. Others have not lost their homes but have been forced to 'diversify' in their search for income following the closures. *Roger* offers quite detailed portrayals of two such people, both women, in ways which raise questions about the kinds of relationship being set up between portrayal and audience and therefore about the more general viewing relationships mobilised in the film. We can contrast the portayals of these two women with the portrayal, over several sequences, of Deputy Ross carrying out his eviction duties. It may be useful to pursue this issue further by examining the relevant scenes in turn.

The 'Pets or Meat' woman

The 'Pets or Meat' woman (anonymous throughout) is first visited by Moore using the 'investigative vérité' mode. He knocks on her door and then, playing naive in order to extract a full description, inquires about what precisely the sign outside the house means. He is taken to the rabbit cages and told about the owner's 'business' routine ('I butcher the babies when they reach four or five months old') and about people's preferences for 'fryers' to (older) 'stewers'. The woman says she also raises Doberman pinschers, and her combined activities bring her a modest weekly supplement to Social Security.

In the second visit, a little later in the film, the woman is shown with a rabbit in her arms. She says she has had a visit from Health and Safety officers, who have required a number of changes to her conditions of business, considered 'unhygienic' at present. Off-camera, Moore asks of the rabbit: 'what's going to happen to him?' and she replies, laughing and rubbing the rabbit's ears, that she is going to eat him for supper. The next scene shows her killing the rabbit by hiting it on the head with a stick and stringing it up on a tree branch for skinning. Whilst performing the skinning, she continues to talk to the off-camera Moore about her activities and plans.

There are two elements at work here which deserve attention. First of all, the element of the oddball, of the freaky, in the depiction of the woman herself and her attitude towards the rabbits. Secondly, the calculated 'shock' value of the rabbit-killing and skinning shots. Moore's attitude towards the woman in the initial visit sequence is managed in such a way as to optimise the sense of observed oddity. For instance, his own responses to her remarks about the 'butchering' and the 'fryers' and 'stewers' are calculated as *performance* to camera; the bonding with the viewer serves to objectify the woman as weird in a way which is also darkly comic. She is positioned within the scene to play this role, with little if anything by way of an empathetic viewing relation being developed through Moore's presence alongside her. The later sequence amplifies this mode of depiction, playing with the ambivalence of the 'butcher' cuddling the 'pet', and then goes directly for a shock effect with the killing and the skinning shots.

Whatever kind of connection with the themes of social deprivation and individual despair is made by the film's two visits to this woman, the depiction is also angled off towards the category of the *grotesque*, a category which is essentially individual (freaky) rather than social. It is a category in which the *remarkableness* of behaviour is amplified to the point where it blocks any serious interest in *causes*.

The 'colours' woman

The second sequence which also raises questions of this kind, questions about the social relations of portrayal, concerns 'Janet', identified in Moore's voice-over as a married woman attempting to supplement the family income as the closures increasingly threaten her husband's job at the plant. Janet's attempts involve the home-merchandising group Amway, which has promoted itself successfully in Flint since the closures started. She has become a 'Colour Consultant', using her home as a demonstration room and a studio in which to identify the particular 'season' of an individual and then to offer suggestions about appropriate colour combinations for clothing. In the principal sequence, we see her demonstrating 'wrong' and 'right' seasonal tonings to a group of women, using a volunteer. However, Moore's voice-over then links us through to a second sequence, some weeks later. In the intervening period, Moore tell us, Janet has telephoned him in some distress, having discovered that her own 'season' was wrongly identified right at the start of her new career and that, acting on this incorrect information, she has therefore been offering faulty interpretations to other women. Janet provides a brief account of this 'error' in interview speech, after which Moore notes his sympathy for her on voice-over, and his willingness to be 'colour tested' himself in order to ease her distress. The shot shows him seated, swathed in a white smock and with a white cloth around his head, as Janet uses coloured fabrics to perform the test – 'we were the same season', he notes in a final voiced-over comment.

Here, in a rather different way from the 'Pets or Meat' sequences, we once again have the development of a certain level of 'bad faith' towards the participant. Once more, it is true, we have an individual whose efforts at supplementing her income appear to connect her story back to the film's main themes. But there is a considered deflection of that link, a deflection which here routes this sequence straight through into the openly comic rather than, as earlier, into the grotesque. For Janet's activities are rendered as silly within the film's account and Moore's initial presentation of her expression of concern over her 'error' and subsequent willingness to be a 'client' himself function to project this silliness with optimum effect. His closing comments ('we were the same season') merely modulate the deadpan through into an obviously insincere sentimentality. Concern for Janet as a 'case-study' within the *social* context of the economic anxiety afflicting the town (admittedly she is less of a victim than those who we see being evicted) is played off against her interest value as comic footage. The terms of this comic representation are emphatically individualised. *Roger's* concern about sustaining viewer engagement, its nervousness about appearing to embrace 'dull' documentarist values, produces this kind of sideshow effect without ever fully taking the film off track or slowing its main chronological impetus. I shall say more about this at the end of the chapter, when I discuss the extensive critical debate on the film's ethics and effectiveness.

The Deputy Sheriff

Deputy Sheriff Ross is first seen 'observationally', forcing an entry into someone's house, with the purpose of eviction. Subsequent scenes show him involved in the eviction of several (mostly black) individuals and families, their furniture and personal belongings piled up on the pavement awaiting collection. Despite being thus aligned with 'authorities' as against 'victims', his portrayal is probably the most positive one in the film, establishing that he had himself worked in the plant until the routine wore him down and that he sympathises with those he has to evict; that they have at least 'someone to talk to' when he does his job. He outlines his wryly realistic approach in location interview, from both outside and inside the homes he has called upon in the course of his duties. He is simply an agent of higher authority, a means of the inevitable. Though many of those he calls upon have hit on hard times following the closures, it is his view that several of them have spent what money they had foolishly, heedless of the need to pay the rent. More than any other figure apart from Moore himself, the Deputy provides the viewer with a guide to interpreting the events in Flint at the human level. His mixture of cynicism and cheerfulness, efficiency and sociability, is therefore a major factor in the film's overall project, serving among other things to add a counterbalancing 'realist' voice to the self-consciously 'radical' tone of Moore. Unlike the two women discussed above, then, his portrayal is not just 'placed' as the object of interpretation (delivering appropriate measures of weirdness and comedy). It exerts an organising effect *upon* interpretation, and I shall return to the question of what the final consequence of this effect might be.

Promotional speech

One of the ways in which *Roger* develops a resonance beyond the particular problems of Flint is by catching at the duplicity of 'promotion', as this is articulated through a variety of personal styles. These styles range from that of Miss Michigan (subjected to what she clearly finds to be a potentially compromising line of questioning by Moore, immediately following her appearance in the carnival motorcade), through the smooth, thoughtless 'affirmations' made about the town by singer Pat Boone, long-time GM promoter, to Roger Smith's Christmas message (contextualised by intercut shots of people being evicted), which is projected as the epitome of bad faith. At other points, professional 'civic boosters' have their say, dissembling and enthusing with varying degrees of inauthenticity. An hilarious training film about Flint tourism, intended to coach promotional staff, shows a family stopping off at a garage on the outskirts of the city, hardly able to contain their excitement at the range of recreational possibilities awaiting them. A friendly pump attendant offers tips as to where to go first.

Many of these sequences of promotionalism merely offer 'soundbite' opportunities to people who are already adept at offering either instant concern ('Oh it's tragic, tragic', says the Governor of Michigan about the Flint lay-offs, rapidly turning off his initial smile at the camera) or folksy remedies (of the 'you can get back on your feet if you try, treat each day as a new start' variety). Indeed, hortatory comments paying testimony to the extraordinary resilient qualities of the people of Flint (who, according to some views, might almost regard the lay-offs as a lucky opportunity for the display of character) appear in different form throughout the film.

One strong exception to the mode of deadpan presentation by which the film generally relays promotional speech is the interview with Miss Michigan at the carnival, an interview which puts the 'promotional mode' under question. In the view of some critics, it does so by placing unfair pressure on the speaker herself. Moore's tactic here is to set up the interview as a conventional post-event celebrity chat but then to shift to questions which cannot but be seen as 'awkward' ones from the point of view of the interviewee. Committed to a glowing smile and to talking about how wonderful the day has been, both for her and the people of Flint, Miss Michigan shows increasing uneasiness with the line taken by Moore's enquiries about her response to the lay-offs, and to the high level of local unemployment. With evasion no longer an easy option, given Moore's persistence, she makes moves towards responding appropriately ('I feel sad for them, but let's hope it's only temporary'). Pushed yet further on her attitude, she tries, desperately, to return to affirmation: 'How do I feel? – I feel like a big supporter – does it matter of what?' Recognising the increasing likelihood of the interview going wrong, she then puts in a comment direct to camera: 'I'm trying to stay neutral here, I'm going to Miss America in two weeks.' Sticking resolutely within this frame, she then misreads Moore's final question to her: 'Have you got a message for the people of Flint?' and responds with: 'Just keep your fingers crossed for me as I go for the gold in two weeks.'

Moore's tactics in this sequence are familiar from earlier 'investigative vérité' interview formats, both in Britain and the United States. The line of questioning is designed to 'wrongfoot' the interviewee, switching them into a line of inquiry which they have neither prepared for nor find it convenient to respond to. Repetition and emphasis reduce the opportunities for playing safe and introduce further harrassment into the improvisation of answers.

Undoubtedly, the sequence is highly effective in the 'deconstruction' of a learnt, promotionalist perspective, one radically inadequate to the general circumstances surrounding this civic event and the speaker's role in it. The cost is, once again, a degree of 'bad faith' in portrayal. Miss Michigan to some extent mediates between the world of ordinary people and the world of corporate promotionalism. Unlike many of the people who appear in the film, she is not so much the calculating author of promotional speech as its awkward device. But within terms of *Roger*'s project – its troubling of the discourses of rationalisation and self-justification both at national and local level – her temporary on-screen discomfiture might be seen to be justified.

Having looked at some principal features of the structure of the film, and at particular thematic elements, I want now to look at how *Roger* has been discussed by critics. As I noted at the start of this chapter, there is a large and growing body of writing which makes reference to the film, a fact which must in part be due to the extensive publicity which followed its general release. The critical debate about *Roger*, whilst it is concerned with much that is specific and novel in the film, also interconnects with a number of more general questions about the nature and direction of modern documentary.

Roger and the critical debate

I observed that the public impact of the film as a generic rarity – a feature documentary with a socially critical theme distributed on general release – served to give a distinctive public character to much discussion of it.

Although there had been enthusiastic critical appraisal of *Roger* at its early festival screenings, perhaps one of the most influential items in that discussion was a lengthy interview which Moore gave to Harlan Jacobson in the issue of *Film Comment* for November/December 1989. Jacobson starts out with a generally sympathetic account of the film's project. However, he then moves on to discover some 'disquieting discrepancies' in the chronology of the events depicted in the film. Essentially, there are four items here:

1 Ronald Reagan, depicted visiting laid-off auto workers, was a presidential candidate, not the President, when he made his visit. (The film does

not describe him as President, but the assumed chronology of the scene and the projected effect of the footage works with the idea that he is.)

2   The evangelist who is depicted visiting the city after the *Great Gatsby* society party in 1987 actually visited in 1982, several years before the crucial 1986 lay-offs.

3   The three big civic development projects which are seen in the film as more or less concurrent attempts to counter the effects of the 1986–87 lay-offs (Hyatt Regency Hotel; Autoworld theme-park; Water Street shopping pavilion) had all closed before these lay-offs.

4   The number of jobs lost during the 1986–87 closures seem to be far less than indicated in the film. The spread of losses from 1974 onwards is closer to the film's estimate. (The figure of 30,000 is given in an edited clip from a *CBS* news broadcast – which may be referring to motor industry closures of which those in Flint are a *part*.)

When confronted with these 'discrepancies' by Jacobson, Moore show himself to be well aware of the true dates of the civic developments and of the spread of the losses across a number of years. The film's chronology is an implicit one (few sequences are actually dated in the commentary) and it is clear that Moore has drawn from events happening throughout the 1980s, reorganising chronological sequence to maximum thematic and narrative effect. This becomes evident in the following extract from the interview (Jacobson's questions in italics):

> *The impression that one has from the movie is that there was a single felling blow, directed at Fisher Plant 1, which cut loose 30,000 people from employment, resulting in immediate and massive devastation to which the local government responded with fantasy projects. There is no mention that those projects existed on the boards back to 1970 ... maybe/maybe not, back to 1978 ... maybe/maybe not, but certainly no mention that they opened up, ran their course, and closed prior to the cutbacks which form the spine of your movie.*

Right. Well, first of all the movie never says that 30,000 jobs ... that this one announcement eliminated 30,000 jobs in Flint. The movie is about essentially what has happened to this town during the 1980's. I wasn't filming in 1982 ... so everything that happened happened. As far as I am concerned, a period of seven or eight years ... is pretty immediate and pretty devastating.

> *You may be right in spirit but you're playing fast and loose with sequence – which viewers don't understand is happening.*

I just don't think so. I think it's a document about a town that died in the 1980's, and this is what happened.

> *I think that's true. And I think that it is incredibly powerful and makes its point.*

Good.

> *It is unquestionably true that you made a film about a town that died in the 1980's, a town that that was in one company's hip pocket, just like all of the towns that have ever been in one company's hip pocket, back to the railroads which built company shacks and company stores. But I think that is also useful to address the question of the sequencing.*

What would you rather have me do? Should I have maybe begun the movie with a Roger Smith or GM announcement of 1979 or 1980 for the first round of layoffs that devasted the town, which then led to starting these projects, after which maybe things pick up a little bit in the mid '80s, and then *boom* in '86 there's another announcement, and then tell the whole story? ... Then it's a three hour movie? It's a *movie*, you know; you can't do everything. I was true to what happened. Everything that happened in the movie happened ... If you want to nit-pick on some those specific things, fine but ...

It's not a nit-pick, and I'll tell you why I don't think it's a nit-pick. You call it a movie; it has the form of documentary. We all know that documentaries have points of view ... what goes into the documentary, even down to the camera angle, has a bias. But we expect that what we are seeing there happened, in the way in which it happened, in the way in which we are told it happened.

(Jacobson 1989:22)

Although the exchange goes on to cover other issues, I think this extract indicates the key conflicts of substance and perspective which were widely picked up in subsequent writing on the film. According to the writer's perspective, these were either seen as constituting a devastating exposé of Moore's bad practice or demonstrating a remarkable naivety on the part of Jacobson. In a strongly critical account of the film in *The New Yorker*, Pauline Kael noted of Moore (whom she described as a 'Gonzo demagogue') that he had:

'[C]ompressed the events of many years and fiddled with the time sequence ... The movie is an aw-shucks, cracker barrel pastiche. In Moore's own jocular pursuit of Roger, he chases gags and improvises his own version of history. (Kael, *New Yorker*, 8 January 1990)

Kael's review was photocopied and circulated by GM promotional staff in their attempts at 'damage control' (Cohan and Crowdus 1990:26). It has been suggested that a further consequence of this backlash was the film's omission from the list of Oscar nominees for 1989 (Cohan and Crowdus 1990:25). Meanwhile, other critics (mostly working from within radical and academic circles rather than writing for the general public) defended *Roger*, taking it as a test case in the inadequacy of traditional generic conventions and the need for a more honest recognition of the nature of documentary representation. For instance, Carley Cohan in *Cineaste* suggests that 'Moore has crafted one of the most literate and hilarious pieces of freewheeling populist journalism ever screened' (Cohan and Crowdus 1990:26). Gary Crowdus, in the same double feature, judges the arguments about chronology to be 'grossly overstated':

Anyone looking carefully at the newspaper headlines featured in the film's occasional montages will often see early Eighties' publication dates. Besides, does it really matter that televangelist Robert Schuller made his sponsored 'inspirational' visit to Flint in 1982, in response to an early wave of layoffs, rather than those in 1986 or 1987? Or that

Reagan's visit to the city, when he took out a dozen unemployed auto workers for a pizza and advised them to look for work in Texas, took place in 1980 when he was a Presidential candidate, and not actually President yet? ... Even the more serious charge – that the auto theme park, the luxury hotel and convention center and the shopping mall – had all opened and had either essentially failed or been closed before Moore began filming – doesn't change the basic fact ... [about] wasteful expenditures. (Cohan and Crowdus 1990:28)

In Crowdus's judgement, the main shortcomings of the film can be found in what he calls its 'cheap-shot' strategy of going for laughs at the cost of 'the sort of contextual information or analysis of issues that any good documentary provides'. This is a criticism not so much of impropriety but of inadequacy. Crowdus's defence of the main chronological transformations ('Does it really matter' ... etc?) is based on a rhetorical appeal to his readers and it would, indeed, be interesting to know how far and in what way members of the broad 'intended audience' for *Roger* viewed its temporal adjustments with concern. This would not by any means conclusively resolve the question as to its 'integrity' but it would at least contextualise this question in terms of public expectations. These expectations need to be recognised by documentary film-makers, even if their subsequent plan is, openly or otherwise, not to meet them.

For some of the more theoretically-engaged commentators, what the debate signalled most clearly was the awkwardness and sometimes the indefensibility of the division between documentary and fiction. Placing *Roger* in the broadened context of a cinema which included feature fiction seemed to these critics to render most of the 'debate' sterile and beside the point, although this still leaves open the question of expectations (as raised above) and of tactics in relation to these. Linda Williams (1993) puts a subtle brake on a celebratory approach to *Roger*'s rule-breaking in noting the way in which Moore actually *appears to stick to the rules* of strict referentiality and linear causal connections. *Roger*, in her view, is not a film which openly addresses itself to the 'documentary problematic':

> Moore betrays the cause and effect reverberation between events by this reordering. The real lesson of this debate would seem to be that Moore did not trust his audience to learn about the past in any other way than through the vérité capture of it.[2] He assumed that if he didn't have footage from the historical period prior to his filming in Flint he couldn't show it. (Williams 1993:16)

Williams's recommendations are for a bolder, more openly convention-challenging approach to the visual depiction of historical affairs. However, it has to be questioned whether the kind of format implied by her comments would engaged the popular audience in the way *Roger* managed to do. In that sense, the idea of 'trusting the audience' becomes acutely problematic, with the film-maker trying to work somewhere in between an unquestioning reproduction of conventional (and suspect) propriety and a vanguardist dismissal of this which risks inaccessibility and rejection.

Conclusions

In any assessment of *Roger and Me*, certain aspects of its construction immediately come to the fore, to be accepted or criticised according to the broader criteria for judging documentary work. That the attempt to engage Roger Smith in personal communication about the closures is merely a device for allowing Moore to do what he wants to do is clear. That Moore's on-camera persona is deliberately honed to fit the theatricality of the 'small guy takes on the big guys' structure is also true. To complain about either of these features of *Roger* seems to me to be working with a very unrealistic set of assumptions about what documentaries routinely do; about even what they *can* do. That Moore has deliberately worked to produce a film which is comic as well as critical is obvious too, and there is no doubt in my mind that at times this search for the comic or the weird makes for some questionable decisions in his use of interviewees. Finally, Moore's own interview comments show that the way in which various events which happened in Flint during the 1980s are structured into a narrative of optimum impact is fully intentional in its breaking with strict chronology. This is a more problematic 'transformation'. We can take the view of several of the more radical reviewers and see the film as, in a sense, 'licensed' by its intended audience to be creative in the interests of greater *watchability*. We can also take the view that the quiet manipulation of certain causal relations gives *Roger* a stronger propagandist value than would be possible if it stayed strictly to the events in the order they happened. In one model, the reorganisation increases accessibility and pleasure without substantially, if at all, affecting the general 'truths' of the film. In the other model, the break with historical sequence is an act of bad faith towards the audience, providing them with a degree of 'bad knowledge' (through conscious deception), however much this may be offset by other things in the film. Certainly, we can assume that if 'adjustments' of this kind had been made by a television unit shooting a documentary, and of course there have been cases which bear a similarity, then they would have been widely seen to have broken the conventions of good practice. But *Roger* operates outside television's rules, its discourse is not anchored in the institutional proprieties of professional journalism and this contributes greatly to its appeal. It does not mean, however, that it is free of obligations towards its audience in respect of conventions of accuracy and honesty. As I suggested above, the question is partly one of expectations – what the audience thinks it is getting and then how it assesses this – and partly one of documentary's own sense of propriety as a form of public communication, one grounded always in particular historical and social contexts.

Moore's attempts to be widely popular, critical of corporate policy and also anti-conventional in the form he uses puts *Roger* at an intersection point unique in recent documentary history. He is quoted as saying that he didn't want to make 'another "Dying Steel-town" documentary' but 'wanted to tell a somewhat offbeat, funny story about what the richest company in the world has done to its hometown' (cited in Cohan and Crowdus 1990:27). Perhaps, as some critics have judged and I have suggested myself, telling the 'funny story' sometimes takes Moore off into dubious territory, but pronouncements about the film's lack of effectiveness (e.g. 'Moore has made a film which fails because it is ultimately harmless' (Harkness 1990:131)) frequently beg too many questions about the nature and disposition of the popular audience to convince. When critics point to Moore's success in achieving Warner distribution for the film as a clear indication of its lack of critical power, then my feeling is that we are operating within the very limited (but famil-iar) discourses of cultural vanguardism. Although it may not have much 'news' to offer the radical viewer, *Roger and Me* brings a whole new range of tones to the depiction of contemporary capi-talism and it will be suprising if its contribution to popular docu-mentary does not continue to be recognised at the same time as its methods and forms provoke further debate.

Handsworth Songs (1986)   **10**

Handsworth Songs was made in 1986 by members of the Black Audio Film collective and directed by John Akomfrah. It quickly attracted a considerable amount of critical attention and won a number of awards, among them the British Film Institute's Grierson award. *Songs* is a one-hour-long, multi-stranded 'essay' on racial inequality and unrest in Britain, starting out from, and regularly returning to, the 1985 disturbances in Handsworth, Birmingham.[1] These disturbances involved intense street conflicts, riot policing, injury to persons and damage to property. Television news images drawing on the familiar iconography of 'urban riot' (police with shields, overturned cars on fire, scuffles and arrests) are employed regularly throughout the film, their 'naturalism' often displaced by slow motion and a soundtrack using distorted musical noises and rhythms.

Songs makes extensive use of archive footage, showing, for instance, the arrival of immigrants on the ocean liners, and establishing a history of the black community's presence in post-war Britain against which to set contemporary disturbances. Although its structure is a complex one, involving several levels of articulation and a degree of repetition and re-statement, the film can be seen essentially to consist of two interrelated projects. There is, first of all, a documentation of recent events, which draws on actuality footage and a number of interviews and discussions with various members of the black community. This constitutes a more or less conventional strand of documentary reportage, involving a degree of objectification and objectivity, a measure of analytic distance. Then there is a more essayistic and self-consciously 'subjective' strand to the film, drawing on the archive material and using the 'songs' as voice-over. These are short sections of commentary, spoken as poems across the images. They have a lyrical intensity and a strongly metaphoric construction. Not only do they reach out beyond 'documentation' to a wider (and historical) context, they also reach inwards, to questions of experience and of aspiration. The term 'excavation' has been used to describe what is going on in *Songs*; this excavation 'discovers' both a social history of dislocation and relocation, within specific terms of toleration, inequality and prejudice, and an experiential history, a voicing of selves.

The great amount of interest shown in the film on its release was not only due to the importance of its theme but was also a result both of its formal organisation (connecting back to the lyrical realism of the 1930s documentary movement but also showing the influence of anti-realist work like that of Godard) and its sense of function and audience (what was its purpose? To whom was it addressed? What was the political character of its 'reading'?). An early review by Salman Rushdie (*Guardian*, 12 January 1987) criticised the film for its failures of 'language' and set a marker for subsequent debate, which often indicated sharp disagreements over much broader issues of cultural politics and black self-representation. At several points in this chapter I shall draw on published materials from the debate.

The closely intertwined strands of *Songs*, generating an associative pattern across past and present, across different voices of exposition and of reflection, make it unproductive as well as difficult to offer a detailed shot sequence. I shall therefore follow the procedure which I have adopted in several other chapters, first of all offering a broad descriptive account of the organisation of the whole film and then looking in more detail at particular sections.

Structure and organisation

Songs does not so much develop an argument as carry out a selective 'trawl' of aspects of black, and particularly black immigrant, life in Britain since the war. The mixing of footage from 'past' and 'present' events is one key dimension of its project (moving the viewer regularly from 'now' to 'then' and back). Another important dimension is the sense of reflective subjectivity introduced into the film by virtue of the 'songs' – registering outer events through a spoken articulation of feeling which is made reflexive by the self-conscious poetics of its composition and performance. It is notable that there is no conventional commentary speech in *Songs*, no strand of speech which can act as a unifying position for reading the other elements. Some of the 'songs' serve a semi-commentary function but, although they invariably promote positive viewer alignment and empathy, they are often registered as voices 'captured' by the film or assembled by the film rather than the voice *of* the film itself. As we shall see, this has the effect of giving *Songs* a more 'open' and perhaps in some cases more enigmatic nature than a containing commentary, even if only an intermittent one, would permit.

I have noted that there are two interrelated projects discernible in the film, one concerned with contemporary events, one with the past and with memory. We can identify a number of different discursive modes at work in the constitution of these projects. Taking visual and verbal elements separately, the principal ones are as follows.

Visuals

(a) Archive footage (monochrome and colour) of immigrants arriving in Britain and of their life in Britain as portrayed in film and documentary footage. This material, highly varied, constitutes a visual plane of 'excavation', over which much of the 'song' material is spoken. A sequence from an early 1980s television interview with the then Prime Minister, Mrs Thatcher, speaking about immigration and the dangers of Britain being 'swamped', can be included under this heading.

(b) News footage of disturbances. This material, sometimes used in slow motion, draws on a number of different events involving civil disorder, including those in Southall, London, but focuses on the Handsworth events of 1985.

(c) Interview material with people involved in, or witness to, the disturbances, most frequently with the interviewees in shot, as individuals or as a group, within a location setting.

(d) Actuality sequences, shot for the film. Scenes of, for instance, a Rastafarian disco; heavily policed city streets (shot from a car window); and the setting-up in a local hall of a television current-affairs debate about the disturbances would all come under this heading. A montage sequence of various newspaper headlines and features on the Handsworth events might also fit best within this category.

(e) Sequences used primarily for symbolic effect. This includes, for instance, the recurring shots of birds in the tops of trees and a shot of a mechanical clown's face intercut with riot footage. If they are not archive footage (despite being in black and white), the opening and closing sequences featuring a black bus conductor in a Birmingham museum, walking around huge items of old industrial machinery, are at least partly to be placed within this category (I discuss these important sequences below). There is also symbolic use of 'found' footage from feature or early documentary material (for instance, a silent cinema sequence, using intertitles, of chainmaking processes).

Soundtrack

(f) Actuality sound (including that from archive materials). This includes a variety of reporter speech, interviews and voice-overs.

(g) The 'songs'. These are mostly spoken by a female voice, across archive and contemporary visuals.

(h) Music. A mix of rhythms and tunes from black musical forms, often radically distorted, is heard throughout *Songs*. The musical soundtrack is a key component of the film's overall discursive character and of the local organisation of both the documentarist and the more essayistic aspects of the film.

In order to provide a better sense of the local texture of the film, I will look at how it begins and develops a multi-stranded account, and then at how it concludes. Here is an indication of the opening section (nine and a half minutes) of the film, with approximate timings for each sequence:

1 (Black and white.) Shot of a large steam pump engine in museum. Black bus conductor in uniform walks around it. Music – a slow, mechanistic rhythm (electronically produced). Titles. (26 seconds)

2 Tops of trees silhouetted against sky (dusk/dawn). Birds in the tree-tops and bird noises. (9 seconds)

3 Slow-motion shots of streets and police vehicles seen through haze of fire. Sounds of disturbance. (8 seconds)

4 Mechanical clown moving face from side to side (medium close up). (11 seconds)

5 Riot footage. (13 seconds)

6 Shots of statues of early engineers Watt and Priestley. (10 seconds)

7 Clown face (waving hand). (12 seconds)

8 Birds in treetops. (8 seconds)

9 Police; crowds; overturned cars on fire. (18 seconds)

10 Clown face (close-up on eyes). (10 seconds)

11 Home Secretary Hurd on 'walkabout' visit to streets in disturbance area. Talks to white residents ('it must have been scaring') and to members of crowd (part actuality sound, part 'song' voice-over which tell us that he is heard to say to accompanying journalists: 'these are senseless occasions, completely without reason', and that a member of the crowd says: 'the higher the monkey climb, the more he will expose'). (45 seconds)

12 Further riot footage. Milk float passes up and through 'police lines'. (15 seconds) Youth running down street pursued by group of police. Police catch him and, in a scuffle, bring him to the ground and arrest him. (30 seconds)

13 Two Rastafarian witnesses to disturbances describe to camera what they saw and why it happened. (2 minutes)

14 Montage of headlines and features from national newspapers about 'the riots' (e.g. 'The Bleeding Heart of England'). (1 minute 15 seconds)

15 Police vans going down road. Long line of parked police vans by roadside (slow motion). Strains of the hymn 'Jerusalem' mixed on soundtrack. (30 seconds)

16 Large photographic images (wedding shots) of people in black community, exhibited in art gallery as hung posters (camera tracks down line of them). Waltz music. (30 seconds)

17 Archive film (black and white – 1950s?). A dance with senior councillors present, wearing chains of office. Black and white people together. Intercut shots of cane-harvesting and fieldwork in Caribbean (1 minute); 'song' voice-over (female).

This sequence breakdown gives a clear indication of the 'montage' character of the film's construction – a movement from shot to shot or sequence to sequence which trades primarily on the associative meanings which it generates, using repetition for rhythm and for emphasis. The familiar referential markers of 'trouble' (television news images) are introduced only after an associative network has begun to form. This network makes connections with Britain's industrial past, with the imagination and skill of its engineers. It picks up on both the continuities and discontinuities suggested by the bus-conductor's admiration for the museum machinery. Its imaging of birds in the treetops and the clown's face serve to provide an associational field within which the more tightly referential material generates expanded meanings. As in later sequences, the symbolic project of *Songs* is achieved through a variety of means, including directly non-literal visualisations, the 'de-literalisation' of what was initially literal–realist footage (from old documentaries and from current news), and the aestheticised elements of the voice-over. In talking of the strategy adopted in the film, Director John Akomfrah noted:

> Our task was to find a structure and a form which would allow us the space to deconstruct the hegemonic voices of British television newsreels. That was absolutely crucial if we were to succeed in articulating those spatial and temporal states of belonging and displacement differently. In order to bring emotions, uncertainties and anxieties alive we had to poeticise that which was captured through the lenses of the BBC and other newsreel units – by poeticising every image we were able to succeed in recasting the binary oppositions between myth and history, imagination, and experiential states of occasional violence. (Gilroy and Pines 1988: 7)

This comment provides a useful insight into some of the ambitious shaping ideas that went into the making of *Songs*.

I have referred above to the importance of the aestheticised speech of the 'songs' themselves, presented almost as discrete, performed poems. Here is the transcription of the 'song' which is heard in sequence 17 above, over archive shots of the civic dance and scenes of work in the fields of the Caribbean:

> He said to her, 'remember Bonney Henriques and Gretta Borg and Lady June Barker? Remember Countess Koblanzka with her black velvet top, her skirt of figured net over satin? It's about time we had our own child. Our own Master George Hammond Banner Bach.'
>
> That night I moved from an idea to a possibility. I was born in a moment of innocence.

This sense of a recollection, both personal and social, being impressed over the film's documentary imagery, thus reinflecting its initial objectification or, in other scenes, setting up a tension between this objectification and what is said, is a recurrent feature of *Songs*. In the next such sequence, where the speech is placed over archive film of a building site, labouring work and of black community life in the 1950s, before ending over a colour shot of a mural (after Picasso's *Guernica*), the language becomes even more dense and metaphoric:

> Once there was land to be cleared and bones to be rebuilt from ashes. They say bones must be given breath and bones will breath life into the soil. There was sand to shift, dry wood to sweep away. And they said to each other: 'here we will be shoulder to shoulder and we will survey the world in ascension, and one day the world will come to us.'

I have already noted how the question of the relationship of the present to the past, indeed to the dead, becomes in *Songs* a central theme.

I want now to look at how the final sequences of the film are organised, how its various depictive strands come together to form a 'conclusion', however provisional this may be. Through the last five minutes, the sequence is as follows:

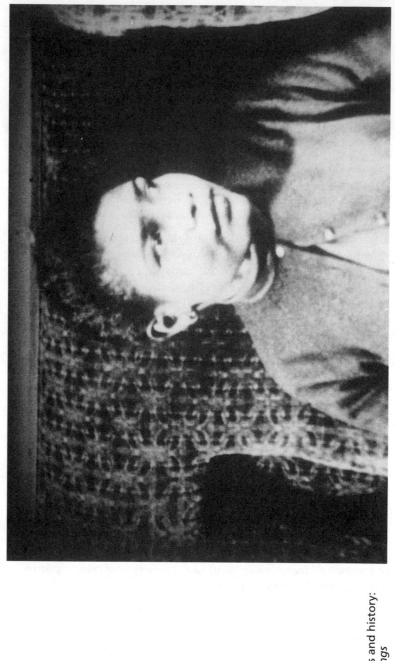

Individual hopes and history:
Handsworth Songs

1 Pan left to right across exterior 'cubist' mural (noted above in description of opening). Figures in distress within this. Distorted, rhythmic music. (40 seconds)

2 Television footage of demonstration march following the recent (and ostensibly 'accidental') shooting in her London home of a black woman, Cynthia Jarrett, by police officers. Radio account of incident, followed by voices of three radio interview witnesses, intercut with microphone address of leaders of the demonstration and, finally, with march scenes again, including close-ups of marchers. (2 minutes 12 seconds)

3 Bus conductor in museum. Walking around exhibits. Voice-over:
It is still good for a West Indian to come here and taste the mature atmosphere of the age of civilisation. England is so rich with the culture of the past that nothing the living can do can destroy the vast wealth of accumulated tradition over the years. Anybody can come in and take no notice of the living. We can be at ourselves, learning from the dead. (40 seconds)

4 Car on fire in street. (6 seconds)

5 Mural (close-up of crying face).

6 Shots of archive film, Asian woman and queues of children awaiting innoculation. Shift to colour film of immigrants arriving from ships and at railway stations. A final shot of a woman walking slowly down a small street alongside a railway viaduct, now become overgrown. Old, abandoned industrial buildings in background. 'Song' voice-over (female) across this:
The fear wouldn't go away. And she began to feel that these thoughts would die before her, die trying to be heard. She didn't understand them but she feared the savage state of death more than ignorance. So she opened the doors and slowly the words came alive and began to speak to her saying: 'these are for those to whom history has not been friendly, for those who have know the cruelties of political becoming. Those who demand in the shadows of dying technology. Those who live with the sorrows of defiance. Those who live among the abandoned aspirations which were the metropolis. Let them bear witness to the ideals which in time will be born in hope. In time let them bear witness to the process by which the living transform the dead into partners in struggle.'

The intertwining of different depictive modes can once again be clearly seen, the contemporary and the past being linked and made to inter-associate. Anger and a more reflective aspiration are overprinted on each other. Learning from 'the dead' (including the white dead) becomes part of the way forward. The extraordinary scene involving the bus conductor in the museum, used to start the film, then returned to in the middle before being used at the end as described above, projects this quieter sense of hope, sharply juxtaposed here against a shot of a blazing car. Within one perspective, what the bus conductor says might be seen to be completely undercut by what follows it. However, within the discursive density of *Songs* this clearly does not happen, not only because of what has come before in the film but also because of what comes afterwards, in the final 'song', where a similar wish is expressed to connect with the 'dead' in finding a new way of advancing the 'struggle'.

A phrase repeated in two of the 'songs' in the film is 'there are no stories in the riots, only the ghosts of other stories'. Again, it is a sense of going 'behind', of carrying out an archaeology which produces a complexity of clues rather than any single body of hard evidence, which is suggested. Comments by the film-makers themselves confirm this:

> The central ideal ... is in some ways to put across a multi-layered text which, if it doesn't specify, at least hints at the possibility that there is no singular origin to the disturbances ... . So the aesthetic quest was in some ways to put across an impressionistic collage of a series of moments, a series of becomings, a series of moments of solitude, ostensibly, which as they threaten to be moments of solitude are recuperated into race and become racial questions. (Akomfrah, cited in Gilroy and Pines 1988:9).

The film-makers have elaborated further on the nature of these 'moments of solitude':

> In archival texts we were confronted with fragmented residues of histories of migration, memories of the joys and pains of settlement, of the grim possibility of having to consolidate the experiences of arrival and often of how best to make sense of rejection in the face of hostility and social indifference. (Auguiste 1988:5–6).

Another theme recurring throughout the film, and visualised here in the final section by the disused and overgrown viaduct of the last shot (shot 6 above) is that of Britain as a country of industrial decline and of infrastructural collapse (see the discussion in Chapter 6 of the imagery in Grigsby's *Living on the Edge*).

From these observations on the film's structure and content, it can be seen that *Songs* is formally ambitious, attempting to represent the complexity of its historical and sociological themes through a form which breaks decisively with the conventional and stabilised ways of depicting racial politics.

I now want to examine the form/theme relationship more closely, drawing out those points around which critical discussion of the film often developed.

Form and theme: the terms of criticism

I have established how *Songs* was positioned as a 'debatable' text not only because of the political and cultural character of its themes but because of its formal approach. In fact, it is interesting to note the way in which different and sometimes conflicting assessments of *Songs* reflect broader differences in the 'politics of documentary' and, more widely still, the 'politics of representation'. So, for instance, *Songs* has been criticised for being too 'conventional' a text in its refashioning of elements from the poetic realism of the 1930s (see, for instance, McCabe 1988:32 on its 'outdated aesthetics'). It has also been seen as damagingly predictable in its iconography of race as a result of its use of television images from the riots, whilst at the same time it has been taken to task for its vanguardist 'difficulty', for its elitist lack of concern for questions of audience and accessibility.

As I have noted earlier, it is Salman Rushdie's comments in the *Guardian* which have served as a marker for much of the published debate about the film. It is worth quoting from his review more extensively:

> There's a line that *Handsworth Songs* want us to learn. 'There are no stories in the riots', it repeats, 'only the ghosts of other stories'. The trouble is, we aren't told the other stories. What we get is what we know from TV. Blacks as trouble; blacks as victims. Here is a Rasta dodging the police; here are the old news-clips of the folks in the fifties getting off the boat, singing calypsos about 'darling London'.
> Little did they know, eh? But we don't hear about their
> lives, or the lives of their British-born children. We don't hear the Handsworth songs.
> Why not? The film's handouts provide a clue. 'The film attempts to excavate hidden ruptures/agonies of 'Race'. It 'looks at the riots as a political field coloured by the trajectories of industrial decline and structural crisis'.
> Oh dear. The sad thing is that while the film-makers are trying to excavate rupture and work out how trajectories can colour fields, they let us hear so little of the much richer language of their subjects. (Rushdie 1987).

In a letter of response, also published in the same newspaper, Stuart Hall defended the film's attempt to find a 'new language' and questioned the terms of Rushdie's interpretation:

> The most obvious thing to me about the film is its break with the tired style of the riot-documentary. For example, the way documentary footage has been retimed, tinted, overprinted so as to formalise and distance it; the narrative interruptions; the highly original and unpredictable sound-track; the 'giving voice' to new subjects; the inter-cutting with 'the ghosts of other stories'. (Hall 1987).

Rushdie's complaints about the use of 'riot' images do show a surprising failure to recognise the transformative work performed upon the footage by the kind of practices which Hall describes.[2] However, it also clear that his critique is in part born of an impatience with the discursive ambition of the film in attempting to make connections across diverse materials rather than, more simply, to 'let the people speak'. In interview, John Akomfrah identifies what he sees to be the dangers of the 'ethnographic' approach:

> In the end, what Rushdie and other critics found really objectionable about the film, and some audiences found problematic, is precisely that anti-ethnographic bias – that you can't use the film to construct other knowledges about Handsworth. (Gilroy and Pines 1988:14)

Elsewhere, he has re-stated his commitment to the project of depicting *dis*-unity:

> The triumphalist vision of race and community operates on the assumption that there is essentially a core of affect that is structured around oratory, around song – giving it an irreducible unity – which wasn't present in the film. (Fusco 1988:62)

In an early review of the film for the *Monthly Film Bulletin*, Pam Cook picked up on the way in which something like a 'core of affect' is, nevertheless, constructed within and across the various sequences, with unfortunate consequences:

> But in spite of the film's deliberate attempt to avoid a homogeneous message or the predominance of a single voice, an overview does emerge from the conjunction of vox-pops, newsreel and elegiac commentary. This tends to present the ethnic communities as innocent victims of promises made but not kept, as dreamers betrayed, helpless to affect their own destinies. To a certain extent, this is contradicted by images of organised political action, scenes of anger and resistance, and instances of individuals speaking and acting on their own behalf. Nevertheless, the commentary's mourning of a lost innocence, spoken by a female voice-over and evoking images of suffering motherhood, betrayal and disappointment, remains a powerfully emotive thread knitting together disparate and conflicting discourses. In view of the fact that it is mostly men who are seen to be actively involved in political struggle, the effect is to make women's role once more one of passive endurance. (Cook 1987:78)

The decision taken by the members of the Black Audio Film Collective to operate in 'the Griersonian spirit' (Auguiste, 1988:35) and yet at the same time to work with a de-centred, multiple sense of their topic rather than any overarching Griersonian unity, seems to lie behind much of the criticism which the film has received.

As the discussion offered above illustates, *Songs* not only reaches back into history and memory in order the more fully to situate the present, it accesses activist voices addressing the urgency of immediate events at the same time as it works a more reflective discourse across the television images of civil disturbance. By including a strand of direct reportorial engagement with specific events (the discourse of the eye-witness; the discourse of the local representative committee) the film perhaps runs the risk of making its more indirect sequences look diversionary, perhaps even aesthetically self-indulgent. And Pam Cook is surely right to draw attention to the way in which the male activism contrasts with the largely female-voiced 'philosophy' which the film articulates and which provides its various deconstructions with a consistency of position even if, finally, this stops short of the 'unity' which Akomfrah rejects.

Handsworth Songs is a work of provocative originality, working for tones and vibrancies of the political beyond the discourses of the declarative and the directly evidential. Its contrasts and shifts of mode and mood serve to open up the topic, to create a disturbed sense of disturbance all the more impressive for the overall 'coolness' with which its elements are contained. Both the film and its problems will remain an important marker in the attempt to use film as a medium of political exploration and the attempt to confront questions of race and nation in Britain.

Documentary futures

11

In this final chapter, I want to consider some present trends in documentary television and speculate a little on the future of the genre within broadcasting. At other points in this book I have indicated how the current situation is a period of reconstruction for documentary and, on occasion (see, for instance, Chapter 3), I have observed how particular methods and formats have become transformed in the mid-1990s. Some of this reconstruction is institutionally imposed as a result of reduced budgets and a perceived need to be more attractive to audiences in the context of multi-channel choice. At their worst, the pressures here threaten to reduce the presence of documentary within broadcast schedules and to modify programming by the requirements of 'lightness' and 'watchability' achieved on minimum expenditure. It is clear how projects with a lengthy research and shooting phase are likely to suffer under such a regime. However, at the same time it is apparent that, in Britain certainly, documentary work is showing a vigorous re-imagining of both its visual and verbal language. It would be hard to find another period when so many different styles of documentarism were being broadcast. This more positive aspect of the current situation has certain links with the shift towards increasing competitiveness, in so far as the latter appears undoubtedly to have been a factor in encouraging at least some of the innovation which is apparent. The related shift towards commissioning more work from independent production companies has also had an influence here. It is far too soon to gauge how these developments will work in combination and it may well be, as the pessimists are already saying, that despite a certain flowering of new directions at the moment, the net effect of much current change will be to the detriment of serious new work.

Hybridisation across the 'conventional' generic range of television is a marked feature of new programming and, although quite directly commercially driven in many cases, the releasing of new depictive energies which often follows from boundary-crossing has been a clear gain which may well outlast its more cynical audience-building applications. Documentary *needed* a measure of re-imagining, and although one might have wished it a good deal more benign a context than mid- to late 1990s multi-channel competition is likely to provide, I have more faith in its survivability than some commentators, without wanting to minimise the present need for vigilance and a degree of protective action on its behalf.

In writing elsewhere on the question of documentary directions (Corner 1995a), I drew a semi-facetious distinction between developments in 'cooked' and 'raw' formats, following Levi-Strauss's classic use of these terms. It seemed to me to be interesting that documentary work was developing a new symbolic density (often borrowing from the self-conscious and 'cool' style vocabularies of advertising, pop videos and fiction cinema) at the same time as other tendencies were moving beyond 'neo-vérité' (see Chapter 3) towards newer forms for the direct presentation of reality ('Reality television' in the somewhat undiscriminating though widely-employed usage). These vectors of change might be seen as oppositional but they might equally be seen as complementary; indicative of broader, destabilising shifts in cultural representation, and to some extent playing off each other.

Looking at the present period, and allowing for simplification, I think three lines of innovatory work have been marked in Britain, although I also want to say something about quieter shifts. These most noticeable lines are:

1   The use of dramatic reconstruction and vérité material in multi-item programmes about emergency services (the BBC's *999* (1992) and ITV's *Blues and Twos* (1994) are indicative).
2   The emergence of the 'do-it-yourself' documentary shot on camcorder, first of all in *Video Diaries* (BBC 1991–) and then in a range of formats, including BBC's *Video Nation* project of mini-programmes and the entertainment-led format of *The Real Holiday Show* (1995).
3   The use of hidden micro-cameras in order to obtain footage by disguise. This was pioneered in Granada's *Disguises* (1993) and has been followed by a successful series of the Channel Four's *Undercover Britain* (1994).

The social relations implied by these three developments differ (for instance, 2 initially had a strong 'access' orientation, whereas the dramatisations of *999* were part of a bid to provide high-ratings 'infotainment' with a public-service conscience). However, as hybridisation continues, the initial connections with specific depictive goals are likely to become more tenuous as the range of applications/modifications increases.

Among the 'quieter' changes I would note is that, mentioned earlier, towards presenting a more visually elaborated and intertextually rich depiction of place, person and even action. This involves a rather stronger authorialism than is conventional in television documentary, one which is often connotatively playful and aware of the kind of 'look' which its images are providing for viewers. I would also identify a shift in 'mainstream' investigative documentary towards a greater permeability of its conventions and an increased use of dramatisation and marked styling.

It might be useful to look in a little further detail at the three main lines of innovation identified, before commenting more generally on the kinds of reshaping which documentary is likely to undergo in the next few years.

The 'emergency services' genre

The use of dramatic reconstruction to provide multi-item feature programmes with greater viewer appeal has a long lineage in television, particularly in the United States. In Britain, *Crimewatch UK* (BBC 1984–) was an important and controversial development in the routine use of dramatic and calculatedly exciting footage in support of notional 'public-service' values – here, the enlisting of public help in the solving of crimes (see Schlesinger and Tumber 1994).

There is no doubt, however, that both in America and in Britain (and also in much of the rest of Europe) a 'new wave' of actuality formats developed as 'infotainment' series emerged in the late 1980s. Kilborn (1994a) points to NBC's *Unsolved Mysteries* as one of the earliest series, starting in 1987, but Fox's *America's Most Wanted*, CBS's *Real Life Heroes* and *Rescue 911* were other significant programmes (see also the comparison of US and European 'reality' programming in Bondebjerg 1996).

The breakthrough in Britain occurred with the BBC's *999*, the first series of which was screened in 1992. The format for this highly successful programme, though directly derived from *Rescue 911*, included a number of 'adaptations' to fit the BBC's sense of what the optimum approach would be within the British context. The programme includes a number of items in each episode, some of which are shot using lightweight cameras in the new urgent, dramatically projected, actuality mode. In Chapter 3 I used the term 'neo-vérité' to describe the hybridised elaborations which had developed around the core features of 'fly-on-the-wall'. Perhaps these more recent modes might be described as 'ultra-vérité' – highly intensive in immediacy values and usually employed in the form of a 'reality segment' rather than a whole programme. However, *999*'s major items use dramatic reconstruction, given novelty by the extensive use of the original participants in the simulation and, where possible, by the intercutting of emergency services and amateur video within the newly shot footage. With a music soundtrack and a narrator build-up to each incident, the story and implications of which are then rendered through narrational segments, *999* provides an interesting example of hybridised 1990s television (see Corner 1995a for a detailed analysis of its communicative structure and Fairclough 1995 for an examination of its language use). The use of a respected journalist and newsreader (Michael Buerk) as its presenter provides 999 with a 'public-service' warrant which is clearly designed to mark the programme as 'serious' rather than 'trivial'. This articulation is reinforced by the extent to which the programme concerns itself with the *procedures* of each rescue which it reconstructs, where appropriate, giving the audience advice on what to do should similar circumstances befall them. The overall symbolic economy of 999, grounded in the vicarious witnessing provided by the reconstructions, is thus balanced between a strongly informationalist function and the production of excitement and pleasure.

Carlton's *Blues and Twos*, screened on the ITV network, (the name indicates the flashing blue light and the two-tone horn of emergency vehicles) is conceived within the same broad perspective but has a significantly different depictive organisation. Here, 'ultra-vérité' rather than reconstruction provides the primary footage (a point emphasised in the programme's spoken introduction). Presentation to camera is not used: instead the viewer's relationship to on-screen action is regulated through a dramatically inflected commentary (its urgency in relation to the actuality footage contrasting with the more measured tones of Michael Buerk's exposition in 999). Of course, the scopic field of *Blues and Twos'* 'caught' material is much more limited than 999's directed reconstructions, so editing and commentary have in part to compensate for the lack of the kind of shots (tight close-ups, reaction cutaways, well foregrounded action) which the other programme routinely offers.

How do we judge the appeal of this new form of documentarism? What broader indications does it carry for factual television? Among television critics as well as academic commentators, there is no doubt that 999 in particular (partly because it is a BBC programme) has been viewed with suspicion as a move on to the 'slippery slope' of tabloid television, a move largely prompted by market considerations (see Kilborn 1994a, and Bondebjerg 1996 for good reviews of recent criticism). Its selective interest, indeed one might say its obsession, with particular kinds of misfortune and practices of survival and rescue, might be seen to put further marginalising pressure on topics which visualise less easily and which carry less potential for strong narrative and drama.

The fascination of dramatic action combined with procedural detail is a long-established factor in 'popular documentary' (applications involving the armed forces and the police as well as the emergency services go back a long way).[1] However, it is possible to see the engagement with risk and danger, and then with rescue and release, around which 999's depictions are structured as indicative of a more recent cultural tendency, an emergent 'affective order'. Within this order, the psychodynamics of anxiety and insecurity become principal terms of the viewing relationship. Such a reading is, of course, highly speculative but it seems to me to be worth consideration and further inquiry (Nichols 1994 develops a strongly negative account of the 'perversity' of Reality television).[2]

'Do-it-yourself' documentary

Perhaps the development in factual television which has received the most critical attention in Britain over the last few years has been the strand of camcorder-shot 'amateur' footage first employed to full effect in BBC's *Video Diaries* series, which started in 1991. The first 'diary' was a fan's account of the 1990 World Cup in Italy, an account which worked both as a personal record and a piece of amateur reportage (documenting, for instance, problems in ticket allocation and crowd control as well as the sometimes rowdy behaviour of the fans themselves). Since then, the series has included a very wide range of topics and perspectives whilst keeping to the basic idea of providing a non-professional with the equipment to film aspects of their lives over a given period, the resulting tapes being edited at the BBC in line with the wishes of the participant/director. Keighron (1993) notes that only about one in fifty applications gets on to the screen and that the BBC were at one point receiving an average of eight applications a day, with an even higher submission rate during periods when programmes were being broadcast. He also notes that extraordinarily high shooting ratios, approximately 150:1, are standard.

Although it quickly became both a critical and a ratings success, the *Video Diaries* format was in fact developed by the BBC's Community Programmes Unit and was an idea emerging out of the long history of the Unit's involvement in 'access' television, in ways of getting a wider range of perspectives and opinions on to the screen (see Corner 1994 for a general analysis of access form). There is no doubt that many earlier experiments in wider participation, often involving studio-based work, have been regarded as worthy but dull by the popular audience. However, *Video Diaries*, with its particular mix of vérité-style footage, intensely personal mode of address and often highly novel topics, themes and settings, engaged audiences in ways which suprised even the members of the Unit. A number of other projects involving 'DIY' camcorder material have followed, as I indicated earlier, and more are to be expected.

Appraisal of *Video Diaries* and the kind of trend it began is interestingly split, though the general significance of the series for television in the 1990s is something upon which most commentators agree. One line of judgement has been to see the whole range of camcorder formats as 'opening up' television in ways which cannot but finally be democratic in consequence, even if specific projects fail or become compromised in different ways. Some critics have pointed to the value of simply having different forms of mediation on the screen, different ways of rendering subjectivity through image and speech. *Video Diaries*, for them, has 'resocialised' television documentation in progressive ways (I take this line in Corner 1994).

However, others have either been suspicious of the format from the start or have become so as a result of what are detectable shifts towards more 'engaging' topics, towards more entertainment. Criticisms have been made of the way in which the series, despite its genuine interest in creating new possibilities for public depiction, is nevertheless yet another generic commodity, one which is increasingly being assimilated within the television system, where it can quite easily be turned into a matter of *style* (to be imitated, for instance, in advertising, thus bringing about a resocialisation). The degree of self-absorption which many 'diary' programmes display has also been viewed as unhealthy by some writers (see Fraser 1992). A broader reservation, related to this, is that the whole DIY trend may indicate a shift away from analysis and argument in factual programming towards revelation and novel forms of 'showing' (a reservation which has also been made about the very different mode of emergency service programme discussed above).

Not suprisingly, debate about the *Video Diary* phenomenon has often broadened out to engage with a much more general set of questions about 'camcorder culture'; questions about voyeurism, exploitation and surveillance as well as about the incorporation of material in various kinds of 'access' format. Many of the worst fears expressed are informed by aspects of camcorder usage and abusage in the United States (see Goodwin 1993). At the same time, the earlier, much more positive note has continued to be sounded – that by 'demystifying' the techniques and devices by which reality is depicted on the screen the wider availability of the camcorder and of camcorder footage will serve to lessen the 'pull' and therefore the social power of mainstream broadcast television. Within this perspective, the activities of video diarists, and indeed of all amateur camcorder users, work as a kind of 'punk television', enthusiastically subverting sophistication in the interests of specific and direct communicative goals.

Hidden camera formats

This third area of development resembles the other two in so far as it is an attempt to provide strong immediacy values and a more intensive viewing experience. With the emergency services programmes, this is achieved as a consequence of the nature of the events being filmed in combination with different devices of dramatic shaping (including full dramatisation). In *Video Diaries*, it is the high levels of authenticity claimed by the depiction, together with the depth and mode of personalisation, which attracts. The use of hidden micro-cameras to obtain footage that would otherwise be either difficult or impossible to obtain combines a direct voyeuristic appeal (watching those who are unaware of being watched) with the sense of role-play and risk associated with disguise.

This is not to deny that the use of micro-cameras presents investigative reporting with a useful supplementary tool, but it is to register the way in which the emergence of the format has to be seen in terms of providing the viewer with a novel 'look', a novel mode for having access to 'the real'.

Although hidden cameras have been occasionally employed in documentary and entertainment programmes for many years (the popular series *Candid Camera* is the classic British instance of their use for 'fun', one with many international variants), it was the Granada series *Disguises*, first broadcast in 1993, which pioneered the use of micro-cameras as a principal series idea. Since then, the Channel Four series *Undercover Britain* has developed the format further.

In *Disguises*, the core footage – shot clandestinely by reporters in disguise – made up only a small proportion of each programme. The main exposition was still largely carried by the conventional devices of a filmed report, using commentary, interviews and presenter address. Within this modality of 'realism', the clandestine footage was offered as a further penetration into an event's or topic's truth. Its distinctive veracity was underwritten aesthetically by the poor lighting, lack of composition and often incomprehensible sound-track (subtitles were used extensively) which necessarily followed from its manner of shooting. So, for instance, in an episode concerning itself with the activities of hunt saboteurs, one short, micro-camera scene shows a female reporter, disguised as a hunt supporter, entering and then being dismissed from a public house in which the other supporters quickly suspect her of affiliation with the saboteur group. As in other new formats, the play-off between serious expositional objectives and the devising of competitively 'watchable' material is clear.

Channel Four's *Undercover Britain* applied the same broad approach to a range of investigative projects, radically reducing the emphasis given to 'dressing up' and generally giving far more emphasis, through interviews (sometimes anonymous), to the views of those living and/or working within the social realm to which the viewer was given temporary access. On occasion, this series extended beyond the use of professional reporters and developed its accounts through having recordings made by implicated 'ordinary' people.

Kilborn (1994a) rightly points out that the use of micro-cameras raises a number of ethical questions which have yet to be properly addressed. This is particularly the case if, as seems likely, the 'hidden footage' approach develops a more strongly sensationalist tendency, growing out of, but then departing from, the investigative design of the first programmes.

Generic continuity and change

The three areas which I have briefly explored are points of marked (and I think significant) change. Just what impact they have on the overall character of 'documentary culture' as this responds to new contexts of funding and production will take a few more years to assess. They all represent the movement towards new kinds of 'raw' depiction, although I have noted how documentarists have also developed more elaborated, self-consciously aesthetic devices, the 'hybridisation effect' here drawing on narrative fiction and the new forms of publicity and music television. *When the Dog Bites*, the subject of Chapter 8, is an example of an attempt to extend documentary language through an ambitious intertextualism which, in contrast to the search for a new 'directness', invites the viewer to consider its own mediations. I commented on the problems of accessibility which such stylisation could cause for a general audience, and therefore the limitations which such work had as public communication. In my discussion of documentary theory in Chapter 2, I looked at how increased self-awareness and intertextualism had frequently been urged by critical commentators as just about the only way for documentary to escape the legacy of 'realism', increasingly seen as a handicap to its conceptual and discursive status and development. Again, though, the possible misfit between ideas derived from a critical concern with formal innovation and the existing and possible sets of social relations within which broadcast documentary operates is apparent. Of course, a shift towards greater symbolic density and a richer visualisation need not be accompanied by a foregrounding of mediating devices. It is quite likely that a number of documentary projects will depart from the codes of realism and immediacy not in order to become more self-aware, discursively decentred depictions but in order to address the viewer from new, tightly integrated and fully centred positions of engaging portrayal. It will be interesting to see what options for rhetorical closure as well as rhetorical openess emerge from more intensive stylisations.

What of the 'mainstream' investigative documentary, grounded in feature journalism? Perhaps the most worrying possibility here is the reduction of budgets to the point where long-term enquiries can simply not be pursued, with a subsequent loss to the range and scale of independent critical surveillance within society. There have been signs of a new stylistic perkiness here too, however. For instance, a recent programme in the Granada *World in Action* series, about the Middle-East business interests of the Conservative MP and Cabinet Minister Jonathan Aitkin, was entitled 'Jonathan of Arabia' and had a title sequence of deserts and camels, which immediately set up a kind of spoof narrative parallelling the serious investigation. This extended to the use of episodic inter-titles, imitating silent cinema, and to the widespread use of a form of 'tableau dramatisation' in which, for instance, the figure of a Western businessman in a suit was seen greeting a traditionally dressed Sheikh in the setting of a tent, opulent in its fabrics and furnishings. Such a depictive device stopped short of 'dramatisation' proper but its approach to narrative and visualisation indicates a new freedom and a new playfulness, even in areas which have the most established conventions. Provided this goes along with the continuation of investigative and expositional qualities, it would be wrong, I think, to view such shifts pessimistically. The whole realm of audio-visual depiction, inside and outside broadcasting, is undergoing change (if not quite so radically as many vanguardists would suggest), and even those documentarists who refuse 'experimentation' will have to adjust to the different contexts in which their portrayals will be circulated and watched.

One area of mainstream work which has shown a continuing strength is the historical documentary. The combination of archive images (including still photographs) with interview testimony from those involved and with read documents (including letters and diary extracts) has frequently produced programmes which have had widespread popularity as well as being serious contributions to historical research. They have often made extensive use of commentary to provide continuity and to give disparate materials a firm structure. The best work of this kind has opened out into questions not usually addressed by conventional historical scholarship, using sources and images in a way which has both originality and critical force. In Britain, a number of programmes have reviewed the 'national heritage' in such areas as the family, sexuality and childhood in a manner which has proved to be deeply questioning and disturbing. On both sides of the Atlantic, experientially direct and demythologising engagements with war have also been undertaken (including both world wars, Vietnam and the Gulf conflict).

As I write, in 1995, Channel Four is screening Ric Burns's *The Wild West*, a six-part series looking at the development of the American West and at the human and environmental cost of this. Burns's programmes, using some of the same methods employed in his earlier, highly successful series on the American Civil War, show the general format at its most accomplished. Contemporary photographs and paintings are placed against commentary and read accounts, interspersed with evaluation from different historians. Perhaps the most important element to the overall feel and effectiveness of the series, though, is the frequent use of present-day filmed images of the landscape. The subject, composition and duration of these images combine direct aesthetic appeal (e.g. the beauty of cloud formations over the Western plain) with strong national and historical connotations (the sense of national place; certain landscapes as constituting a kind of capacitor of national feeling, both of pride and of guilt). Such depictions give the programmes their steady pace and allow the viewer time for contemplation, providing a visualisation which both generates its own meanings and helps to connect and deepen those emerging from surrounding material. It is interesting, too, that the series also employs occasional 'dramatic' markers (e.g. wagon wheels turning in the snow to match a narrated account of an Indian war party returning to camp) of a kind parallelled in recent British material. This understated, 'metonymic' level of dramatisation, providing narration with increased imaginative intensity, is a part of that more general symbolic reinforcement of documentary language to which I have referred.

At many points in this book I have noted how documentary in the mid-1990s is at a point of transition as both television itself and, more widely, the nature and means of public information undergo quite rapid change. Both positive and negative aspects of this transition can currently be seen. Even at the most general level, whilst multi-channel competition places increased value on the immediate attractiveness and 'cost-effectiveness' of documentary work, a cable channel like *Discovery* can dedicate itself almost entirely to a broad range of work in the genre.[3]

Documentary practices, and the definition of what constitutes documentary, have changed radically since the time when the Griersonian case for a documentary cinema was made. Documentarism has become a central element in broadcasting's performance of its public informational and critical roles as well as a general source of knowledge and pleasure. Within the independent cinema and video sector, it has for many years been an area producing substantive criticism and formal innovation. Though national conventions still exist, documentary work has increasingly shown an international awareness at the level both of themes and styles. In this book, I have looked at examples of good and significant work in documentary from the 1930s to the 1990s. At several points, the question of 'generic stability' has been addressed. I have noted the factors making for *in*stability and the arguments of those who would regard further instability as progressive. My view has been that a strongly referential and indeed evidential dimension will be a major component of any 're-imaginings' and will be retained, if in modified form, within the heightened discursive self-awareness which many documentarists feel is desirable. I would also want to suggest that, as a public form, documentary has the capacity to survive both postmodernist scepticism and the constraints of the audio-visual market (the latter presenting considerably more potent a threat than the former). Whatever, it is certain that around its future are assembled some of the most important issues of audio-visual form and public culture.

Notes

Introduction

1 Harvey (1989) remains a valuable source of interdisciplinary commentary on postmodernism both as a condition and as a perspective. The essays in Renov (ed.) (1993) variously discuss the implications of postmodernism for documentary, as does Winston (1995).

2 For a thorough, critical account of how earlier theorists and practioners of the cinema viewed its 'realist' potential, see the early chapters of Winston (1995). Winston makes connections with realist painting. Williams (ed.) (1980) is an excellent general account of ideas about cinematic realism, with extensive citation.

3 Grierson was reviewing the film *Moana*, by the American director Robert Flaherty, for a New York newspaper. Too much simplisitic emphasis has been placed on the 'coinage', however, and Winston (1995:8–14) is a good corrective to this tendency. I have also found Rosen (1993) very useful on the definition of documentary and the continuing difficulties which it presents.

4 A comparison of Orwell's diaries with his final prose accounts is instructive in terms of 'selective transformation'. Orwell's intellectual affiliation with the 1930s documentarists is also instructive. I have not space fully to argue the point about the status of prose description as documentary, but see the comment on indexicality below.

5 'Indexicality' refers to the way in which certain representations are formed from the physical trace of that which is represented. The cultural power of the photograph, the sound recording and the cinematic and electronic image is largely a product of this distinctive relationship. See the discussion in Nichols (1991:149–55).

6 Sontag (1978) is a classic account of the referential powers of photography. Stott (1973) is a detailed and justly celebrated study of documentary photography in a specific historical context. See Scannell (1986) for an account of developments in the documentary potential of radio.

7 Of the Soviet directors, Dziga Vertov is perhaps the most important in this respect. See the chapter on 'Kinopravda' in Winston (1995:164–9). Nichols (1994) argues that film history has shown a tendency to under-recognise Eisenstein's contribution to the documentary idea, in particular the skilful and effective way in which he self-consciously blurs boundaries; his influence on the development of narrative fictional cinema being seen as more significant. The broader international tradition of critical work is well reflected in Rosenthal (ed.) (1988), though with an understandable bias towards North America.

1. Documentary theory

1 Apart from the major scholarship of Sussex (1976), Low (1979a and 1979b) and Aitkin (1990), there is a very large literature of articles. Higson (1995) contains excellent bibliographical reference to these.

2 An important influence on the development of the British school as well as having international significance. Hillier and Lovell (1972) contains a general appraisal.

3 Winston (1995) is always illuminating on the relations between depictive convention and technology. See for instance his Chapter 25, 'Technologising the documentary agenda'.

4 I raise this point in relation to the more general problems of media studies inquiry in Corner (1995b). The question of how meaning (particularly visual meaning) acts to manage viewer evaluation in ways which are implicit remains high on the agenda, despite the recent emphasis on interpretative variation (for a comprehensive treatment of which, see Morley (1992)).

5 Aitkin (1990: Chapter 7) discusses these tensions. Throughout, Winston (1995) takes a more critical view of Grierson's general position and working assumptions.

6 See Windlesham and Rampton (1989) for the published account of the Inquiry, which contains revealing information about the researching and production of investigative television.

7 In 1986, the offices of BBC Scotland were raided by Special Branch policeman, who confiscated material relating to a series of six programmes, entitled *Secret Society*, about national defence and security. One of these programmes, on a British spy satellite code-named Zircon, was eventually banned. The 'Zircon' affair, as it became known, is discussed in Barnett and Curry (1994:42–4).

8 A very recent review of the situation is given in Kilborn (1996).

9 Anthropological film-making has been widely drawn on in recent discussion of 'alternatives'. Loizos (1993) is a good general study of work in the field. Nichols (1983) attempts to show what lessons can be learnt from anthropological practice.

10 This point is taken up, with examples, in Corner and Richardson (1986).

2. Action formats: drama-documentary and vérité

1 Vaughan (1983) and Higson (1995) discuss some of these wartime films usefully, noting points of style and of production method.

2 Again, Winston (1995) is exemplary on the question of technological limitations and technological development.

3 I first mooted this distinction in Corner (1979). Caughie (1980) uses a comparable differentiation and develops further the discussion of documentary-drama.

4 Laing (1986) documents this for *Z Cars*; the social (and sociological) origins of *Coronation Street* are well explored in Dyer *et al.* (eds.) (1981).

5 See Arrowsmith (1981) for a perceptive study of the film. Tracey (1978) gives the best account of the behind-the-scenes events leading to its banning.

6 Caughie (1980) brings this aspect out very well, along with its implications for viewer alignment and knowledge.

7 This is taken from the opening remarks of a talk given by Woodhead to students at Liverpool University in spring 1992, although he has used the phrase quite widely in interviews and writing.

8 Stratton and Ang (1994) look at the series with these questions in mind.

9 Spencer Chapman, the series producer, gave a very spirited defence of it before a group of students and staff at Liverpool University in spring 1995. An ambitious mixture of series aims and then disappointments and realignments in attempting to achieve them were apparent.

3. Coalface and Housing Problems (1935)

1 Chapter 3, 'Grierson's Aesthetic', of Aitkin (1990) documents the broad ideas about depiction behind the group's work, citing some of the films from abroad which they were seeing and talking about. He notes that, with one or two exceptions for particular artists, Grierson was a critic of Modernism for its ethical irresponsibility.

2 Scannell (1986) looks at contemporary experiments in radio features. See also Chaney and Pickering (1986) on modalities of the 'factual' in the Mass Observation movement, which connected with the broader literary cross-currents of the 1930s. Miles and Smith (1987) give a useful account of these latter. The 'poetry of statistics' is to be found in a range of works of the period. In film, the use of stock-market figures as soundtrack in Basil Wright's *The Song of Ceylon* (1935) is a particularly striking example.

3 Higson (1995:195) uses 'metonymy' suggestively to indicate the way in which a film sequence can very quickly generate a wide range of themes and sub-themes.

4 A recurrent theme in the work of the 1930s. See, for instance, the dramatic and contrastive placing of the fisherman against the sea in Grierson's *Drifters* (discussed in Aitkin (1990:110)).

5 His critique of Modernism hinged on this point (see note 1 above). He often expressed doubts about films which in his view over-emphasised their aesthetic organisation.

6 His comments on a work sequence in Wright's *Cargo From Jamaica* are very instructive here (Hardy (ed.) (1979:27–9).

7 Assessment of the movement's politics continues, although all future commentary will have to note the sustained critical judgement of Winston (1995).

4. Look In On London (1956)

1 The historical development and modes of the interview deserve further attention. In this book, several chapters engage at length with specific questions raised by its use, from *Housing Problems* in 1935 through to its various employment in contemporary television.

2 These questions, pursued across a number of genres, form the basis of the collected articles in Corner (ed.) (1991).

3 The terms within which ITV constructed its 'popular' provision, involving what was to be a major advancement of market principles into the sphere of public information, have been the subject of much discussion in the light of recent (1990) changes in British broadcasting funding and regulation. In particular, debate has focused on the degree of cultural closure or, alternatively, of accessing of previously subordinated forms involved in its commercial strategies. See the introductory essay and selected chapters in Corner (ed.) (1991).

4 One important exception to this is the strong early tradition, discussed in Chapter 2, of studio-based 'story documentary' work, which followed many wartime documentary feature films in leaking exposition through the dialogue and situations of an acted narrative. For a detailed history of this and other strands of television documentary before 1955, see Paddy Scannell (1979:97–106) and Elaine Bell (1986:65–80).

5 The emphasis on interviewing as a central feature of documentary presentation and the shift to 'actuality' from studio settings were also undoubtedly influenced by developments in radio features. No detailed study of the methods and forms of post-war radio journalism exists, but see Paddy Scannell's valuable discussion of pre-war output (Scannell (1986:1–26)).

6 The quotation also indicates clearly that the transference of the documentary project from cinema to television did not bring many changes, if any, to its dominantly masculine character. Despite the domestic dimension both of the system and its conventions, the public sphere constituted by 'serious' television was nevertheless a sphere of male concern and debate whose information needs were served by male enquiry and presentation.

7 The *BFI Distribution Library Catalogue 1978* gives dates of 1956, 1957 and 1958 but the Associated Rediffusion files indicate that after 1956 all schedulings were of repeats.

8 An account of the ideas behind this programme, which was quite quickly networked and became important to the development of television feature journalism, is given by Bernard Sendall (1982:355–6). The more light-hearted 'magazine' approach is clearly evident in *Look in on London*.

9 A remark of Norman Swallow is relevant here. 'What was missing from television documentary before the mid-fifties was, quite simply, people' (quoted in Scannell (1979:104)).

10 Besides the direct development out of *This Week*, there might have been influence from the BBC's television magazine programme about the capital, *London Town*, which began in 1949 and featured Richard Dimbleby. See Elaine Bell (1986) on this and also Jonathan Dimbleby (1975:219-21) for an account of the programme's artful mixing of studio and actuality material.

11 Outside broadcasts were prevalent in 1956. The BBC's very popular *Saturday Night Out* broadcast from a submarine and a helicopter and took a television set out as a present for the crew of the South Goodwin lightship.

12 More generally, the extent to which a 'classless, buoyant Britain' is seen to describe present or imminent circumstances rather than a goal for political struggle seems crucial to the kinds of accommodation which television makes with the burgeoning, Conservative theme of 'affluence' after the 1955 general election. Through its funding, ITV is obviously more directly linked into this emerging economic and ideological configuration than is the BBC. The point is touched on again later.

13 Though a contemporary manual for writers wanting to work in television is interesting here. Talking of documentary material it notes: 'the programme should shock, surprise and even develop the occasional "twist"' and, on the organisation and *scripting of interview responses*, 'I always try to make three main points, two interesting and one (if possible) surprising' (Swinson (1960:113)).

14 The 'anthropological' view, with its implied social relations, has often been commented on in respect of documentary depictions of work (see the discussion of *Coalface* (1935) in Chapter 3.

15 Good examples of the (highly effective) use of this method in Mitchell's work are *In Prison* (BBC, 1957) and *Morning In the Streets* (BBC, 1959). Both are discussed in Corner (1991a).

16 Though regional accents were occasionally to be heard. It was seen to be a strong point in favour of Robert Reid, the reporter for *Special Enquiry*, that he 'had a slight northern accent, [which] added to his earthy, no-nonsense appearance' (Swallow (1966: 73)).

5. Cathy Come Home (1966)

1 Paget (1990:91) comments on this, referring to the founder of Shelter, Des Wilson's, own judgement that although the programme helped, Shelter would have been established anyway. Sandford (1973, extracted in Goodwin *et al.* (eds) (1983:19)) describes the changes in council thinking prompted by the programme, noting the decision by Birmingham to stop separation of husbands and wives. Another useful retrospective is Sandford (1976), in the preface to the published playscript.

2 Discussed briefly in Chapter 2. Hill (1986) is the best detailed study.

3 Wilson (1993:140–1) perceptively explores the formal and pyschological character of this effect.

4 Banham (1981) gives a good general discussion of the programme's structure and its address to the viewer.

5 Sandford (1973) uses a charge made by the critic Paul Ableman (Ableman (1972)) that *Cathy* was a 'just a huge commercial', as its title. Ableman was worried by the possible distortion of proper public debate which he thought the affective strategies used by Sandford might introduce.

6. Living On The Edge (1986)

1 Petley (1987a:168) notes this influence in a brief but suggestive review of the film and draws comment on it from Grigsby himself in interview (Petley 1987b:169).

7. The Life and Times of Rosie the Riveter

1 The idea of giving personal experience time for a full recounting and reflection, and for a measured contrast against official discourses, is central to feminist media practice. *Rosie* provided a particular model for doing this. For instance, in the mid-1980s, the Channel Four 'Eleventh Hour' slot screened the series *Women and the Welfare State* – a workshop production from the North-East which mixed biographical testimony with archive informational films and a popular song soundtrack to bring out the continuation of patriarchy in the postwar formation and projection of the Welfare State.

2 The process is a filmic version of the more general project of 'consciousness-raising' as a feminist goal. The kinds of discursive relationship implied in such a project and the connection with more general questions of ideological reproduction and its 'countering' are, of course, points around which considerable controversy has developed.

3 Wartime propaganda aimed at women has been the subject of historical analysis both in the United States and Britain. See for instance Rupp (1978) for a comprehensive review of this issue for the period 1939-45. The 'Rosie' myth is dealt with in detail.

4 White (1995) asks similar questions of the film and is not satisfied with the answers. She charges *Rosie* with repressing key aspects of the distance between 'past' and 'present' in a way which exerts an undue closure on the former, thereby articulating a politically regressive spirit of 'progress'.

8. When The Dog Bites (1988)

1 The celebrated single-take opening shot of the Welles film establishes the night-time milieu of the town's main street with a marvellous mixture of tracking and composition, its marked durational values providing an effective preliminary to the action which shortly ensues (the explosion of a car bomb). *WTDB* does not follow it precisely but stays close to its general organisation and therefore to the kind of narrative 'entry point' it provides. See the director's own comments on this in the interview transcript following my analysis.

2 Conducted by the author, July 1995.

9. Roger and Me (1989)

1 In Britain, Roger Cook's move from radio 'consumer investigations' to *The Cook Programme* (BBC) saw the rapid development of this style (causing, among other things, a number of parodies in comedy programmes). Since his success with *Roger*, Michael Moore has continued his 'formula' in *Michael Moore's TV Nation*, which is now screened in Britain (BBC2) with British items intermixed with ones from the United States. Not suprisingly, the recipe of irony, farce, radical critique and 'plain guy' appeal often falters a little within the constraints and expectations of the series format.

2 'Vérité' doesn't seem quite the right word here – *Roger* is grounded in the discursive, connective probity of journalistic inquiry and exposition rather than the particularistic, indexical evidentiality of the vérité method (with its emphasis on the onlooking and overhearing relationship). Brian Winston, in a helpful comment on a draft of this chapter, has alerted me to the full complexity of the questions raised (or begged) in any attempt to assess Moore's approach, and my own later comments are made with this in mind.

10. Handsworth Songs (1987)

1 The incident, together with others of the same period, drew an extensive commentary from sociologists and race relations researchers. See, for instance, Augustine *et al.* (1970).

2 Among these practices are those drawing upon 'scratch' video, the deliber-

ately disorienting and thematically subversive juxtaposition of very different types of 'found footage' and the extensive use of repetition. See Cubitt (1991:94–5) for a brief discussion of 'scratch' effects.

11. Documentary futures

1 The pioneer 'outside broadcast' transmissions of the BBC regularly drew on this in the 1950s (army parachuting, naval submarine exercises, lifeboat crews, fire-fighting teams, etc.). Of course, what could be delivered to the audience by way of a visual experience was radically constrained by camera technology. An emphatic and near-continuous commentary was one way of attempting to compensate for this.

2 Some kind of audience research with regular viewers would be a necessary stage in the advancing of this argument, though by its nature it could not be *directly* evidenced by such means.

3 Dedicated narrowcast channels are not a substitute for the widespread public distribution of current affairs and documentary material, however. There is also, currently, a good measure of extremely tacky, sensationalist and (occasionally) hilariously incompetent material on the *Discovery* channel (e.g. hurriedly assembled 'Special Forces' compilations, 'Shark Weeks', all told a general overplaying of the male adventure theme).

References

Ableman, P. (1972), 'Edna and Sheila: two kinds of truth', *Theatre Quarterly*, 2:7, 45–8.

Aitkin, I. (1990), *Film and Reform*, London, Routledge.

Arrowsmith, S. (1981), 'Peter Watkins', in G. Brandt (ed.), *British Television Drama*, Cambridge, Cambridge University Press, 217–37.

Auguiste, R. (1988), 'Handsworth songs: some background notes', *Framework*, 35, 4–8.

Augustine, J., R. Holman and J. Lambert (eds.) (1970), *Race in The Inner City*, London, Runnymede Trust.

Banham, M. (1981), 'Jeremy Sandford', in G. Brandt (ed.), *British Television Drama*, Cambridge, Cambridge University Press, 194–216.

Barnett, S. and A. Curry (1994), *The Battle for The Beeb*, London, Aurum.

Bell, E. (1986), 'The origins of British television documentary: The BBC 1945–55', in Corner (ed.), *Documentary and the Mass Media*, 65–80.

Bondebjerg, I. (1996), 'Public discourse and private fascination', *Media, Culture and Society*, 18:1.

Branigan, E. (1992), *Narrative Comprehension and Film*, London, Routledge.

Caughie, J. (1980), 'Progressive television and documentary drama', *Screen*, 21:3, 9–33.

Chaney, D. and M. Pickering, (1986), 'Democracy and communication: Mass Observation 1937–43', *Journal of Communication*, 36:1, 41–56.

Cohan, C. and G. Crowdus (1990), 'Reflections on *Roger and Me*, Michael Moore and his critics', *Cinéaste*, 17:4, 25–30.

Collins, R. (1986), 'Seeing is believing: the ideology of naturalism', in Corner (ed.), *Documentary and the Mass Media*, 125–38.

Colls, R. and P. Dodd (1985), 'Representing the nation: British documentary film, 1930–45', *Screen*, 26:1, 21–33.

Cook, P. (1987), 'Handsworth songs', *Monthly Film Bulletin*, 638, 77–8.

Corner, J. (1979), 'Television's "real life" dramas', *The Media Reporter*, 13:1, 30–2.

Corner, J. (ed.) (1986), *Documentary and the Mass Media*, London, Edward Arnold.

Corner, J. (1991a), 'The interview as social encounter', in P. Scannell (ed.), *Broadcast Talk*, London, Sage, 31–47.

Corner, J. (1991b), 'Documentary voices', in Corner (ed.), *Popular Television in Britain*, 42–59.

Corner, J. (ed.) (1991), *Popular Television in Britain: Studies in Cultural History*, London, British Film Institute.

Corner, J. (1992), 'Presumption as theory: realism in television studies' *Screen*, 33:1, 97–102.

Corner, J. (1994),' Mediating the ordinary: the access idea and television form' in M. Aldridge and N. Hewitt (eds), *Controlling Broadcasting*, Manchester, Manchester University Press.

Corner, J. (1995a), *Television Form and Public Address*, London, Edward Arnold.

Corner, J. (1995b), 'Media studies and the knowledge problem', *Screen*, 36:2. 147–55.

Corner, J. and K. Richardson (1986), 'Documentary meanings and the discourse of interpretation', in Corner (ed.), *Documentary and the Mass Media*, 141–160.

Corner, J., K. Richardson and N. Fenton (1990), *Nuclear Reactions: Form and Response in Public Issue Television*, London, John Libbey.

Cottle, S. (1993), *Television News, Urban Conflict and the Inner City*, Leicester, Leicester University Press.

Cubitt, S. (1991), *Timeshift*, London, Routledge.

Dimbleby, D. (1975), *Richard Dimbleby*, London, Hodder & Stoughton.

Dyer, R. *et al.* (eds.) (1981), *Coronation Street*, London, British Film Institute.

Edgar, D. (1981), 'The treasured possession of the creators of dramatic fiction ...', *The Listener*, 1 January, 10–11.

Fairclough, N. (1995), *Media Discourse*, London, Edward Arnold.

Feuer, J. (1983), 'The concept of live television: ontology as ideology' in E .A. Kaplan (ed.), *Regarding Television*, Los Angeles, American Film Institute/University Publications of America, 12–21.

Fiske, J. and J. Hartley, (1978), *Reading Television*, London, Methuen.

Fraser, N. (1992), 'The frames people play', *The Sunday Times* (Supplement), 20 September, 8–9.

Fusco, C. (1988), 'An interview with the Black Audio Film Collective', in *Black Film/British Cinema*, London, British Film Institute/Institute of Contemporary Arts, 60–2.

Gilroy, P. and J. Pines, (1988), 'Handsworth songs: interview with the Black Audio Collective', *Framework*, 35, 9–17.

Goodwin, A. (1993), 'Riding with ambulances: television and its uses', *Sight and Sound*, 3:1, 26–8.

Goodwin, A. *et al.* (eds.) (1983) *Drama-Documentary: BFI Dossier 19*, London, British Film Institute.

Graef, R. (1974), 'Skeletons on the box', *New Society*, 27 June.

Grierson, J. (1932–34), 'First principles of documentary' in Hardy, (ed.), *Grierson on Documentary*, 19–30.

Guynn, W. (1990), *A Cinema of Nonfiction*, Rutherford, NJ, Associated Universities Press.

Habermas, J. (1989), *The Structural Transformation of the Public Sphere*, Cambridge, Polity Press.

Hall, S. (1987), 'Songs of Handsworth praise', letter, *Guardian*, 15 January.

Hardy, F. (ed.) (1979), *Grierson on Documentary*, London, Faber.

Harvey, D. (1989), *The Condition of Postmodernity*, Oxford, Blackwell.

Harkness, J. (1990), 'Roger and me', *Sight and Sound*, 59:2, 130–1.

Higson, A. (1986), 'Britain's outstanding contribution to film' in Charles Barr (ed.), *All Our Yesterdays: 90 Years of British Cinema*, London, British Film Institute, 72–88.

Higson, A. (1995), *Waving the Flag*, Oxford, Oxford University Press.

Hill, J. (1986), *Sex, Class and Realism: British Cinema 1956–63*, London, British Film Institute.

Hillier, J. and A. Lovell, (1972), *Studies in Documentary*, London, Secker & Warburg.

Jacobson, H. (1989), *Michael and Me*, interview, *Film Comment*, 25:6. 16–26.

Kael, P. (1990), 'Roger and me' review, *New Yorker*, 8 January.

Keighron, P. (1993), 'Video diaries: what's up doc?', *Sight and Sound*, 3:10, 24–5.

Kilborn, R. (1994a), 'How real can you get?: recent developments in reality television', *European Journal of Communication*, 9:4, 421–39.

Kilborn, R. (1994b), 'Drama over Lockerbie. A new look at the drama-documentary debate', *The Historical Journal of Film, Radio and Television*, 14:1, 59–76.

Kilborn, R. (1996), 'The new production context for documentary in Britain', *Media, Culture and Society*, 18:1.

King, N. (1981), 'Recent political documentary', *Screen*, 22:2. 7–18.

Kuhn, A. (1980), 'British documentary in the 1930s and independence' in D. Macpherson (ed.), *Traditions of Independence*, London, British Film Institute.

Laing, S. (1986), *Representations of Working-Class Life 1957–1964*, London, Macmillan.

Loizos, P. (1993), *Innovation in Ethographic Film*, Manchester, Manchester University Press.

Low, R. (1979a) *The History of the British Film 1928–1939: Documentary and Educational Films of the 1930s*, London, Allen & Unwin.

Low, R. (1979b), *The History of the British Film 1928–39: Films of Comment and Persuasion of the 1930s*, London, Allen & Unwin.

McCabe, C. (1988), 'Black film in 80's Britain', in *Black Film/British Cinema*, London, British Film Institute/Institute of Contemporary Arts, 31–2.

Mamber, S. (1974), *Cinéma Vérité in America*, Cambridge, MA, MIT Press.

Miles, P. and M. Smith (1987), *Cinema, Literature and Society*, London, Croom Helm.

Morley, D. (1992), *Television, Audiences and Cultural Studies*, London, Routledge.

Murdock, G. (1993), 'Communications and the constitution of modernity', *Media, Culture and Society*, 15:4, 521–39.

Neale, S. (1979), 'Triumph of the will: notes on documentary and spectacle', *Screen*, 20:1, 63–86.

Nichols, B. (1983), 'The voice of documentary', *Film Quarterly*, 36:3, 17–30.

Nichols, B. (1991), *Representing Reality*, Bloomington, Indiana University Press.

Nichols, B. (1994), *Blurred Boundaries*, Bloomington, Indiana University Press.

O'Kane, M. (1994), 'There's a fly in my soap', *Guardian*, 9 March.

Paget, D. (1990), *True Stories? Documentary Drama on Radio, Screen and Stage*, Manchester, Manchester University Press.

Petley, J. (1978), 'John Grierson and the documentary in Britain in the thirties', *BFI Film Catalogue*, 5–13.

Petley, J. (1983), 'Parliament, the press and Death of a Princess', in Goodwin *et al.* (eds), *Drama-Documentary*, 89–105.

Petley, J. (1987a), 'Living on the edge', *Monthly Film Bulletin*, June, 167–8.

Petley, J. (1987b), 'Out of the perpetual present' (interview with Mike Grigsby and John Furse), *Monthly Film Bulletin*, June, 168–9.

Petley, J. (1996), 'Fact plus fiction equals friction', *Media, Culture and Society*, 18:1.

Platinga, C. (1991), *The mirror framed: a case for expression in documentary*, Wide Angle, 13:2, 41–53.

Rabinowitz, P. (1994), *They Must Be Represented*, London and New York, Verso.

Renov M. (1993), 'Towards a poetics of documentary', in Renov (ed.), *Theorising Documentary*, 12–36.

Renov, M. (ed.) (1993), *Theorising Documentary*, London and New York, Routledge.

Richardson, K. and J. Corner (1986), 'Reading reception: transparency and mediation in viewers' accounts of a TV programme', *Media, Culture and Society*, 8:4, 485–508.

Rosen, P. (1993), 'Document and documentary: on the persistence of historical concepts', in Renov (ed.), *Theorising Documentary*, 58–89.

Rosenthal, A. (ed.) (1988), *New Challenges for Documentary*, Berkeley, University of California Press.

Rotha, P. (ed.) (1956), *Television in the Making*, London, Focal Press.

Rupp, L. (1978), *Mobilizing Women for War*, Princeton, NJ, Princeton University Press.

Rushdie, S. (1987), 'Song doesn't know the score', letter, *Guardian*, 2 January.

Sandford, J. (1973), 'Edna and Cathy: just huge commercials', *Theatre Quarterly*, April, extracted in A. Goodwin *et al.* (eds.) *Drama-Documentary*, 16–19.

Sandford, J. (1976), *Cathy Come Home*, London, Marion Boyars.

Scannell, P. (1979), 'The social eye of documentary', *Media, Culture and Society*, 1:l, 65–80.

Scannell, P. (1986), 'The stuff of radio' in Corner (ed.), *Documentary and the Mass Media*, 1–26.

Scannell, P. (1988), 'Radio times: the temporal arrangements of broadcasting in the modern world', in P. Drummond and R. Paterson (eds.), *Television and its Audience*, London, British Film Institute, 15–31.

Schlesinger, P. and H. Tumber (1994), *Reporting Crime*, Oxford, Oxford University Press.

Sendall, B. (1982), *Independent Television in Britain, Volume 1: Origin and Foundation 1946–62*, London, Macmillan.

Shubik, I. (1975), *Play for Today: the Evolution of Television Drama*, London, Davis-Poynter.

Silverstone, R. (1985), *Framing Science: the Making of a BBC Documentary*, London, British Film Institute.

Sontag, S. (1978) *On Photography*, Harmondsworth, Penguin.

Stott, W. (1973) *Documentary Expression and Thirties America*, Oxford, Oxford University Press.

Stratton, J. and I. Ang (1994), 'Sylvania Waters and the spectacular exploding family', *Screen*, 35:1, 1–21.

Sussex, E. (1976), *The Rise and Fall of British Documentary*, Berkeley, University of California Press.

Swallow, N. (1956), 'Documentary television journalism', in Rotha (ed.), *Television In The Making*, 49–55.

Swallow, N. (1966), *Factual Television*, London, Focal Press.

Swinson, A. (1955, 2nd edn 1960), *Writing for Television*, London, Adam & Charles Black.

Tracey, M. (1978), *The Production of Political Television*, London, Routledge.

Turton, D. and P. Crawford (eds.) (1992), *Film as Ethnography*, Manchester, Manchester University Press.

Vaughan, D. (1976), *Television Documentary Usage*, London, British Film Institute.

Vaughan, D. (1983), *Portrait of an Invisible Man*, London, British Film Institute.

Vaughan, D. (1992), *The aesthetics of ambiguity* in Turton and Crawford (eds.) Film as Ethnography, 99–115.

White, M. (1995), 'Rehearsing feminism: women/history in *The Life and Times of Rosie The Riveter* and *Swing Shift*', in D. Carson, L. Dittmar and J. Welsch (eds.), *Multiple Voices in Feminist Film Criticism*, Minneapolis, University of Minnesota Press, 318–29.

References

Williams, C. (ed.) (1980), *Realism and the Cinema: A Reader*, London, Routledge/British Film Institute.

Williams, L. (1993), 'Mirrors without memories', *Film Quarterly*, 46:3, 9–21.

Windlesham, Lord and R. Rampton, (1989), *The Windlesham/Rampton Report on 'Death on the Rock'*, London, Faber.

Wilson, T. (1993), *Watching Television*, Cambridge, Polity.

Winston, B. (1988), 'Documentary – I think we are in trouble' in Rosenthal (ed.), *New Challenges for Documentary*, 21–33.

Winston, B. (1995), *Claiming the Real*, London, British Film Institute.

Young, C. (1974), 'The Family', *Sight and Sound*, 43:4, 206–11.

Zheutlin, B. (1988), 'Documentary: a symposium' in Rosenthal (ed.), *New Challenges for Documentary*, 227–42.

Index